CULTURE SHOCK!

Hungary

Zsuzsanna Ardó

D0465744

Graphic Arts Center Publishing Company
Portland, Oregon

In the same series

Illustrations by TRIGG

© 2001 Zsuzsanna Ardó

This book is published by special
arrangement with Times Media Private Limited
Times Centre, 1 New Industrial Road, Singapore 536196
International Standard Book Number 1-55868-530-8
Library of Congress Catalog Number 00-102146
Graphic Arts Center Publishing Company
P.O. Box 10306 • Portland, Oregon 97296-0306 • (503) 226-2402

Printed in Singapore

To my father,
Pál Ardó

NOTE TO THE READER

Hungarians very often refer to Budapest as simply 'Pest'. Similarly, in this book, 'Pest' refers not to the county of Pest but the city of Budapest. It may refer to the whole city, including Buda, or just the Pest side of Budapest, depending on the context.

CONTENTS

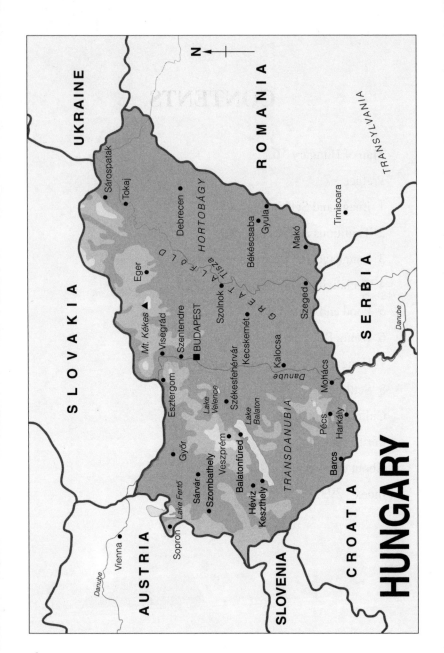

N

UKRAINE

ROMANIA

TRANSYLVANIA

SLOVAKIA

SERBIA

AUSTRIA

SLOVENIA

CROATIA

HUNGARY

Sárospatak
Tokaj
Debrecen
HORTOBÁGY
Gyula
Békéscsaba
Makó
Eger
Szeged
Mt. Kékes
Visegrád
Szentendre
BUDAPEST
Szolnok
Kecskemét
Kalocsa
Mohács
Esztergom
Lake Velence
Székesfehérvár
Lake Balaton
Pécs
Harkály
Győr
Veszprém
Balatonfüred
Barcs
Sárvár
Szombathely
Hévíz
Keszthely
Sopron
Lake Fertő
Vienna

TRANSDANUBIA
GREAT ALFÖLD
Tisza
Danube

Timisoara

Danube

PREFACE

"Úgy kell néznünk a nemzetet, amelyhez tartozunk,
mintha kívülről néznénk;
úgy kell magunkba tekintenünk,
mintha idegen szemmel tekintenénk."

— Illyés Gyula

"We must look at the nation to which we belong
as if we're looking at it from the outside;
we must look inside ourselves
as if we're looking with foreign eyes."

— Gyula Illyés, translated by Zsuzsanna Ardó

"Dehát mikor felnőtt egy nép?
Ezt nagyon nehéz megmondani.
Én azt hiszem, hogy egy nép akkor felnőtt,
amikor nemcsak iróniára, hanem öniróniára is képes."

— Örkény István

"But when does a people enter adulthood?
It is very difficult to say.
I believe a people enters adulthood
when capable of not just irony but self-irony as well."

— István Örkény, translated by Zsuzsanna Ardó

Confucius tells us that "All people are the same. It's only their habits that are different." At times of birth and death, love and hate, delight and dismay, we may often feel how true Confucius rings.

And in many different ways this is not surprising at all. The somewhat fuzzy notion of the 'universality of the human experience' is being underpinned by the fussy facts of biology. As I am tapping these letters on my keyboard to make up the words to configure my thoughts, another sequence of letters is being worked on by scientists: the sequence of the three thousand million letters of the DNA alphabet which makes up all us humans. The language of the genes supports the ancient Chinese philosopher's dictum – we are indeed the same.

Having said this, most of us have also experienced the direct opposite of this. The peculiar sense of fascination alternating with alienation as we dip our toes into the culture of a different person, family, neighbourhood or region – let alone a different country – may not be altogether unknown. As Horace Walpole puts it so vividly: "What strikes me the most upon the whole is the total difference of manners between them and us, from the greatest object to the least. There is not the smallest similitude in the twenty-four hours. It is obvious in every trifle."

Just like Confucius, Walpole probably also resonates with feelings we recognize as familiar. In fact, at least as much, if not more. So where have all those universal features faded? If we are indeed the same, how come the unsettling gap between them and us can apparently open up so deep and wide? Is Confucius or Walpole right then? Well, as it is often the case, probably neither. Or rather: both.

Culture Shock! Hungary sets out to dance between these two impressions of the human experience, taking both in turn. It is also about the dynamic dance between cultures and their perceptions. Its rhythm oscillates between the sense of cosy comfort of the 'familiar' and the challenging unease, even a sense of alienation or frustration, triggered by the 'other'. *Culture Shock! Hungary* initiates you into some of the important steps and routines of the dance called Hungarian culture. It makes you aware of local patterns so that you can avoid misconstruing them and aim to recognize individual variations on the cultural theme.

Once you know the steps of this dance, you will not step on others' toes just because you assume that your usual, well-worn way of dancing – your frame of reference for interacting, thinking, being – is the be-all and end-all. You will not fritter away precious energy on fearing others stepping on your toes either, because you will learn how to side-step them elegantly if need be. Instead, you will be free to enjoy the flow of the dance of Hungarian culture, appreciating it and feeling part of it, even if you are relatively new to it perhaps. And when you have learnt how to orient yourself on the dance floor, once you have a feel for your dance partners, you are bound to enjoy improvising. So come and hit the floor, let's feel the beat!

Zsuzsanna Ardó
ardo@pobox.com

Chapter One

IMAGE AND SELF-IMAGE

"**Hungary.** A mania with a population of ten million. It is now generally regarded as curable, though this would take away much of its charm."

— István Örkény

For all aspiring Europhiles, trying to forge a European identity has been a very bumpy ride – a frequently exasperating process that has so far proved elusive. It is an exorbitantly expensive process given the amount of red tape involved, the cost of running the pan-European bureaucracy, marketing the idea and translation/interpreting costs in several languages. Is it not high time to admit, critics argue, that the approach hasn't worked: that creating a mosaic from competing countries and cultures is much too tall an order?

The alternative solution is glaringly obvious. Instead of endlessly trying to reconcile many different cultures across the continent, the straightforward option is to take one's cue for Euro identity formation from a country which considers itself to be right in the centre of Europe. Indeed, as Hungarians often like to say endearingly, Hungary is the belly button of Europe. So there you have it.

HUNGARIAN SELF-IMAGE

Europeans Par Excellence

To the casual observer, Hungary may appear to be towards the east of Europe. This is not so for Hungarians. They see themselves as the very heart of Europe, and argue their case geographically: if Turkey and Romania are Eastern Europe and Germany is Western, then Hungary is the Central European country per se. Thus, Hungarians long for the day when it finally dawns on the world that it has got the geographical centre of Europe all wrong. It is in fact in Hungary where indeed it should be. Simple, really.

The country's claim to being at the very heart of Europe is made even stronger by a long and torturous cultural-historical argument, more of which will be seen later.

How Hungarians Like to Be Seen

Generous, warm, friendly, hospitable and sophisticated are qualities taken for granted as far as their own self-image goes. But this is only the beginning. Unless they are fully satisfied with the breadth and depth of your awareness about the Hungarian genius, Hungarians will be eager to point out to you that when appreciation of talent is not language-dependent, as with their literature (see more under *Literary Cornucopia*, page 235), Hungarian genius abounds and graces the world.

Talented in Music

You can do considerable damage to yourself if you are not sufficiently well versed in the ins and outs of Hungarian music talent. You can demonstrate your impressive knowledge of this subject, if you refer to Liszt and Lehár as Ferenc, rather than Franz, to Reiner as Frigyes rather than Fritz, Dohnányi as Ernő rather than Ernest, to Ligeti, Kurtág and Solti as György rather than George, and so on. These are an internationally renowned selection of Hungarian composers and conductors.

Hungarians have a straightforward view of consistency: if Mozart could retain his 'proper' first names, i.e. in the original language, then so should Hungarian composers, as is the case with Béla Bartók and Zoltán Kodály. Note that the diacritics are by no means optional; indeed, the fact that often foreign publishers, programme notes and even the BBC are cavalier about their proper use is a constant source of aggravation for Hungarians. (See more about this in the chapter on Language.)

13

A trombone lesson at the Zeneakadémia Ferenc Liszt Academy of Music, which is the Hungarian training centre for musicians from all over the world, and also a concert hall rich in Art Nouveau interiors. Many famous musicians, including Bartók and Kodály, have taught here. Music is an integral part of the Hungarian educational system.

Never mind that Liszt, for example, did not speak Hungarian. Just remember that to Hungarians, once a Hungarian, always a Hungarian. In any case, Liszt was born in Hungary and founded the present Academy of Music in his own flat – not to mention his music, which speaks clearly enough, does it not?

Your first attempts at pronouncing Hungarian names will naturally generate irrepressible giggling among Hungarians.

Talented in Sport

Hungarians truly wish the world at large would recognize their pre-eminence in sports.

Football (soccer) is considered an indigenous Hungarian sport, and before the English would claim it otherwise, they should swiftly recall Puskás and his team in the famous match of 1953 when

Hungary beat England 6 – 3 at Wembley Stadium. This may seem irrelevant today, but with the Hungarian fixation on history, it is a well-preserved memory, one regurgitated ad nauseam by Hungarian braggers and English masochists alike. Naturally, other events of that year, such as Queen Elizabeth's coronation and Hillary and Tenzing's conquest of Everest, pale in significance compared with the ignominy of England's first-ever defeat at Wembley. Just to rub it in, a year later, in the rematch in Budapest, Hungary won even more convincingly, 7 – 1. Magnanimous as they are in victory (infrequent as it is), and as an example of their concern to protect the vulnerable English ego, Hungarians will rarely ever refer to this second massacre.

Having been the number one country in football in the 1952, 1964 and 1968 Olympics, Hungary currently has a 48th standing or thereabouts in the world rankings. This position generates wide-ranging discussion in the Hungarian media about possible scapegoats for the present 'glorious' state of affairs. A steady flow of trainers come and go, including the semi-mythical figure Puskás, who persevered for as long as two months! One thing, however, Hungarians will not do, and that is to reconsider their obsessive belief that they are destined, ultimately, to be number one in world football!

In line with Hungarian versatility in general, they make their mark in a great variety of sports, mental and physical alike. Who but three Hungarians, the young Polgár girls, could become *la crème de la crème* of the chess world?

And then there is the Hungarian contribution to that great parade of sporting talents, the Olympics. To back up their argument, Hungarians boast a long list of gold, silver and bronze medal winners. They will point out to you just how tiny their population is compared with other countries which win the most medals, not to speak of the dire shortage of funds to support sports in Hungary. Then, moved to tears, they demonstrate how, out of the 150 plus participating countries, Hungarians have consistently been in the top 10 nations with the highest number of Olympic medals over the years. They show particular eminence in fencing, wrestling, pentathlon, swimming and canoeing, all of which provide convincing evidence of how successful Hungarians have been in sublimating their roaming, rambling and raiding skills from their Great Migration period.

Hungarian excellence at international competitions illustrates the exceptional Hungarian talent in sports, even though the majority of the population does not do any sports whatsoever. That is altogether a different matter. In any case, it only strengthens their argument that if all Hungarians unexpectedly launched themselves into some daily exercise, it would be quite unfair. There would obviously be no medals left for anyone else!

Talented in Science

But should you care neither for music nor sports, Hungarians will still not abandon the hope of redeeming you from your blissful ignorance of Hungarian genius. Beware: Hungarians will immediately button-hole you, and there is no escape until you fully recognize the astounding preponderance of scientists of Hungarian extraction.

Ah ... so you take Vitamin C every day, do you? Who else but a Hungarian, Albert Szent-Györgyi, got a Nobel Prize for his work on that!

What do you write with? A biro? It is named after its Hungarian inventor, László (Leslie) Biró.

Has Rubik's Cube driven you sufficiently crazy? Thank the Hungarian, Ernő (Ernest) Rubik for that.

Do you fancy holographic badges, games and art? Naturally, the Nobel Prize winner for that was Hungarian, Dénes (Dennis) Gábor.

Do you use a computer? Or game theory in economics? János (John) Neumann, a Hungarian mathematician, was closely involved in the development of these.

And the controversial, but pivotal, research on nuclear energy and the atom bomb? More Hungarians: Ede (Edmund) Teller, Jenő (Eugene) Wigner and Leó Szilárd.

And the list goes on.

Many of these outstanding scientists and inventors actually became famous abroad and not, with the exception of Rubik, in Hungary. Though Szent-Györgyi did get his Nobel Prize in Hungary, he too continued his work overseas.

HUNGARIAN IMAGE ABROAD

"If we look at the aura created for a foreigner today by the word 'Hungarian', independent of a Hungarian in the particular or Hungary as a political entity, the first thing we have to say is that everything decorated with the adjective 'Hungarian' belongs almost without exception to the field of the exotic, and in particular to the type we could call the 'European exotic' ..."

— István Bibó

In many parts of the world, street performances of Liszt's *Hungarian Rhapsodies* or Brahms' *Hungarian Dances* draw crowds swinging in an enthused trance to the romantic Romany rhythm commonly (mis)taken for authentic Hungarian culture par excellence. Part of this romanticized image of Hungarians foregrounds exotic glamour. Once such expectations dip into Hungarian reality abundant with 'exotic glamour', the fanciful image chases its froth.

Where could this popular, heady cocktail come from?

—"You bring out the Gypsy in me!"
—"Cos I'm Hungarian, ja?"

Well, listen to Gershwin's *Crazy for You*, for example. In this zesty classic, the all-American heroine falls for Béla Zangler, the charismatic Hungarian showbiz producer/director from New York – perhaps a Broadway alter ego of Hungarians such as Adolf Zukor and György (George Dewey) Cukor, just two of numerous outstanding Hollywood personalities of Hungarian origin? To be precise, his all-American friend impersonating Béla sweeps her off her feet.

17

And what's the attraction in the synthetic 'Hungarian' for the all-American girl? Much the same as for the riveted crowds in Covent Garden market, immersed in the Romany melodies of *Hungarian Rhapsodies* or *Hungarian Dances*. Brahms and Liszt it is not, but her heart grows tipsy as she makes it quite clear: "You and you alone bring out the Gypsy in me!" And what triggers off that wildfire? Simple: "Cos I'm Hungarian, ja?" The all-American boy explains his (non-existent) 'gypsy qualities' by his (nonexistent) Hungarian genes, with, to boot, a German question tag to create an authentic aura of the Austro-Hungarian monarchy in a New York theatre.

Then again, in Leowe's *My Fair Lady*, one of the major cathartic points of the piece is when an outsider to English high society, an eccentric Hungarian 'linguist', knowingly breaks the news that the other quaint outsider at the ball, the charismatic Eliza, is, of course, none other than Hungarian.

And if it is not a ball in London, then it is a seductive casino in Paris with – what else? – a name with a Hungarian aura, Transylvania, to conjure up the exotic in Massenet's *Manon*.

Charming Mystery and Mysterious Charm

It sharpens your interpretation of frazzled reality just to bear in mind that uncharted characters who flaunt flair and ooze mysterious charm are bound to have Hungarian genes. Well, sort of. If not, simulating the stereotype may work even better. Remember, the *echt* American boy feigning the exotic Hungarian is more attractive to the heroine in *Crazy for You* than Béla, the authentic Hungarian counterpart.

Similarly, in Strauss's *Die Fledermaus* (The Bat), when the heroine, a Viennese lady of mainstream ordinariness, decides to seduce her own husband to prove his disloyalty, she goes for the disguise she knows will work like a charm. And it does, without a hitch: the impersonation of a (nonexistent) exotic Hungarian countess, who, when challenged about her identity, rebuts with the music of her 'native country' – convincingly stoking 'Hungarian fire' in her breast with her *Csárdás* (Czardas).

18

Hmm ... could it be then that it is not the authentic but the simulated Hungarian which is the epitome of exotic glamour?

HUNGARIANS: WHO ARE THEY?

The word 'Hungarian' misleads innocent outsiders who, by default, tend to take things literally. This will not do in Hungary where almost everything is tantalisingly complex, or at least people love to act as if this is the case; if not, every effort is done to make it so.

Huns and Hungarians

Again, in the case of the word 'Hungarian', things are rarely as straightforward as they might appear to be. As a novice to Hungarian culture, you could possibly be forgiven for thinking that the name 'Hungary' refers to the ancient Hungarians. Recalling the 'Scourge of God', a.k.a. Attila the Hun, you might cheerfully deduce that Hungarians are descended from the Huns and thereby feel you have safely pinpointed the origins of all Hungarians.

Not necessarily. Both the Huns and the descendants of the people now referred to as Hungarians arrived from Asia to enthusiastically embark on the grandest European tours ever undertaken. So far, so good. However, there was a negligible time lag of several hundred years between the two ostentatious ramblings, and the same hiatus before their eventual upshot. The first – the great horse-nomadic Hun empire and its powerful king Attila – disappeared around AD 453 only to resurface in an eponymous Verdi opera and in the first syllable of the name 'Hungarian'. Now this term, however, refers to the second group of happy wanderers who eventually settled down in Central Europe in AD 896 or thereabouts.

Magyar, Magyarok, Magyarul and Magyarország

They and their progeny call themselves *Magyar* (singular), *Magyarok* (plural), with *Magyarul* meaning 'in Hungarian' and *Magyarország* (Magyarland) standing for the country 'Hungary' itself. Relax – no extra titbits to denote gender. The name Magyar supposedly means 'speaking man' from the Finno-Ugric *mon* (speak) plus *er* (man). But the Magyar was just one, albeit the leading one, of the seven tribes of the *Magyar Törzsszövetség* (Hungarian Tribal Federation) between the 6th and 10th centuries. You can come across the names of the other tribes in Hungarian first names, surnames and place names: Kürtgyarmat, Jenő, Kér, Keszi, Tarján and Nyék.

'Hungarian' and its many variations are only used by and in communication with foreigners. Indeed, this is probably how the name stuck, as a result of some popular misconception on the part of outsiders about the Magyars being the Huns. The outsider references to Magyars such as Ungarn, Ungherese, Hongrois, Ungroi, Hungarian, etc, are all supposedly derived from On Ogur, a Turkic name for 'Ten Tribes', to name the alliance between the seven Hungarian and three Kabar (Turkic Khazar) tribes later joining them.

The first to equate the Huns and the Hungarians were the Western chronicles in the 9th and 10th centuries. Most of the references were a tad uncomplimentary except for the ones in the *Nibelungenlied* (Song of the Nibelungs) of the 12th century, which is not very surprising considering the leadership roles German tribal kings played in Attila's multi-ethnic – Turkic, Germanic and Slavic – empire.

Gesta Hungarorum (Deeds of the Hungarians)

This confusion is, however, not the exclusive privilege of foreigners, past and present. Attila (the ever-popular Hun emperor, in case you'd forgotten) is still a very fashionable first name in Hungary, no doubt given to denote being 'authentically Hungarian'. And for a good reason too. One of the 13th century chroniclers, Simon Kézai, used the sources of *Gesta Hungarorum* (Deeds of the Hungarians), his own chronicle of the Hungarians, rather creatively. He reinterpreted the Western chroniclers' mostly negative references to the Hungarians as Huns, and took them as compliment rather than insult, and thus incorporated them into his text.

Hungarian Historical Consciousness

Kézai's (the royal chaplain-cum-storyteller) construction of the Hun-Hungarian relations has made a lasting impression on the Hungarian consciousness. His ideas were picked up by the cultural nationalism of the 19th century, when cultures were frantically searching for their own unique *Volksgeist* (national spirit), thanks to Herder's theories and admonitions about national soul and identity. Historical, musical, literary traditions and so on, if found lacking or deemed insufficient, were projected into the past, and then back into the present for conjectures about the future.

Attila and Árpád

Soon poetic inspiration and historical documentation, fact and fiction became impressively and (almost) irretrievably blurred. Thus Hungarian collective memory holds that Attila was in fact a Hungarian hero, directly linked with Prince Árpád. It also places Attila's burial place, a triple sarcophagus of iron, silver and gold, right in the Hungarian River Tisza, where else? By the way, Attila is not to be confused with an *atilla*. Although the latter is the derivation of the former, the connection is a touch tenuous since atilla is a term of fashion denoting a braided military jacket, typical of the *huszárs'* (hussars), which also metamorphosed into the high-fashion world of balls and galas.

Do not be surprised either if *Magyarország* (Hungary) is referred to not just as *Pannonia* (a reference to Roman times) but also as *Hunnia*, especially in Hungarian literature, lore and trademarks. One literary example is *Buda halála* ('The Death of Buda'), the first part of the epic poem *Hunnic Trilogy* by János Arany, the great Hungarian poet of the 19th century, about Attila and Buda, his brother.

Rege a Csodaszarvasról (Legend of the Wondrous Stag)

According to *Rege a Csodaszarvasról*, the 'Legend of the Wondrous Stag', Hunor and Magor (Magyar) were the sons of King Nimród and his wife Eneth, so they were blood relations to start with. Then they shared a primary bonding experience: they were lured far away by a wondrous white stag only to find their would-be brides to mate with. The Huns and the Hungarians are thus the offspring, so the story goes, of this magical 'post-stag-party' experience: two nations of direct blood relations and shared experience.

Although the legend is supposed to be about the origins of Hungarians specifically, in fact the stag story is paralleled in other cultures around the world. Just like the 'tree of life', the stag and its antlers – which are cyclically shed only to regrow – reflect the pattern of nature, and are the universal symbol of rebirth, long life, sexual drive, the light and sun and so on. From the Finnish *Kalevala*, Celtic, Buddhist, Chinese, German, Scandinavian and Scythian legends to Greek and Christian mythology, the stag is a potent mythical symbol across many cultures.

Thus the legend of the wondrous stag is significant partly because it relates Hungarian culture to universal mythology and symbolism. At the same time, it ingeniously establishes Hungarian legitimacy for Árpád's conquest of the Carpathian Basin, the heart of the Hunnic empire. If Árpád is a descendant of Attila, then Hungarian tradition holds they simply took a few hundred years later what used to be in the family in any case, so to speak.

Compelling as it is, the degree to which this legend is accepted varies wildly from unquestioning enthusiasm to a view that it is romantic but somewhat absurd. Theories abound, expeditions to the Orient come and go, academic debates continue. Certainly, Hungarian folk tales and the pentatonic nature of Hungarian folk music support the consensus that Hungarian origins are Oriental; but the question remains – just how Oriental?

HUNGARIANS IN AND OUTSIDE HUNGARY

You cannot but bump into Hungarians wherever you go; you will find them everywhere even if you (or they themselves) are unaware of their roots.

Even the British Royal Family is supposed to have some Hungarian blood, and, lo and behold: the palace itself has confirmed this rumour. And the family connection is not even that obscure: it is *Rhédey Carola Grófnő* (Claudine Countess Rhédey), the paternal granny of Queen Mary (Queen Elizabeth II's grandma). This Hungarian lady from Erdőszentgyörgy in *Erdély* – 'Transylvania', now part of Romania – is the Hungarian bond with the Royal Family.

Transylvania has a particular place in the Hungarian psyche – you would do well to tread with extra caution here. You will make a lasting impression if you casually demonstrate your knowledge that the Hungarian name for the town of Cluj (now in Romania and currently called *Cluj-Napoca* in Romanian) is *Kolozsvár* (Kolozs Castle). The same town was called *Claudiopolis* in Latin and referred to in German as *Klausenburg* by its Saxon inhabitants. This is by no means unique – there are many other examples of local place names in three or four different languages – and gives you an inkling of the shifting tides of Central European history. (See more under *Erdély* on page 27.)

To start with, in neighbouring countries around Hungary there are ethnic Hungarians numbering around one third of the population of

Hungary itself. This gives you an insight into the impressive Central European complexities of the relationships between nations and states, and consequently, languages, cultures and identities. You are likely to score Brownie points in a conversation with Hungarians by dropping a few empathic comments about the Hungarian communities in Austria, Croatia, Romania, Serbia, Slovakia, Slovenia and the Ukraine.

Similarly, ethnic minorities within Hungary include Croats, Germans, Romanians, Serbs and Slovaks. Their numbers used to be very significant indeed in the multi-ethnic Hungary with a population of around 18.2 million. After the Trianon Treaty in 1920, however, the population of Hungary was reduced to little more than 7 million.

Hungarians have also been emigrating from Hungary for at least the last five hundred years. Some of the greatest emigration waves were in the wake of lost revolutions and wars – not an entirely unfamiliar concept in Hungary. Such fundamentally political emigrations took place after the anti-Habsburg Rákóczi War of Liberation (1703–11), the March Revolution led by Lajos Kossuth (1848–49), the Communist-Socialist Revolution (1918–19) and the Hungarian Revolution of 1956. The turn of the 20th century witnessed a grand-scale exodus motivated by economic rather than political reasons. Then the 1930s and post-World War II triggered off respective emigration waves of a mostly intellectual and political nature. Thus, in the last two centuries alone, around one million ethnic Magyars, and all in all more than twice as many Magyar citizens settled down in many different countries around the world, though mostly in the United States.

Sense of Loss, Self-pity and a Soupçon of Superiority

Some countries have grown larger in the course of history, some have disappeared, and others, like Hungary, have successfully managed to go through the traumatic process of seeing their territory shrink dramatically, with corresponding ego implications. The psychological burden of deep resentment felt at having lost 70 per cent of her territory and around 60 per cent of her population to neighbours after World War I still haunts Hungarians, some more than others.

To be a Hungarian, you must not be disturbed by the argument that in spite of large swathes of Hungarian communities in the lost territories, 52 per cent of Greater Hungary was, in any case, not Hungarian. Besides, even eminent Hungarians would be hard-pressed to argue that the relationship between themselves and the various ethnic minorities within Greater Hungary was historically any better than is generally the case in such complex situations.

As far as Hungarians are concerned, they are dramatic losers in the game of history, and they consider the world to be definitely worse off for that. As a novice Hungarian, make sure you cultivate an abiding sense of loss in your subconscious.

As with most Central European cultures, a loser you may be as a Hungarian, but this should not prevent you from perceiving yourself with a soupçon of superiority. As a Hungarian, you must learn to act exuberantly which could appear to some as arrogant, assertive and proud. All of these are engineered by way of compensation for the great sense of self-pity and sulking at having been so misunderstood and ill-treated by the rest of the world.

A European preoccupation indeed.

LOVE THY NEIGHBOUR

Not unlike most peoples, Hungarians have the truly admirable gift for irritating their neighbours. Some Hungarians can outdo most others by far, when they really set their mind to it.

10 Million Versus 15 Million

The first post-1989 Hungarian prime minister's comment about being the 'soul' prime minister of 15 million Hungarians, rather than the piffling 10 million within Hungary, rivals de Gaulle's provocative statements about Quebec. Surely an outstanding bid to improve neighbourly relations?

A Touch of Phobia for the 'Other'

All in all, to become an insider to Hungarian culture, you will need to be infected by the widespread disease of seeing yourself as rather superior to other nationalities, in particular those in close geographic proximity. This should not be too difficult since ignorance followed closely by fear, and, consequently, hatred of 'them' as opposed to 'us', is a preoccupation in many cultures of the world.

The business of acquiring the sophisticated systems of prejudice and long-standing resentments among countries in Europe, offers a decent challenge for any neophyte European. However, if you are to be a truly notable European, you would be much better off going Hungarian. What a weird, wonderful, unmatched variety of phobias!

Forget the petty grudges of, for example, the English against the Welsh (lazy), the Irish (volatile), the Scottish (mean), the French (dirty), the Germans (domineering), the Swiss (plain boring), the Americans (successful) and so forth.

For some Hungarians the mild phobia of the 'other' does not need constant and specifically targeted justification: an intensely vague discomfort or inarticulate ethnocentricity will suffice. Engaged in a conversation about such issues, the most a Hungarian might venture to say is that the particular ethnic group in question works, eats, sleeps, or does whatever is being discussed, either too much or too little. And, in any case, they are different from Hungarians, who are, of course, the only valid point of reference. Ethnocentricity, at home in most places around the world, is no stranger in Hungary either.

As a guideline for up-and-coming aficionados of Hungarian culture, a useful starting point is to love thy neighbour as you dearly love your own minorities. For example, warmly embrace the Germans because they work too much; the Gypsies because they do not work enough; and the Jews because it is a tradition. Hold close to your heart the Tartars, Turks, Austrians, Germans and Russians because they came to Hungary, fancied staying, and did; and the English and the Americans because they did not.

SPECIAL RELATIONSHIPS

One of the best ways of getting an insight into the workings of Hungarian culture is to understand how the rich tapestry of relationships with various other peoples has been woven over the centuries. The following are some of the pivotal relationships that provide important points of reference.

Erdély (Transylvania): the Land Beyond the Woods

As earlier indicated, *Erdély* (Transylvania) is a particularly sensitive issue in the Hungarian psyche, its roots going back hundreds and hundreds of years.

To have even an inkling of what this special relationship is about, you will need to know a few things about Erdély more than it being the homeland of Count Dracula. And on that score, here are four nuggets of information that might also surprise you, dear reader.

Firstly, the Irish writer's (Bram Stoker) *Dracula* is not simply a figment of the imagination but based on a 15th century figure, Vlad III, the Impaler. Secondly, Transylvania was not the territory he terrorized; rather it was in Wallachia (now southeastern Romania) that he did his dastardly deeds until King Matthias of Hungary threw him into jail. Thirdly, Dracula means – guess what – 'Son of the Devil' or 'Little Devil', the diminutive form of *Drakul* (Devil). And fourthly, the Hollywood character of the shadowless vampire, universally symbolising sadism, that does not die until a stake is driven through his heart (note the connection with Vlad the Impaler), was made famous by Béla Lugosi, a Hungarian American actor.

Apart from (mistakenly) associating Dracula with Erdély, some will also have heard about its majestic landscape – like an intimate version of the Scottish Highlands. The name Erdély is from *erdő* (forest), and appropriate it is to describe the place of dense woods and mountains rich in natural resources; a rural paradise where ancient villages nestle amidst steep valleys, babbling brooks and lush meadows, with folk traditions preserved over the centuries.

But for Hungarians, Erdély is more than Arcadia; it is a primary repository of Hungarian culture. A significant part of Hungary and Hungarian history, Erdély was apportioned to Romania at the end of World War I as a result of the Trianon Treaty in 1920, which has caused not a little resentment.

As is generally the case in Central Europe, Erdély's history is a rather complex ballgame of various invasions, migrations and nationalism. It became part of the Kingdom of Hungary after the Árpádian conquest in the 9th century. In the 12th century, the Hungarians and the Hungarian-speaking Székelys were joined by the Saxons of Transylvania, and around the 13th century by the Wlachs (now called Romanians) from the Balkan peninsula. In the 15th century, the Hungarians, the Székelys and the Transylvanian Saxons formed a federation ruled by Hungarian princes, with a Hungarian-speaking Diet. When it languished in other parts of Hungary under the Turks and then the Habsburgs, most of Hungarian culture survived right here. This was the case even during the population resettlements carried out under Ceausescu, a period fraught with tensions and conflict due to (still) unresolved minority issues. Around two million people in Transylvania, a third of its population, are ethnic Hungarian. The landmarks of Erdély are found in what Hungarians eat, for example *Kolozsvári rakott káposzta* (Kolozsvár layered cabbage); in street names in Hungarian cities; in many folk songs and dances; in Hungarian history and literature; and in the music of Bartók and Kodály.

A significant part of Hungary's contribution to European culture is, strictly speaking, from Erdély. For example, many of the world-famous Hungarian composers were born here, such as Béla Bartók, György Ligeti, György Kurtág and Péter Eötvös; so was the famous mathematician Farkas Bólyai, the father of non-Euclidian geometry, along with many prominent figures in Hungarian culture and history.

So, beware: the Hungarian-Transylvanian special relationship can be a considerably emotive subject for Hungarians, even though individual feelings vary. You are well advised, therefore, to proceed with a generous amount of empathy and sensitivity.

A cigányok (The Gypsies) vs the Roma (Romany)

First of all, let us get the name right. As is often the case, *cigány* (Gypsy) is a label that got stuck by outsiders' reference to a particular group. The Magyars are referred to as Hungarians simply because ages ago they were mistakenly identified with the Huns, which was an already familiar, therefore handy, category at the time. Similarly, when the nomadic groups from northern India first made their appearance in Europe, they were thought to be Egyptians – hence the name Gypsy and its countless versions in various languages such as *Cigány, Cyganski, Gitan, Zigeuner*, etc. Not surprisingly, the insider name for the group is different, and much preferred: Roma (Romany), meaning 'human'.

By way of clarification: *Roma* (Romany), *Roman* and *Romanian* are three quite different terms denoting three separate concepts, which are not interchangeable. *Roma* (Romany) refers to the Gypsy people from northern India and their language, and *Roman* to the citizens of ancient Rome and its empire, whereas *Romanian* (also spelled *Rumanian* or Roumanian) is the adopted name of the citizens of Romania, a neighbouring country of Hungary.

The Hungarian Gypsies, the Romungro, have been living in Hungary since the early 15th century. However, they have not been exactly quick to abandon their traditional nomadic lifestyle, and therefore their integration into European societies, including Hungarian, has also not been speedy. It has not been without tensions and conflicts either. It is an ongoing, often very painful process, marred by prejudice and discrimination in Hungary just as much as elsewhere in Europe.

Some of the Roma speak one or more of the Romany dialects, but most of them speak Hungarian, and tend to see themselves as Hungarian. At the same time, their cultural revival in the 1990s, such as the formation of the Roma Parliament and recordings of traditional Romany music among other things, indicates a need to reassert their ethnic identity.

Although trends are changing, many of the Romas have been traditionally linked with the Hungarian Gypsy music industry. Do not rush to the conclusion that Hungarian Gypsy music must then be either authentic Hungarian or Romany folk music or perhaps a combination of both. This is a very common misconception both in and outside Hungary. Remember, distrust labels and take no meaning for granted, especially if they make perfect sense at first glance. The fundamentally string-based, pseudo folk music that you hear, especially in touristy restaurants, is the product of various 19th century composers, and it is Gypsy to the extent only that a lot of the time the musicians playing it have been Romany. Their own traditional music is essentially vocal and percussive.

A zsidók *(The Jews)*

The Jewish-Hungarian relationship dates back to the time of the Hungarian conquests of the Carpathian Basin. Apart from there being Jews living in the area at the time of the conquest, the beginning of the Hungarian-Jewish relationship came through the Khazar empire (7th–10th centuries) of a Turkic people, the ruling class of which converted to Judaism in the mid-9th century. Now three tribes of the Khazars, the so-called Kabars, joined Árpád's team of seven tribes to form The Alliance of Ten Tribes, which is credited with the superb job of finding the new home for the Magyars in Hungary.

The first relatively large Jewish immigration was in the wake of the Tartars' devastating visit to Hungary in the 13th century: King Béla IV, the then Hungarian king, invited Jewish groups from the west to settle in parts of Buda, Óbuda and other towns. Jewish immigration continued over the centuries from different places, including Austria, Bohemia, Moravia, Spain and Poland.

Jewish integration into Magyar culture was speeded up after the emancipation of the Jews in 1867, i.e. when they finally acquired full Hungarian citizenship rights. It did not take too long before they became an important part of the Hungarian urban middle classes. As elsewhere in Central Europe, they have contributed very significantly to the urbanization and industrialization of Hungary, to its scientific and cultural development. Many of them identified with Hungarian patriotism and its issues with enthusiasm even though their assimilation was, at times, viewed with anti-semitism by some.

Hungarian-Jewish relations were not helped by the so-called Numerus Clausus Law in the wake of World War I and the three Jewish Laws enacted in the run up to and during World War II (1938–41). The Numerus Clausus Law set quotas of ethnicity and nationality which kept Jewish students in particular, and minority students in general, out of Hungarian universities. The goalposts shifted as to who qualified, i.e. was defined, as a Jew, but they were consistent in their purpose: to increasingly disqualify Hungarian Jews first from

31

Reading the papers while taking a rest in a park in Szilágyi Erzsébet fasor with a statue by Imre Varga commemorating Raoul Wallenberg, the Swede who saved thousands of Jews in Budapest during World War II.

selected professions, then from integrating into society by outlawing mixed marriages and sexual relationships. In the first Jewish Law, you were defined as a Jew if you were of the Jewish faith. Then the business of gene counting kicked in – you qualified as a Jew if you had one Jewish parent or two Jewish grandparents regardless of their faith according to the second law. Predictably, the third law synthesized the 'scientific' criteria of both the first and second laws, and you had the privilege of being labelled a Jew either on the basis of your faith or if you could flaunt at least two, say, grannies, of that religious disposition.

All the hard work of the Hungarian legislators did not satisfy Hitler. So, when one fine spring night in 1944, his troops presented themselves in the country, they started their own way of doing things, with a little help from Hungarian fascists. Together they worked hard, not least on the 'final solution': around half a million Hungarian Jews died in the Holocaust.

Anti-semitism has not entirely vanished in Hungary. Surprising as it may sound to the uninitiated, the words *kozmopolita* (cosmopolitan), *urbánus* (urban) and *liberális* (liberal) are sometimes used – with negative connotations – by some as code words for Jews. The scars of the relationship seem to be healing, and there is a Hungarian Jewish cultural revival, especially in Budapest. Also, most Hungarians are very proud of their world-famous expats, many of whom, ironically, are of Jewish origin. Ironically too, they often achieved fame or fortune at least partly because they had to continue their studies or work abroad. The famous Jewish Hungarians include most of Hungary's Nobel Prize winners, film business successes like Adolf Zukor, George (György) Cukor, William Fox, Joe Pasternak, Alexander Korda, Leslie Howard (László Steiner) and others, an endless list of prominent musicians, scientists and so on.

A németek (The Germans)

German-Hungarian contact goes back to the 9th century. Their relationship has fluctuated over the years: they have sometimes been friends, at other times, foes. To get an idea of the nature of this relationship and some of its underlying issues, it helps to understand its context. In Central Europe the theme of Western cultures defending themselves from Eastern cultures is a fundamental one. It started at least with the Limes, the strategic defence points set up by the Romans in the first century AD against the uninvited guests from the East, kindly called Barbarians, a Greco-Roman term. The Hungarian tribes coming from Asia also started their European career in this category.

The Hungarians continued their visits to France, northern Italy and Germany which were deemed barbarous raids from the Western hosts' perspective, but in their own view simply adventures as a way of life. When they lost the Battle of Lechfeld (in Germany) in 955, it finally drove home the message that a paradigm shift in their nomadic, hunting, pagan lifestyle was in order.

To start with, in practical terms this meant that Szent István (Saint Stephen), their first king, got himself Gizella, the sister of the Holy Roman Emperor, Henry II, and a Bavarian princess, as his wife. He also got himself crowned by the Pope in 1000, and set about the business of Christianizing and settling the Hungarians, often with the help of various 'consultants' from the West, many of them Germans and Italians. (See more under *Italians* beginning on page 39.) In brief, during this period Hungarian culture made its momentous move from the Oriental orbit to the Occidental cultural sphere.

Germans from different parts of the Holy Roman Empire (962–1806), mostly German, Italian and Czech principalities, continued to settle in Hungary, especially in the 12th and 17th–19th centuries. The Habsburgs, multi-tasking as both monarchs of many lands and emperors of the HRE, were also involved in the settlement policies in Hungary after 1526 when they ruled Hungary as well.

Various German ethnic groups – such as the Saxons and the Swabians – contributed significantly to Hungarian urbanization and industrialization; their legacy is still felt, among other things, in the Hungarian educational and administrative system, in technology and science. Many of them assimilated into Hungarian society and by the 20th century became an important part of the middle classes.

However, World War II marred the German-Hungarian relationship in complex and tragic ways, and this trauma remains part and parcel of the Hungarian consciousness. Many Hungarians feel they actively defended Western civilization in 1989, once again without being properly appreciated for it. They see themselves as having virtually dismantled the Iron Curtain when they let East Germans through the Hungarian-Austrian border, thus facilitating Germany's reunification and the subsequent collapse of the Soviet Empire.

Az osztrákok (The Austrians)

The decades of the Austro-Hungarian empire (1867–1918) and the preceding periods of the Habsburg empire are distant enough for Hungarians to be able to afford some bittersweet nostalgia, albeit tinged with resentment.

Yet the Habsburgs used to be silly enough to provoke the Hungarians by imposing German as an official language, as, for example, Emperor Joseph II tried to do in 1784. Although forcing a shift in the use of language – from Latin to German – for his multi-ethnic, multilingual empire was part of his modernizing drive, it certainly did not go down too well in Hungary, a budding nation with already a powerful hang-up about survival and language. *Nyelvében él a nemzet* (the nation survives through its language) is a saying which still has great clout in Hungary.

Deep down, Hungarians know full well that they are smarter and much more fun than their northwestern neighbours who speak funny German are. Unfair as it is, Hungarians have also come to terms with the fact that Austria picked the Jolly Joker card by sheer virtue of being geographically a wee bit further west of the centre of Europe, i.e. Hungary.

Since Hungarians got 'prime choice' of the various waves of gate-crashing guests from the East – Tartars, Turks and Russians – it is only understandable if Austrians resent being unfairly deprived of the unpredictable excitement and 'character building' that Hungarians experienced over the centuries.

Time has moved on and tables have been turned. Borders and power relations have shifted. Rather than a threat, Austrians are now seen as important partners by Hungarians, out of pragmatism as well as nostalgia, or perhaps even heartfelt admiration by some. The "we shall not give an iota from the 48!" – no compromise is possible on the demands of the March Revolution (1848–49) – attitude towards Austrians has mellowed much. This is quite significant considering that being mellow is not always characteristic of Hungarians, for many of whom compromise traditionally tends to be a despised concept.

Taken in the round, though, Austria has traditionally been Hungary's first and direct link to Western cultures, and therefore the relationship between them is rather special. Business, economic and political sense, along with a shared enthusiasm for operettas, balls and coffeehouses with their delicious, albeit not exactly healthy cakes, also do their job of bonding the two neighbours.

A few Hungarians, including the Hungarian Smallholders' Party, took this mellowing-cum-nostalgia towards the Austrians to Royalist proportions in 1990. Inviting Otto von Habsburg – a German citizen and heir to the nonexistent throne of Hungary – to be the king or at the very least president of Hungary is, however, something dismissed by most as a ridiculous notion. The offer was declined by Otto himself, a political philosopher fluent in Hungarian (rather than expecting Hungarians to speak German) and taking an interest in all matters Hungarian: in short, one of the more charming political stars in Hungary's nascent democracy.

A törökök (The Turks)

When you relax in the high-domed steam baths or sip your steaming *kávé* in one of Budapest's coffeehouses, you are enjoying some of the legacies of the Turks. Along with paprika and tomato, many national dishes and styles of Hungarian cooking stored in the collective memory actually made their entrance into Hungarian dietary habits during Turkish times.

The first Turkish attempts to make themselves at home in Hungary go back to the 14th century. But to orient yourself within the labyrinth of Hungarian culture, the really important dates you have to remember are 1526, the *mohácsi csata* (Battle of Mohács), and 1541, *Buda bevétele* (conquest of Buda) by the Ottoman army.

If you really want to get down to the nitty-gritty of Hungarian sensitivities, then remember that, as far as Hungarians are concerned, historically it is the Turks who take a lot of responsibility for the general and lamentable lack of awareness that Hungary is in fact the centre of European culture. After the Turks' gate-crashing in the early 16th century, Hungary was partitioned into three sections – military, economic and administrative, the central part coming under direct Turkish rule. The Habsburg and Ottoman empires, representatives of Western and Eastern cultures respectively, played out their battle for hegemony for more than 150 years, Hungary being the stage for the unending drama or indeed tragedy.

When the drama was finally over in the late 17th and early 18th centuries, the stage was more than devastated, and not much of the population was left. Even today, two centuries later, you can clearly see the outlines of the theatre by looking at the settlement and development patterns of the country. From the Hungarian perspective, the Turks seriously dislocated the development of Hungary, particularly from a cultural and socioeconomic view, from its Occidental orbit, just as the Tartar's visit did earlier, and the Russians' later in the 20th century.

The extended Turkish visit also had a major impact on the ethnic composition of the country. The depopulated Hungarian villages were often resettled by other ethnic groups, which led to Hungarians being in the minority within Hungary itself. This in turn contributed to a complex and tenuous situation, and later to the Trianon Treaty in 1920, for which at least some of the responsibility is often attributed to Turkish rule and the Austrian-Ottoman power play on the Hungarian stage.

In this extensive drama, most Central European players, for example the Serbs (Kosovo, 1389) and Austrians, have also performed the role of being the bulwark of Christendom. Nonetheless, the Hungarian psyche holds Hungary as the primary defender of Western culture against the Turkish invasion. Having demonstrated their membership credentials at the very foundation of European identity, it is little wonder they so much begrudge the big ado about

Hungary's admission to the European Community. Now there is irony for you.

A szlávok (The Slavs)

It may help to look at the term itself briefly. *Szláv* (Slav) is an umbrella term which includes many peoples, including the western Slavs, including Czechs, Slovaks, Poles; the eastern Slavs such as the Russians, Ruthenians and Ukranians; and the southern Slavs, for example Bulgarians, Croats, Slovens and Serbs.

Now the Slav-Hungarian relationship goes back to the Árpádian Magyars' arrival in the Carpathian Basin, parts of which were already being populated by Slavs at the time. Perhaps the closest Magyar contact with Slavs has been with the groups called *horvát* (Croatian), *rutén* (Ruthenian) and *szlovák* (Slovak), but to a varying degree also with the *szerb* (Serbian), *cseh* (Czech), *lengyel* (Polish) and *bolgár* (Bulgarian) groups as well.

Although their relationship has not been without conflict, the Hungarians and the Slavs substantially influenced one another's lives, language and culture for a thousand years or so. For example, although Poland and Hungary are not neighbours now, they used to be for many centuries, often sharing kings, and at times even national heroes such as the Polish *Bem Apó* (Father Bem), the legendary general of the Hungarian revolution of 1848–49. Ironically, Bem survived the failed revolution by fleeing to Turkey and reinventing himself as Murad Tevlik, a Muslim pasha. Thus, this Hungarian-Polish national hero died as the Turkish governor of Syria. On the other hand, many Serbs survived by fleeing from the Turks and finding a home in Hungary – as many of their churches bear evidence in Budapest, Szentendre and elsewhere. Or take the Zrínyis and the Frangepans: noble families and prominent Hungarian historical figures of Croatian origin whose names you are bound to learn in Hungary since streets names, squares, buildings and the like are named after them.

The Soviet Union (1922–91), the successor of the Russian empire, took considerable interest in Central and Eastern Europe, and thus in Hungary as well. Russian troops took thorough care of the Hungarian Revolution in 1956, a date etched in the memory of many, not just Hungarians. The tenuous relationship with the ex-USSR was formally terminated after a mere forty-odd years when Russian troops finally bade farewell to Hungary in June 1991. This long-awaited yet somewhat sudden goodbye was something of a surprise to those who assumed that this sojourn, like the gracious visit by the Turks, would last around 150 years.

Others considered the efforts to foster this particular relationship a hopeless exercise from the beginning. While attempts to ruin Hungary's economy and interfere with its political system are not taken too kindly by Hungarians, it is the imposition on their language and culture which provokes them the most. It was a decidedly low feasibility project trying to uproot Hungarians from their Western European traditions. They may have arrived from behind the Urals, or even further away, but Hungarians have come to view their origins with some geographical, historical and psychological distance after a thousand years of hard-earned survival in Central Europe.

Some of the more fun results of this lopsided affair can be viewed in the Sculpture Park in Budapest, the ghetto of 'socialist' art. This is where sculptures from public places were relegated to after the downfall of communism, partly to protect them from being knocked down, and partly to be able to view them together as a gallery of days gone by.

The Italians

The Italian connection goes back two thousand years when the legions of Emperor Augustus made their home in what they called the Province of Pannonia, thus extending the Roman empire to the west of the Danube. Signs of the Roman presence, camps and towns of this civilization, are still visible around Hungary, including in Szombathely,

Pécs, near Tác (then called *Savaria, Sopianae* and *Gorsium* respectively), and Aquincum, which was at the time the capital of Lower Pannonia, and is now Óbuda, or old Buda of Budapest. (See more in the chapter *Settling In.*)

But there are more than ruins to remind you of the Italian-Hungarian cultural connection. One of the most striking and prominent sights in the heart of Budapest is the view of *Gellért-hegy* (Gellért Hill), with a statue on top, often illuminated at night. This image, which is often used as a symbol of Budapest, and even of Hungarian civilization itself, represents a major turning point in Hungarian history, and at the same time is intimately linked with Rome and Venice.

Before the Hungarian tribes made their momentous lifestyle change, abandoning the relentless radicalism of their raids, the uninvited visits of Hungarian horsemen were infamous in Italian, French and German monasteries. Their reputation is evidenced by the words of prayer at the time: *De sagittis Hungarorum libera nos Domine!* (From the arrows of the Magyars deliver us, oh Lord!) But soon *Szent István* (Saint Stephen), the first Hungarian king, established a more formal and cooperative link between Rome and Hungary. He secured his crown from Pope Sylvester II for persuading the restless Hungarians to curtail their enthusiasm for adventures abroad, and instead to settle and to convert to Christianity, whether they liked it or not.

Not all of them heeded his call, as evidenced by the fate of an eminent Venetian, *Szent Gellért* (Saint Gerard). This 11th century patrician left Venice for Jerusalem but found himself busy in Hungary instead in 1015, as the tutor of the king's son and later as the Bishop of Csanád, a pioneer of Hungarian Christianity – and, eventually, a martyr of it. During the pagan uprising in 1046, Gerard was apparently hurled in a barrel from the top of the hill into the Danube – hence the name of the hill in the middle of Budapest in honour of him, and his statue on top of it.

Pannonhalma in Dunántúl Transdanubia in western Hungary, the first Benedictine abbey in Hungary, was founded by Prince Géza in 996, and it continued to be supported by his son, King (Saint) Stephen. Probably the first school in Hungary, it became an important centre of Christian learning.

During the Renaissance, many prominent Italian artists, artisans and scholars came to live and work in Hungary, including Andrea Scolari, Filippo Scolari and Pier Paolo Vergerio. Furthermore, since *Mátyás Király* (King Matthias) married Beatrice of Aragon in 1476, not surprisingly Italian culture, especially from Firenze, was popular and pervasive in his court. The Renaissance splendour of his royal palaces in Buda and Visegrád and his outstanding library of around one thousand illustrated manuscripts are fabled by the Italian humanist historian Antonio Bonfini in his book *The Deeds of the Hungarians*.

— Chapter Two —

TRADITIONS AND VALUES

"The English and the Hungarians are very much alike, except the Hungarians are more so."

— adapted from James Dunne

SOME TRAITS

Joie de Vivre Hungarian Style

Hungarians, as quintessential Europeans, are devoted to the sophisticated art of muddling through in all possible and impossible fields of life. Needless to say, Hungarian muddling-through is a muddling-through with a difference: they passionately nurse the blues *while* muddling through. This is high-tech *joie de vivre* Hungarian style.

In fact, nursing the blues is one of the most cherished Hungarian pastimes and an infatuating indulgence, a national hobby so to speak. Muddling through is an a priori part of this painful pleasure since it generously generates blues to nurse.

Obviously, the stiff upper lip the English pride themselves on while they happily muddle through whatever needs to be muddled through, is just that: stiff, much too stiff, for many Hungarians. They tend to prefer the Hungarian state of mind: rapturous blues-nursing jazzed up with a pinch of manic-depression.

Whether it is momentarily blue, manic, or depressive, the admirable lack of self-irony with which some Hungarian egos indulge themselves by fits and starts guarantees the heavy-duty nature of their state of mind.

The Legendary Hungarian IQ is successfully impeded by a lamentable EQ

Critics may argue that the rather impressive gap between their intelligence and emotional quotient is purposefully designed as well as strenuously adhered to by Hungarians. Committed as they are to fair play, this is their way of giving a sporting chance in life to others.

The dazzling display of demonic powers you may unleash by some casual remark about the value of viewing matters with some degree of EQ can be enthralling. Whenever you feel like making a tentative comment to Hungarians about the advantage of cultivating psychological distance by putting whatever in question into perspective, think thrice ... then do so at your own risk.

Perspective they have, thank you very much, and plenty of it. Or so the national mythology goes.

Nemzethalál (the Extinction of the Nation) vs 'Bouncing Back'

Having remained stuck in arguably the busiest international crossroads for most of their past, Hungarians have an acute sense of history and unfinished business. For the uninitiated, it may feel every now and then like unwittingly sharing a psychoanalyst's communal couch.

Having managed to survive their history so far, Hungarians are highly adaptable and extremely adept at preserving a distinct undercurrent to the various dominant cultures that come and go. This feature of the Hungarian cultural profile, along with its implications, is worth mulling over, especially if you come from a country which has not been invaded since the 11th century, like England, or never been invaded by outsiders at all since its birth, like the United States. People in Central Europe, including Hungarians, tend not to take the survival of their own culture for granted. Most of the forty or so Hungarian generations over the past thousand years have spent their lives focusing on getting adjusted to everyday realities being uprooted and shifting around them. Consequently, training yourself to cope with fundamental disorientation and reorientation in the aftermath of recurring major historical and socioeconomic shake-ups has become a feature of the Hungarian psyche.

The Hungarian revenge on the various bids to take over their culture has been to cheekily resurface and assert their identity again and again. Part of their dogged determination to survive is marked by an in-depth and ongoing analysis of the threat to their existence. "It's good to talk," or as Hungarians like to say, *"Beszéljük ki magunkat jó alaposan!"* (Let's have a heart to heart and get it off our chest!)

Nemzethalál (the extinction of the nation) is certainly one of the well-rehearsed topics: it is a revered Hungarian tradition to seriously chew over aspects of their culture's imminent demise. Fortunately, they expound so much energy on engaging the issue in principle, that there is little danger of it actually happening in practice.

In the light of the above, it is not surprising that Hungarians are keen to keep themselves and their remarkable 'bounciness' shipshape by elevating their everyday life to new epistemological heights. You can join them in this jolly – and possibly addictive – activity by keeping up your daily dose of peering into the existential abyss of whatever is at hand.

This is risky and daring but not terribly strenuous so far. But after the ritual moaning, watch out for the next step in the procedure, which is decidedly not to give in to the anaesthetic of familiarity. Rather than getting sucked into the sweet seduction of despair, they get on with whatever needs to be got on with, and do so with the appropriate mélange of melancholic dynamism and dynamic melancholy. Note: melancholy, yes; despair, no, except for those who rather than using this activity as a regular life-muscle toning exercise, overdo it and opt for embracing the depth of pointlessness once and for all.

Navel-gazing: honfibú, bús magyar sors és társai (Hungarian gloom, doom et al.)

The efficiency of many invaluable Hungarian traits is somewhat undermined by the Hungarians' fatal attraction to navel-gazing. They will endlessly probe their history, which may have been dramatically heroic but not by any standard cheerful. Inevitably, indulgence in self-pity will follow.

The concept of 'recent' history may be different from your own unless yours too is impressively elastic and stretches to, say, the 16th century. You might like to adjust your sense of historical time to feel more at home with the Hungarian version. Their concept of 'recent times' can be flexible enough to include the *mohácsi csata* (Battle of Mohács) in 1526 as a 'recent' point of reference directly and indirectly impacting on the present. (More under *The Turks*, page 36.)

Generally speaking, Hungarians are strongly success-oriented. Therefore, speculating over 'what's to come' is a popular pastime. This does not mean that reckoning with the past is not. On the contrary! Hungarian culture is as Janus-faced between Eastern and Western cultures as it is between the past and the future. Indeed, the past is an all-pervasive protagonist, often hogging the limelight of the present; present grudges flirt and make alliances with the past, once grand and glorious, but mostly bitter.

Since, taken in the round, the Hungarian past is not particularly upbeat, its hovering over the present lends a sense of sophisticated and subtle stoicism to most subjects. In the most unlikely interactions you might find the topic of the moment suddenly wrapped in tangential hints to historical figures, dates and events. The sombre complicity of this organic cross-referencing gives an almost surreal 'fourth dimension' to an otherwise flippant or frothy remark.

Sírva vigad a magyar (Maudlin Merrymaking)

Traditionally, some fine Hungarian wine triggers off, rather sooner than later, the great Hungarian behavioural paradox epitomized by the saying: *sírva vigad a magyar* (Hungarian merrymaking is a tearful affair). The special expression for this unique Hungarian trait, *sírva vigadás*, may be a bit odd to outsiders – after all, how often do you find yourself dramatically shedding tears in the midst of merrymaking?

Sírva vigadás is, however, most appropriate and understandable in the light of behaviour mellowed by 'sacred spirits'. The Hungarian id, in particular when fired up by a few glasses of *Bikavér* (Bull's Blood), may be demonstratively woe-stricken.

This is not to say, of course, that you will not find many Hungarians who react very strongly against this tradition and get irritated by the concept, let alone the practice, of *sírva vigadás*. In any case, you would do well to brace yourself: the amazingly go-ahead Hungarian ego, bubbling with irrepressible energy, is never too far away. Hungarians have a knack for surprising the world with yet another resurgence of vitality at the most unlikely times.

SOME OBSESSIONS

Ethnic Homogeneity

If there were a category for being the ethnically most varied of small nations with the most obsessive claim for being homogeneous, Hungarians could arguably get into the *Guinness Book of Records*. It is quite difficult to see how on earth they, as some proudly claim, could have stayed ethnically homogeneous in the middle of the busy traffic-jam their ancestors decided to settle in a thousand years ago.

To start with, the Magyars installed themselves in Hungary together with peoples who were here already. And others – both from the East and the West – joined them after the conquest to settle the country in the 10th–11th centuries. This pattern continued with several settlement campaigns later on, for example in the 13th–14th centuries and in the 17th–19th centuries.

It is worth remembering though that having bounced back after the Batu Khan-led Tartars' (strictly speaking, Mongols') uninvited sojourn in 1241–42, but before the next guests, the Turks, called in, in 1526 (remember, a date all Hungarians can recite in their sleep), the Magyar population was larger than and possibly even twice the size of England's at the time. As for the physical size of the country around the 14th century, it may give you a rough idea if you recall the space bounded by the Baltic, the Black and the Adriatic Seas. As far as educational developments are concerned, the 14th century also saw the founding of the first Hungarian universities in Pécs and Buda.

Hungarians argue that this foundation for lasting historical success was undermined first by the Tartars and then, especially and irrevocably, by the Turks deciding to overstay their enforced hospitality. Historical 'earthquakes' reworked Hungarian realities on a grand scale: settlements and towns disappeared, socioeconomic development regressed and the population got decimated; for example, about 60 per cent of it was wiped out in 1241–42 alone.

During a period when the European population in general increased substantially, by the end of the Turkish takeover bid lasting a good 150 years, the Hungarian population dwindled to around one third its previous size. These Magyars may have been homogeneous – though this is highly unlikely – but by the time the Turks pulled up their tent pegs and left, they were certainly few in number. So the new guests, the Habsburgs, added to the population here and there, mixed and stirred it, and arguably the concoction they cooked up has haunted Central-Eastern Europe ever since.

Acting as the proverbial bridge between East and West secured Hungarian culture an eventful and colourful history and a genetic background, which is fundamentally the same as the European at large. Were you to set out to find a Hungarian without a mixed genetic background, it would be a challenge to say the least. Most people, not just the Hungarians, share a good part of their ancestors down the line.

Sharing a common language and, via the language, its literature and sense of history, would fulfil the criteria of homogeneity for some cultures. Not so for Hungarian purists. Their attitude demonstrates the truism that the shakier the ground of an argument – here the obsessive claim to an ethnically homogeneous nation – the more forcefully and manically some will argue the case.

But no one can blame Hungarians for rigidity and lack of reasonable compromise. They will flaunt accomplishments in culture, science and history as Hungarian per se, regardless of the dubious ethnicity of the Hungarian who achieved whatever it is they take so much pride in.

Sándor Petőfi, one of the greatest Hungarian poets and national heroes, is a case in point. His father, Petrovics, was of south Slav extraction: Petőfi is the translation of Petrovics, meaning the 'son of Peter', a common name format across many cultures. His mother was originally not Hungarian either but Slovak, and she spoke Hungarian with difficulty. Or take Attila József, another Hungarian literary icon (for many, the greatest of all), who described himself as of *kun* (Cumanian) origin on his mother's side, and a mix of *Székely* (Transylvanian Hungarian) and Romanian on his father's. The poets and heroes from the Zrínyi family were of Croatian origin. János Hunyadi, a celebrated military leader and a major hero in Hungarian history, and his son Mátyás Hunyadi, who became perhaps the most popular and successful Hungarian ruler, King Matthias Corvinus, would be unlikely to count as Hungarian with many sticklers for gene-counting. István Széchenyi, who acquired the epithet 'the greatest Hungarian', wrote his personal diaries in German, and Liszt, the most well-known composer identified with Hungarian culture, did not speak Hungarian.

Contributions to internationally renowned Hungarian achievements are most welcome from any background, whether Croatian, French, Italian, Jewish, Swabian/German, Slovak, Sloven, Serbian, Slav, Romany, Romanian or what have you. Having said that, you may encounter some Hungarians who will turn around with remarkable intellectual dexterity, and try to impress upon you the homogeneity argument.

Language for Survival

Although their ancestors didn't do their offspring any favours by settling in the crossroads of various empires, the Hungarians are an undemanding, grateful lot – they are besotted with them for simply settling at all. Now, considering that in this richly eventful geographical location most other communities vanished without a trace by being completely taken over by more powerful ones, you can understand that, for Hungarians, surviving as a community speaking the same language is a remarkable feat in itself.

The German philosopher and poet, Herder, gave a huge boost to the Hungarian survival instinct when he declared in the 18th century that the Hungarian language, and thus nation, was soon doomed to extinction. His endearing comments spurred the Hungarians into death-defying action to pre-empt *nemzethalál* (the extinction of the nation). To prove him wrong, they got their act together and successfully overhauled the entire language which at the time was in dire need of restructuring.

Surprising as it may seem, the question of survival is not considered passé by some pundits of the nation who go almost as far as to suggest that Hungarians should do themselves a big favour by going forth and multiplying as fast and furiously as humanly possible.

On-side Inside Europe

As far as Hungarians are concerned, since they stopped ravaging

Europe with romantic flair and reluctantly settled down more than a thousand years ago, Hungarians have always been the quintessential Europeans. Therefore, they cannot see how they could reasonably be expected to wait in the corridor, along with ordinary applicants, to be admitted to the European Community. They argue with conviction that they need no admission; they have, of course, been inside all the time. The only snag is that the rest of Europe has either not woken up to, or worse, forgotten this teeny fact.

Rule by Taste Bud

Eating, or better still, feasting, holds a tight control over the Hungarian psyche, given the symbolic importance of land and the people's continuing fascination with the fruits of the soil.

Hungarian cuisine is a demonstrably powerful part of Hungarian identity. Traditionally, Hungarian tourists wouldn't dream of leaving their native soil without adequate supplies of Hungarian sausage and salami. On the other hand, Hungarian emigrants will start growing sorrel, marrow and cherry-paprika, and plant a vineyard long before making any serious attempt to adjust to the eating habits of their adopted country.

Why Live Life Like a Drama
When You Can Live It Like a Tragedy?

As Europeans of old, Hungarians are into catharsis in a big way, and in a dramatic fashion too.

It should not take too much effort for you to get involved with a Hungarian hooked on living life as drama, or, better still, a Greek tragedy. Hungarians have not only preserved this most valuable source of European civilization in its art form but practise it religiously as a lifestyle. Not on their life would they deprive each other of this elevating experience.

If you are lucky enough, you may have your own fair share of infinite series of intense catharses. Just daringly dip in at the deep end and soon you too will acquire the Hungarian taste for cultivating feelings as pointless as they are persistent.

Délibáb Heroism vs
'My Pessimism is More Optimistic than Yours'

Are you an optimist by nature? Well, go easy on it in Hungary where optimism is often conflated with what Hungarians call *délibáb* (mirage' mentality: building castles in the air). Historically, they see *délibáb* heroism as a strategic nonstarter and probably that is part of the reason why they tend to regard the *délibáb hős* (hero of the mirage) with so much suspicion and even condescension. From their point of view, since pursuing pie in the sky and optimism can overlap, why would any reasonable person want to be an optimist and risk being perceived as a *délibáb hős*?

In any case, the general take on this is that optimists are probably not pessimists because they are either not yet sophisticated enough or simply ill-informed. For well-educated, well-informed Hungarians to come across as professional pessimists is almost de rigueur. Make vaguely pessimistic remarks or even just semi-articulated grunts in a sufficiently pessimistic tone to indicate that you are with it. What, 'with it'? In fact, ahead of it all!

Before you rush headlong to the conclusion that now you know what makes Hungarians tick, take a moment to consider the refined recipes offered by the deli of Hungarian pessimism. You can pick and choose from the delectable versions of pessimism available to you to express just the right shade of mistrust in the positive outcome of an event or of the universe in general. Hungarians savour their words as they elaborate about their pessimism being 'deeper than it seems'; how their pessimism is actually 'based on their optimism'; their pessimism is 'more optimistic (or pessimistic) than somebody else's'; and the all-time favourite, 'we should not be overly optimistic'. Listening to Hungarians, you will learn to see optimism, an attitude you always thought was basically positive, in a new light, i.e. as a survival hazard.

The attitude 'Only the pessimists – better still, paranoids – survive' will manifest itself without fail even in relatively minor events, such as everyday greetings. The routine question *Hogy vagy?* (How are you?) will not let you off the hook with a breezy conscience. What you will probably get is the quintessential Hungarian response: *Hát megvagyok ...* (Well, I am still around ...'), with all its historical depth, hint of heroism and existential implications.

SOME VALUES

A Család (The Family)

Two children plus their biological parents tend to be the Hungarian family model in theory and in advertisements. In practice, this model has proliferated and has been producing several alternative family structures. To start with, in around one third of families there is only one child, not two. Couples opting to have an *Egyke* (only child) are not a recent demographic phenomenon, one which is seen by some as a real problem from the point of view of diminishing birth rates, and also in terms of the child's personal development.

At the same time, it is estimated that around one third of marriages in Hungary will end in divorce. Since about three quarters of divorces involve children, this produces a plurality of family setups. More than 10 per cent of parents spent their childhood in single-parent families due mainly to their own parents' divorce. Not surprisingly, the rate for children in such a situation at present is even higher: around 16 per cent or more. Single parent families, as in many other cultures, tend to be the mother living with her children, which in turn often means lower living standards and other disadvantages for them. Nonetheless, some argue that it is not the divorce and its consequences that have the most drastic bearing on children, but the tension they may directly or indirectly experience in their parents' relationship sometimes long before the divorce.

Having divorced, many re-partner or remarry and establish a new family, often producing children from the new marriage, but also accommodating, to a varying degree, children from previous marriages. Judging by the statistics, the institution of marriage has fallen out of favour recently, whereas common-law marriage, and children born into them rather than within the traditional framework of wedlock, has been on the increase. So has the number of parents adopting children.

No Wedlock Deadlock

"Wanting everything instantaneously.
As if life, her life, was a film in fast motion."
— Péter Esterházy

*"Mindent azonnal akar.
Mintha egy gyorsított film volna az élet, az élete."*
— Esterházy Péter

Hungarians' general life strategy is a penchant to live life extensively and intensively, in a rush, as if they were trying not to miss out on something inestimable. To this preamble, a highly civilized (read *rapid*) and easy-peasy divorce procedure is a caveat. No wonder that Hungarian laws are exemplary in their democratic and enlightened attitude to divorce, thereby securing an eminent place for Hungary in international divorce statistics.

Backward European countries, such as England, would have a glimmer of hope in improving their divorce performance if only they had a grain of common sense and followed Hungary. Hungarian divorce laws truly respect the rights of the individual and do not impose unwilling partners on each other. It is only a matter of months before you can freely mess up your life again. This is quite unlike in England, where you can virtually die three times over before, in the eyes of the law, you deserve a divorce. If both partners wish to go their separate ways, it takes a whole year, most likely two (an absurdly long time for a Hungarian), of separate habitation before a divorce will be even considered by the English courts. Should one of the partners delight in hanging on to the other regardless of the other's desire, evidence of a mere five years' strict separation will do the trick.

As for competent Hungarians, this wedlock deadlock is, of course, a ridiculous proposition. Why, they efficiently get through several marriages in the time the English can barely manage to get divorced.

With a Little Help from Family and Friends ...

According to the statistics, the ratio of people living in extended families, for example where one or more relatives live with the family or several families live in a shared household, is low: around 3 per cent. On the basis of living arrangements this may be so, but in practical terms it does not really feel like that. Many families seem to function as extended and relatively closely knit structures.

For example, students during their university studies, and often later on as well, continue to live with their parents; they are not necessarily expected to leave as soon as possible, just to prove that the parents did indeed bring them up to be sufficiently self-reliant and independent. The Hungarian *Nagyi* (granny) and *Nagyapa* (granddad) tend to be institutions in their own right, with often vital roles to play in single-parent setups or in two-track-career families where both parents work full-time.

Family members, friends and sometimes even colleagues may rope each other in to help out in various ways. This can include anything like babysitting for the night; picking up, feeding and supervising children after school; or doing some sort of *kaláka* (voluntary cooperative work) at the weekend: say, mixing cement as part of a team to build a friend's house.

You too can become integrated into this fabric of social togetherness as a family member or a close friend. If you do, it will probably provide you with sustained support. It also gives you the all-important family, friends and connections that may open for you the coveted door or ears. It is a two-way street, though. Do not be taken aback if you are expected to join in and pull your weight, i.e. do what you can to help out if and when necessary. The request may or may not be explicit – anticipating the implicit opportunity to prove yourself helpful is unlikely to go unnoticed.

Whether they are looking for a gynaecologist, a plumber or the appropriate personal tutor for their children, Hungarians tend to grab the telephone directory – mind you, not the Yellow Pages, business directory or listings of professional associations. No, it is their own invaluable directory of friends and acquaintances they tend to investigate as the vital first step. A personal track record does give you a degree of credibility but a personal introduction provides you with authenticity and trust. Personal networks are seen as capital gain.

Siker (Success) – Posthumous Is Best

To be successful in Hungary puts you in a double bind: it's too bad if you aren't, but god – or whatever supernatural powers you happen to fancy – help you if you are.

Successful individuals are best appreciated (read *tolerated*) when they are safely and surely out of Hungary. And the farther, the better. Preferably stiff, tucked away in the realm of no return. This way, they can be freely shaped and explained (away) to suit the frills and frolics of any higher purpose and period of time gone by or yet to come. Why not save the risk, the unnecessary hassle and frazzle triggered off by people interfering and (mis)interpreting you, by just rolling over, and shuffling off this mortal coil?

This practical arrangement suits perfectly both the appointees sitting in judgement and those who are judged. On the one hand, reality is so much snappier to deal with when it has irrevocably become the past. On the other hand, for the individual concerned, once you are dead, it involves markedly less stress to process how you are (mis)perceived and (mis)used.

If you are the high-powered, high-achiever type wishing to go down in Hungarian history as a success of some sort, you'd better count on first having to be out of circulation in this fleeting world of mortals for a wee while – decades, as a mandatory preamble to

Hungarian appreciation, will do just nicely. Dominant discourses with their respective bents and biases will take turns in exclusively defining their favourite filter they like to call 'the truth'. It is a matter of waiting for the discourse matching yours to come around. Should the discourse in power deem you their match, they will exhume and eulogize you to boost their ballyhoo.

Should you be intrigued by the bamboozle of success in a quintessentially Central-European context, you may wish to consult the works of István Bibó, one of the major political thinkers of the 20th century in Hungary.

Anything You Can Do, I Can Do Better ...

The ancient game of 'outsider-insider' is consciously cultivated at all levels; it is done quite as you may have experienced it elsewhere, but possibly with more panache. Eminent outsiders thrive on patronizing insiders; intimate insiders are seen per se as no good from the professional outsiders' point of view. And vice versa.

Then, there have always been some unfortunate Hungarians who just do not fit into this neat little game. Alas, they are cursed by having an unduly acute sense of looking at issues from both outside and inside perspectives. Now, this exercise has mostly been a tad hazardous in Hungary. Indulge yourself in it by all means if your masochism desires the apocalyptic attention of those with hard and fast principles. And there is no serious shortage of this type. Those with no dithering doubts about 'right and wrong' will zero in on you and *zap!* zip you up in no time. How? Bear in mind, Hungary is not an excessively large country blessed with a relative abundance of fine intellectual circles of des belles-lettres and ideological camps. Ignore those who say the two, overall, overlap. Small wonder, then, if the responsibility of the intellectual as prophet and politician *malgré lui* is a very Hungarian topic. Wordsmiths or warmongers? Again, what a cynical dichotomizing of the issue that is ...

A more contextualized view will give credit where credit is due.

In Hungary, there is an admirable compulsion to 'correct' manifestations of almost anything 'other' than oneself, almost as if for some Hungarians self-worth were directly correlated with the correction (cynics argue, the corrosion) of others.

Just try to air your pet theories and see what hits you. It is not really reasonable to get upset if you get the impression that anything you say or do, Hungarians can do better … They certainly believe that they can. And that they do. At least in the context of their own particular monologue which tends to be, after all, one of the more dominant national discourse genres.

Health – Fuming with Anger? Puff It Away!

Hard-liners of biopolitics specializing in health and the right to breathe clean air will meet the challenge of their lifetime if they are to take on Hungarian zealots of the weed.

Challenging gloomy figures of smoking-related early dispatch, Hungarians choose to believe in their own immunity. Should personal immunity let them down, they fall back, with typical Hungarian bravado, on the stock response: "Well, it's just too bad for the facts …" – a not uncommon attitude in other less significant fields of life such as politics and economics.

Traditionally, many Hungarians embrace premature death with gusto. To carry out this mission, many spare no expense on their passion: they dosh out around 60 million forints per annum, i.e. about 6,000 forints per person (1997). If you take away babies and Methuselahs, included for statistical purposes, then the number is even higher. A Hungarian *dohányos* (smoker) will puff away insouciantly on his or her fag – on average almost twenty per day (1999). It is mostly men in their late forties and fifties, and mostly in Budapest, who pursue this self-destructive passion with a vengeance. The picture is not any brighter if you look at a survey of secondary school pupils in Budapest: more than 20 per cent of them smoke, around 25 per cent indulge in drugs, and 30 per cent drink (1994).

Hungarians' lack of care about themselves, like most things they do, is alarming yet disarming. As evidenced in Hungarian films, Hungarians only smoke before, during and after making love. A similarly inflaming experience is to enter a Hungarian elevator and exit a few minutes later transfumed into smoked haddock.

Health – Dispirited? Drown your Blues in Spirits!

Hungarians like multi-pronged approaches to achieving success.

Puffing themselves until they snuff it is one strategy favoured by 27 per cent of the adult population. Priding themselves on a sumptuous diet of anything as long as it is (too) much and explicitly harmful according to the current dietary wisdom (fatty, sugary, salty and spicy) is another alternative passionately pursued by many.

In case this painstaking celebration of life, Hungarian style, still does not precipitate an early enough popping off, the really target-driven back up the process with drowning their blues in spirits. Should you be feeling down, this is a perfect reason to wet your whistle; if you are feeling high, it is even better. Company is not company without a bottle; without company, the bottle is the company for many: almost 70 per cent of the adult population consume alcohol with a varying degree of frequency. Men with relatively little education and earning power tend especially to be in the grip of this drug; professionals are more likely to be social drinkers only.

Around 3,300 forints per year per person is spent on alcohol (1997). To interpret this number, it may be helpful to know that Hungarians spend on average around 87,000 forints a year on food. This means that judging by the statistics more than 10 per cent of the average annual food bill is committed to financing the combined passions of alcoholism and smoking. Sure enough, all that spilling of hard-earned dough to juice oneself up is not wasted. A not altogether unpopular Hungarian mission – self-destruction – is quite successfully accomplished judging by the respectable rate of respite from life facilitated by alcohol.

Below are some of the centres that help those who prefer to battle their problem with alcohol:

Central Detoxication Institute
1084 Budapest, Aurora utca 22/28
Tel: 333 6730

Drug Information Center
1184 Budapest, Thököly út 2/4
Tel: 290 2571

Drug-Stop-Budapest Agency
Telephone help-line
Tel: 267 3344, 270 2766

Depression
Being depressed seems to be a popular activity around many parts of the world, almost a post-modern must. According to the World Health Organisation's predictions, by 2020 depression will be the second most frequent reason, after heart attack, leading to departure from this world. The Hungarian trend seems to conform to the predictions. In 1988, around 24 per cent of those surveyed suffered from depression; less than a decade later, more than 30 per cent did so.

Men approaching their fiftieth birthday seem to be the hardest hit in terms of their general life expectancy, which decreased dramatically between the 1960s and 1990. The most frequent causes of death, including cirrhosis of the liver, lung cancer, heart attack, stroke and suicide, indicate the habits and traditions leading to low life expectancy (alcoholism leading to liver problems, smoking to lung cancer, etc). Whether for a Hungarian man or a woman, life expectancy is likely to be the lowest in Europe.

Life – Top Rank in Suicides

Apart from the exceedingly creative use of diacritics in writing, Hungarians share with the Finns a distinct penchant for suicide, without having the good excuse of long dark days inflicted on the Finns up north. No, Hungarians are responsible, self-reliant people and, as such, manage to sustain their leadership in the league of global suicide rates without the benefit of luxuriously extended northern nights. To call one's life off as a final gesture of project control has been a life management strategy opted for by a relatively high number of Hungarians since the 1870s. This trend continued throughout the 20th century, generally securing the number one place for Hungary internationally, and second place only during the world economic crisis between the two world wars. Traditional behavioural patterns and values have been changing, but relatively heavy drinking, depressive attitudes and suicide undoubtedly have deep roots in Hungary.

Arguably, one of the indications of the degree of alienation and societal crisis in communist Hungary was the suicide rate, which particularly increased between the mid-1950s and mid-1980s: it more than doubled in three decades (18 to 46 per 100,000 from 1954 to 1984). To have some appreciation of the relative value of these numbers it is worth comparing the data from the same period from different countries. For example, in 1981 there were 3.3 suicides per 100,000 people in Greece, 8.9 in England and Wales, 12.1 in the United States, 27.1 in Austria and 45.6 in Hungary. The suicide rate

peaked in 1985 and since 1988 it has been increasingly less of a norm to express one's disagreement with society by rejecting it altogether.

Generally speaking, unlike in the United States for example, in Hungary the traditional pattern of aggression seems to be directed more towards the self than at others at large. In Hungary, you are more than 10 times likely to kick the bucket on your own accord rather than courtesy of another person. In America this ratio is the reverse. Simply put, it seems that while a fatally frustrated American may go out and shoot others, a Hungarian is more likely to shoot himself, whether he lives in Hungary or in the United States (Americans of Hungarian origin tend to lead the suicide rate there as well).

Madness or Models?

"To be a Hungarian is a collective neurosis."

— Arthur Koestler

So how is one to interpret these statistical signals? As a sign of some illness or madness perhaps? In actual fact, just the opposite is the case. Hungarian history guaranteed throughout the centuries that almost each and every generation had a generous mixture of gene variety, thus ensuring a splendid biological variety, which in turn safeguards genetic fitness. So, genetically speaking, there is absolutely no rhyme or reason for the self-destructive tradition in Hungary.

61

Culturally speaking, however, there may be. One of the many reasons could be that suicide traditionally seems to be perceived as an acceptable, even heroic, act of defiance. The role models are clearly there: for example, Count István Széchenyi (1791–1860), often called the 'greatest Hungarian', a reformer, writer and politician whose contributions to Hungarian society are outstanding. Among many other things, his credits include founding the Hungarian Academy of Sciences (1825), the first National Bank (1832), the first shipyard and the first casino. The Széchenyi Chain Bridge (1848) connecting Buda and Pest, which has become a seminal symbol for Budapest and Hungary (see book cover), was also his baby. He started steam shipping on the Danube and on Lake Balaton. He authored many books advocating the social, political and economic modernisation of Hungary. The list of his incredible achievements goes on until it suddenly ends with his suicide in 1860. Then there is Count Pál Teleki (1879–1941), a Transylvanian-Hungarian aristocrat, eminent scholar, president of the Hungarian Geographical Society (1920–21) and prime minister of Hungary (1939–41), who committed suicide as a form of protest against Nazi Germany's invasion of Yugoslavia in 1941. But it is not just politicians who may establish these social norms as acceptable. Take Attila József (1905–37), one of the most outstanding 20th century Hungarian poets whose self-inflicted farewell in 1937 served as a model for a well-known and popular actor many decades later.

Social services to combat this problem are available at:

Life Mental Hygiene Association
1024 Budapest, Fillér utca 11
Tel: 212 4529

The Secret Hungarian Work Recipe: Workaholism Coupled with Navel-gazing

One explanation you may be offered to account for Hungary's respectable place in the international league table of suicides is a nebulous reference to work. The lethal cocktail of exuberant workaholism and melancholic navel-gazing coupled with persistent stress do a top job. Heavy drinking, smoking, a decidedly non-PC diet and emotional frustrations are luxurious add-ons.

Germans may think they have a patent on *angst*, a caveat to European modernity. But just wait and see Hungarian angst – it is done with so much more flair and intensity. Hungarian oscillations between euphoric drives to get ahead and melodramatic soul-tearing driven by paranoid fatalism are sizzling and spectacular.

Some Hungarians spare no pain to do the utmost possible to shuffle off their mortal coil, if not by suicide, then by sheer lifestyle. The English have hobbies like gardening, the French spend their life at the dinner table, and the Germans exercise. Instead of a workout, many Hungarians work themselves out and into the ground. Moonlighting or some smart legal combination of two-three jobs used to be a common hobby substitute. But nowadays competition is so fierce in the job market that often the same amount of energy, or more, is required to hold down one job as used to be required to juggle three before the 1990s.

Then Sunday cometh, but there is no rest for the wicked. It is perhaps as much out of necessity as therapy – or neurosis? – that many Hungarians spend their day of rest slogging their guts out building their house or holiday cottage, or helping their family, friends or colleagues to do the same, or catching up on work, or meeting some deadline ...

Hungarian living is a rigorous routine. No wonder if traditionally Hungarians have no qualms about eating for two if not three people. An expensive but sure way to secure an early respite from all this Hungarian hurly-burly.

A vital component of the Hungarian recipe for this life-shattering shake is profound and uncompromising expectations of European lifestyle – living standards befitting Hungarians' self-acknowledged place in the heart of Europe. For many European cultures, the 20th century, if nothing else, has repeatedly demonstrated how ephemeral bourgeois rites and rituals can be. Hungarians know just how ephemeral. The European citizen's lifestyle, success symbols and achievement patterns are greatly coveted: the more ephemeral, the more coveted.

Death – Fancy a Ceremonial Reburial?

> *"Temetni, azt tudunk ..."*
> "To bury we certainly can ..."
>
> — Hungarian saying

If you are into decorative tombstones and fanciful fences around houses, Hungary is definitely the place to tickle your fancy.

The bigger, the thicker, the heavier, the more ostentatious, the more ornate and monumental, the better. No doubt about it, many Hungarians like to make sturdy statements about boundaries to their private spheres. Awe-inspiring fences around houses whilst alive, and tombstones once dead, are authoritative yardsticks of material success, especially in the countryside.

Besides stating their status clearly by showy fences and tombstones, Hungarians are into ceremonial reburial in quite a big way. The tradition is highlighted by such prominent names as Lajos Kossuth (1802–94), statesman and leader of the Revolution of 1848–49, who died in exile in Italy, and whose official reburial in Hungary was a gesture of defiance. Count Mihály Károlyi (1875–1955), anti-Habsburg liberal politician, prime minister and president of the first Hungarian Republic (1919), died in France and got reburied in Hungary in 1962. Hungarians know that if all else fails, a reburial, such as Béla Bartók's (1881–1945) posthumous journey from the United States back to Hungary in 1988, gets them into the much pined-after focus of the European centrestage. (Béla Bartók is acknowledged as one of the greatest composers of the 20th century. He was also an internationally acclaimed concert pianist and a highly respected music scholar.)

So did the reburial of Imre Nagy (1896–1958), communist politician, prime minister and martyr of the 1956 Revolution. He was executed, on Soviet instruction, in 1958 by the communist government of János Kádár which, in return, deliciously hung onto power for several decades after the event. It took a mere thirty years for Nagy to finally make his way from an unmarked hole in the ground to a tomb bearing his name in 1988. In the meantime, in the absence of the person or even his grave, the name itself became a taboo for decades. There was a time when a sheer reference to the peculiar circumstances of his departure from this world could be sufficient grounds to fire an intellectual from a job, however humble. No reason to grumble, though. It took hardly half a century for Nagy to be elevated to quasi sainthood, after the democratic changes in Hungary in the early 1990s

Just two years after the national ritual of the left-wing Nagy's burial, Hungarians hit the international headlines with the relocation of yet another dead Hungarian body. This time it was the reburial of Miklós Horthy, Hungary's conservative, anti-communist regent of Hungary when it was a kingdom without a king (1920–44). His remains were repatriated from Portugal to Hungary in 1992 and the reburial was attended by senior members of the very same government which turned out to pay its respects to the communist Nagy just two years previously …

Politics – The Revolution Devours Its Own Creations ... and More

Hungarians are deeply embedded in European traditions in most respects; politics is no exception. Arguably, the period of personal cult and show trials in the 1950s within the communist bloc, for example, harks back to a most noble tradition of the French Revolution – to be on the top is the quickest way to the bottom of the pile, furthermore losing one's vital properties, such as one's head, on the rollercoaster drive.

The example of László Rajk (1909–49) illustrates the fine line between becoming famous then infamous, famous again, and back to infamous. Rajk began his chequered career as an engaging young socialist democrat and a student of French literature turned underground communist before and during World War II, with a detour (1937–39) to fight as part of the International Brigade against Franco's regime in the Spanish civil war. So far, so good. However, he then made the trifling mistake of becoming Home Secretary; a rather consequential faux pas in the communist regime of Mátyás Rákosi (a disciple of Stalin, exported to Budapest directly from Moscow), a ravishingly charming and remarkably self-effacing man – not. Now, Rajk was, remember, popular – tall, dark and handsome to boot – and had Western connections. Hardly surprisingly, he was singled out by Rákosi to play the part of chief culprit in the show trials of the early 1950s by memorising and presenting carefully constructed lies fed to him as his own confessions. Apart from being tortured, Rajk was allegedly promised a Crimean holiday with his young wife and baby boy to persuade him to take the star role of the main scapegoat in the show trials. He played his part as agreed; then he was duly hanged, along with many others who confessed to various sins they had never done.

A twist to the story is that Rajk himself fell victim to procedures not very different from the ones he had used as Home Secretary in his ardent communism. The posthumous life of the purger who was in turn purged was just as eventful. First he was denounced as an anti-communist spy, then a few years later he was glorified as a self-sacrificing communist hero. Then, guess what, he was reburied (1956), and a street in Budapest was named after him, only for it to be crossed out a few years later. So when you look at the street sign with his name crossed out, there is a long and winding road behind those short and simple diagonal lines.

Perhaps the only person never to give in to becoming a witness in the sham trials, and thus unwillingly collude with this criminal charade, survived to tell the tale – Béla Szász (1910–99), writer, filmmaker, editor and literary translator. Cynics would bet that this must be the reason why he has no street sign named after him. He left more lasting evidence of his existence though: *Minden kényszer nélkül* (Volunteers for the Gallows), his perfectly riveting personal account of the show trials.

Fame – 'Double-barrelled' Street Signs

In England, street signs are erratic; they may be displayed at corners, but then again, they may not, so you quickly learn to appreciate their occasional presence. On the other hand, Canadians prefer their street signs glaring at them, if at all possible, from the pavement as well as the wall. In Japan, street signs are virtually nonexistent whereas in the United States they are content with mostly puritanical numbers and geographical parameters assigned to streets – keeps the spatially and numerically challenged on their toes.

The Hungarian situation is not due to any sort of confusion on the local council's part but is a simple matter of Hungarians reinterpreting their past in a self-conscious yet demonstrative manner. Double-barrelled street signs (a new street name stuck under, above or beside the old one) have shown themselves to be tangible pieces of evidence for the fragile, fleeting nature of fame in Hungary.

Suppose you wish to find a street in Budapest. Be alert on at least two counts: double-check the year of publication of your map to start with, and then treble-check the street signs themselves which some-

A glimpse of history and change encapsulated in street signs. You can buy a recently published várostérkép *(town map) at most newsagents and bookshops, and sometimes at petrol stations. It is a good idea to check the date of publication of the map.*

times offer a choice of two perfectly acceptable looking names. Or so you would think, except that one, viz. the person who first went down in history then later fell out of favour, will be crossed out. You can pretty much guarantee that the name of the historical figure, concept or suchlike on the other sign is now the flavour of the month. This is how Austro-Hungarian royal figures, such as Empress Maria-Theresa and Emperor Joseph, made their glorious return to the boulevards of Budapest. At the same time, Marx, Engels and Lenin, along with their homespun varieties, have been crossed out after their relatively short-lived (a mere half a century or so) dominance of Hungarian public spaces.

Asking the way is therefore not necessarily a straightforward matter; should you be the cautious sort, arm yourself with all available names for the particular street you want. Otherwise you may well be flabbergasted when people shrug their shoulders in bewilderment regardless of how many times you repeat the address in question, demonstrating your impeccable and most impressive Hungarian pronunciation. Your Hungarian interlocutor may be either too young or too old to know the particular version you've unwittingly picked.

In any case, don't make the mistake of asking a traffic warden or policeman for the information. Your safest bet is probably striking up a chat with a convivial taxi driver who will not only provide you with instantaneous information but serve also as an instant litmus test of current consensus on burning issues, based on a representative cross-section of society, viz. their customers. Once you have initiated the dialogue, brace yourself for exhaustive and exhausting streams of consciousness: idiosyncratic stories will hit you in succession embroidered with the drivers' meta-comments about their own views as well as those of their various clients.

Fortune – Suspect
Wealth, like other forms of success, enjoys a catch-22 status: you are damned if you have it, damned if you don't.

To appreciate this Hungarian tradition, it may help if you considered divesting yourself of some of the old-fashioned reserve regarding private matters and try to cultivate an interest in other people's business. The silver lining to this tradition is that you do not often feel neglected. It is reassuring to know that others around you know what their business should be, i.e. sparing no pains to investigate your business. If you can afford it (whatever 'it' may be), how come you can; if you can't, how come you can't? If they themselves have it (substitute your object of desire), how come you don't; if they haven't acquired one to flaunt, how dare you?

In short, this is a delightful situation to revel in. Just relax and enjoy that for once in your life you don't have to suffer sleepless nights ridden with anxiety about how others perceive you: if you haven't made it, you are suspect; if you have, you are even more so.

Status – One-up, One-downmanship

Hungarians are of the good old European stock with an innate respect for democracy: they practise one-downmanship as well as one-upmanship. The stereotypical view that understatement is an English speciality whereas overstatement is a Hungarian trademark is worth a challenge. Naturally, the fine art of one-upmanship is not unknown in Hungary. However, Hungarians also practise its democratic alternative: one-downmanship.

One-downmanship is all about the Hungarian tradition of highlighting empathy with anyone claiming to be worse off than yourself in whatever respect. If you strike a tone of despair, do not be taken aback if some Hungarians attempt to 'outlament' you. Say you sound a shade plaintive about your boss: you may well find out how fortunate you really are compared with them. Should you have a bone to pick with your neighbours, they will readily commiserate with you by sharing horror stories about theirs. If you are cross with a friend who has just left you in the lurch, you may find yourself comforted by a cathartic narrative of betrayal.

One way of going about this is to gauge the mood of the conversation and then simply take your cue accordingly: briskly opt for either one-upmanship or one-downmanship. Empathy and emotional intensity do matter.

GENDER RELATIONS (WOMAN)

So What's the Big Attraction?

"Desire is fuelled by all but fulfilment."

— Ernő Osvát

"A vágyat minden izgatja, kivéve a teljesülés."

— Osvát Ernő

Hungarian culture is, overall, still rather macho.

To contextualize this, it is worth bearing in mind that not so long ago, well into the 1940s, much of Hungarian society was still agricultural, with the usual traditions that go with this social mode of being. Female and male roles have been defined accordingly. Roles and attitudes are changing, but role conditioning tends not to reinvent itself with the speed of lightning. Public and personal attitudes to gender relations and roles are contradictory and inconsistent, and are often a source of tension in families. For example, since the early 1990s both men and women seem to favour no or only part-time employment for women with children; at the same time many women who do stay at home with the children would prefer to go out to work.

Whether the wife works full-time or part-time or is a full-time homemaker, she is normally expected to do most, if not all, of the household chores, and to take care of the overall management of the home and the children.

Although caring and sharing 'new men' do exist in Hungary, it is much more common for men to think that they have done their domestic bit by bringing in the bacon, buying labour-saving devices and gadgets, and perhaps by helping out occasionally, say by taking

71

out the garbage. Sharing home-related jobs is not the norm. On the other hand, most Hungarian men just love being chivalrous. They may well feel snubbed if you do not give them the satisfaction of doing dangerous and strenuous jobs you could not possibly do yourself such as opening doors, entering public places ahead of you, dealing with the waiter, or helping to put on your coat!

But if good old-fashioned gallantry and machismo don't exactly grab your imagination, there are alternative attractions, more often than not ever so peacefully – not – residing in the same man.

So How About a Hungarian Romance?

"What utter baloney.
Has no one ever noticed
that reading love stories of European literature
should in fact turn us off being in love?"

— Péter Nádas

"Micsoda ökörség.
Nem tünt föl még soha senkinek,
hogy az európai irodalom szerelmi történetei láttán,
valójában el kéne mennie kedvünknek attól,
hogy szerelmesek legyünk?"

— Nádas Péter

Should your ego need a boost, your mind and body shameless flattery, and should you need to be generally doted on beyond your wildest dreams, getting involved with a Hungarian is an almost reasonable risk to take. It is not altogether unlikely that you will come across Hungarians who graciously spoil you and turn your mind into an erogenous zone with their wit. Incidentally, they will probably make it clear beyond any doubt whatsoever that you are the single most momentous event (for the moment, that is) in their life.

You may resist them of course. That is, if you wish to increase the titillation and adoration since your refusal will frantically fuel the flames of courtship (read *challenge*) to unprecedented heights.

Hungary, remember, had the privilege of having been part of the Roman empire like other European cultures of old. Latin temperament, however, rubbed off on Hungarians a touch more effectively than, say, on some Anglo-Saxon cultures.

You are the Tops! But on Top?

The English may be very proud of sending flowers on Valentine's Day – what sort of frequency is that? A predictable enough custom designed to gently bore the pants off you. You will know your lover is the real McCoy, a Hungarian on heat, when humungous bunches of exquisite flora or other surprises hit you at all times and places.

Distance is no obstacle. Indeed, the greater the distance, the more overwhelming the expressions of devotion. They will wake you up at the crack of dawn to buoyantly let you know that they still adore you; call again around 11 a.m. to inform you that they love you even more; then the phone will ring at lunchtime and you will lunch together over the phone; a quick buzz or two in the afternoon and just three marathon ones in the evening are there to reassure you that they love you for ever – more and more. And more.

Their exuberant passion will know no bounds, spare no time, energy or cost to satisfy all your needs. Irrepressible, they will fondle all your follies and fancies; irresistible, their passion will penetrate your privacy and, against all reason and rhyme, touch your heart.

Beware: it is bound to sweep you off your feet, rather sooner than later, and keep you energized and elated.

Veni, Vidi, Vici

"I was a most virile lad at the time and made no bones about the fact that I was a veritable man in my lovemaking. Let her whom I chose for myself also go mad and scream with joy, let her boast of it afterwards."

— Endre Ady, translated by Judith Sollosy

"Én akkor a legszebb siheder voltam belülről, s nem csináltam titkot belőle, hogy bolond vagyok szerelem közben. Bolonduljon meg és örvendően jajgasson, akit én magamnak választok, és dicsekedjék el vele."

— Ady Endre

Having conquered the citadel, Hungarians will flamboyantly flaunt their trophy (i.e., you) as if they themselves had begotten you rather than wanting to do the begetting with you; they will be expansively expressive about their love to all and sundry.

They will be imaginative, inspiring and insightful enough to drive you wild with desire; they will be sacrificing and sensitive with a constancy and consistency that could be termed sheer lunacy.

They'll expect much the same in return: only much, much more. In the quite likely event that you cannot measure up to their expectations, you deserve, of course, what you get: after being pampered in heaven on earth, all hell breaks loose.

Jealousy

"beyond the law, like an animal,
be like that, I'll love you then.
Like a lamp that's turned off, you
mustn't be if I don't need you to;"

— Lőrinc Szabó, translated by Edwin Morgan

*"törvényen kívül mint az állat,
olyan légy, hogy szeresselek.
Mint lámpa, ha lecsavarom,
ne élj, mikor nem akarom;"*

— Szabó Lőrinc

Jealousy is acted out with a sense of operatic climax that would possibly make Italian self-expression pale by comparison.

A seemingly mundane incident, such as checking into a hotel, may rapidly turn into an elevating educational experience on Hungarian double standards governing the gender code of behaviour. To the male receptionist's question, the Hungarian man may say in happy jest: "Yes, a double bed, and a big one at that." His female partner cannot then simply pick up the style of discourse from there and join the banter in similar vein. That would be a fatal faux pas.

Make no mistake, Hungarian romance conforms to and, as usual, self-consciously outdoes other European traditions.

It may help to bear in mind that demonstrating a sense of humour tends to be a male prerequisite; for a woman, it is considered by some almost a taboo. To have a sense of humour is, of course, an absolute must for a woman just to keep her sanity while masochistically indulging herself in a Hungarian romance. But she had better keep her sense of humour to herself, to humour herself – not her Hungarian partner. That is to say, if she wishes to keep the romance tumbling along in a seemingly endless series of spontaneous combustions.

Now, unless she has cottoned on to the double standard at hand, she will be at the receiving end of overwhelming and exhilarating joys of jealousy.

Impressive Physical Theatre

Suppose she continues the discussion tongue-in-cheek about strategies to improve the firmness of the bed. Well, it will suffice for some Hungarian men in jealous ecstasy to pick up the suitcase, storm up and down the staircase while throwing the suitcase wildly about. To this impressive physical theatre he may even provide you with a running commentary. Anyone in a forty-mile radius will enjoy his hullabalooing with gusto about taking sides and betraying intimacy.

To the unwary, this scenario may sound romantic and exhilarating. It is, if only you did not have to fall back on all your reserves of stamina to survive it. No common sense will clinch the argument in such pandemonium. No talk about the unfairness of double standards will cool off such a Hungarian man wallowing in nonsensical but nonetheless (rather, *therefore*) orgasmic jealousy.

It is plain silly to assume words of reason will pacify the pipshriek. Uncouth furore he will brandish as a sign of his true devotion to the undeserving wench. (On such occasions he will prefer to refer to you in the royal third person.)

If you have the good fortune to hit upon such a Hungarian man, reason with him at your own risk. A strategy that may just work to bring this type of emotional Rambo around is lavish, unconditional tender-loving-care ...

The Mega-caring Magyar Farewell: "I loved you so ..."

"When she hates me, I love her,
when she loves me, I hate her.
No other alternative."

— Péter Esterházy

*"Amikor ő gyűlöl, én szeretem,
amikor ő szeret, én gyűlölöm.
Más eset nincs."*

— Esterházy Péter

Some argue that labouring on building and nurturing a consensus-based love relationship with a Hungarian is, overall, like teaching ravens to fly underwater. This is grossly unfair ... to ravens. There is consensus all right as long as you consent to whatever your hero desires. Better still, you should anticipate effortlessly, and without ever a hiccup, even his most enigmatic ideas. Eloquently articulating his ideas for him may also work like a dream.

Now should you beg to differ, let alone stick to your guns – well, chances are that your dogmatic attitude, appropriating Hungarian behaviour patterns, will simply be beyond the tolerance threshold of a self-respecting Hungarian.

The mega-sensitive Hungarian lover may just get up one morning and nonchalantly step out of your life with the mega-caring farewell, "I loved you so ..." Unruffled, he will walk out on the 'one and only love' of his life, no matter how many times he may have solemnly and sincerely sworn to make you his perennial passion he would never give up, not being able to live – let alone breathe – without you. If by then the object of this all-encompassing and preposterously possessive love is bearing some intellectual (or other) fruit of the affair, that is surely and solely your affair.

Relatively popular is to casually let the love of his life know over the phone that his crazy haze is as constant as ever, with the minor difference being that the object of it has changed, and for some time too. The stupendous sincerity in his voice will remind you to respect the individual's right to impulsively shift the focus of eternal love.

Gorgeous Grief Galore

> "It is terrible, I admit that,
> but it is true.
> To love's to have your own heart
> kill or nearly kill you."
> — Lőrinc Szabó, translated by Edwin Morgan

> *"Hogy rettenetes, elhiszem,*
> *de így igaz.*
> *Ha szeretsz, életed legyen*
> *öngyilkosság, vagy majdnem az."*
> — Szabó Lőrinc

If you make the audacious decision to get intimately involved with a Hungarian, it may be wise to be prepared to savour elated moments of high drama. You may look forward to the excitement of perhaps being gallantly deserted on pitch-dark highways in the middle of nowhere. Be ready to welcome deliciously endless arguments in pouring rain and sweet running amuck in style. Besides other such catharsis-generating pleasures.

If you strike it really lucky, your 'fantabulous' Hungarian might do you the favour of restructuring your life by abandoning you at fairly regular intervals and prodigally returning in romantic flames at reassuringly predictable moments. Some might even have the imagination and flair to add further spice to this heady dose of infatuation they tend to call love by commanding you to vanish from their life at their whim only to plead with you to have pity on them and return. In such relationships, what Hungarians might expect in return is that you take the slings and arrows in your stride.

And, more importantly, that you daily, painstakingly, and above all, devoutly polish their halo.

GENDER RELATIONS (MAN)

> "Man, in his eternal egotism, has not noticed the vital difference between the two principal items of life's delicatessen, the woman and the steak; if I bite into a steak, it won't bite back, whereas the woman will."
>
> — Frigyes Karinthy

> "A férfi végtelen önzésében nem vette észre a két főbenjáró élvezeti cikk, nő és rostélyos közti lényeges különbséget: hogy a rostélyos nem harap vissza, ha beleharapok, de a nő visszaharap."
>
> — Karinthy Frigyes

The concept of sexual harassment is making its way into the common Hungarian awareness at an admirably leisurely pace. Hungary provides first-rate gender role models. Yes, of course, things here too are changing but you can still safely relax in the knowledge that gender roles are reliably entrenched, cut and dried.

Hungarian men are rarely emasculated by feminist dictates and dogma. No, most Hungarian men actually prefer to be done in by the myth of their own macho power, a.k.a. domestic bliss. Some Hungarian homemakers pride themselves on being the high-quality clones of their ancient European ancestors, the amazons: they will, by hook or by crook, fiercely enforce their bliss based on the mythical male ability to provide.

Occasionally women will whimper or brag about, depending on their personality, the casual gropings up their thighs they are expected to tolerate or even relish. But the general consensus tends to be that you get what you deserve – and you had better appreciate it!

Feminists are still seen by some, including some women, as glorified bluestocking bitches or bitching bluestockings – well, take your pick.

Sexy Versus Sexist

"Even today, most men practically see women as an object to derive pleasure from and have no more concern for her than for the Wiener schnitzel they eat."
— Ágnes Heller

"A férfiak többsége a nőt ma is gyakorlatilag élvezete tárgyának tekinti s nincs több tekintettel rá, mint a bécsi szeletre, amelyet megeszik."
— Heller Ágnes

A man, however highly educated – the head of a university department, for example – may not think twice about pinching, or even better, slapping the female posterior with zest. This he may be quite happy to do under the blazing attention of colleagues.

Should the lucky lady voice a word of complaint, such as "Now that was a rather *sexist* gesture!", the refined Hungarian gentleman will simply interpret it as *sexy*. To add insult to injury, he will rebut with something as frightfully sophisticated as "Oh, la la ... I didn't know you were in such desperate need, darling!"

Some, such as those terribly misguided PC (politically correct) dogmatists, might be inclined to stigmatize the innocent event as a clear case of sexual harassment.

Hungarians are much too broadminded and tolerant to make such rushed judgements. Thirty-odd colleagues may have been absorbed by the jolly scene but it would be less than smart, indeed quite unrealistic of you to count on the common decency of anyone present to bear witness to it. That is, if you had the gall at all to lodge a complaint about the sexist gesture to start with.

Time to get off your high horse of sensibilities and fairness and start appreciating Hungarian gender relations. Wiener schnitzels and steaks are there to be enjoyed, remember, and not to bite back.

Consuming Life – Consuming Lives

> "I did not learn the ways of love so I would know what love was, but so I could consume it, and burn myself with it, as is only right."
>
> — Endre Ady, translated by Judith Sollosy

> *"Én nem azért tanultam meg a szerelmet,*
> *hogy tudjam, micsoda, hanem azért, hogy fogyasszam,*
> *hamvasszam vele magam, ahogy illik."*
>
> — Ady Endre

Many Hungarian men and women excel in the art of seduction, when they really set their minds to it.

And many sure do. They routinely engage in banter, play with innocent looks, ambivalent words and gesture. Just in case you might be insulted otherwise, many feel honour-bound to make overtures to you, no matter what.

They like to pride themselves on having adventurous and imaginative love affairs, hectic and taxing marriages, and gruesome and gruelling divorces. Some are hot to trot to start the cycle again until popping their clogs finally relieves them from this compulsion.

Many Hungarians, as you may have already gathered, love anything that is challenging and consuming. They cannot possibly have enough of the joys and sorrows of life, including being in love. Or anything that will approximate it. Draining, it must be. If not, it is not worth doing.

Hot-water Bottle, Horizontal Workout, Ecstasy and More ...

"Albeit all humans were born to love,
not everyone is equally good in doing it.
Beside natural talent, loving requires
some theoretical knowledge as well."

— Tibor Déry

*"Az ember ugyan szerelemre termett,
de nem mindenki egyforman ügyes a végrehajtásban.
A természetes tehetség mellé valamennyi
elméleti tudás is szükségeltetik."*

— Déry Tibor

The English may have their proverbial hot-water bottle, coupled with a snug mug of Horlicks to rely on in bed. Arguably, both are underrated. Both are, granted, 100 per cent loyal and reliable but just a pinch predictable for Hungarian liking.

Then again, the Germans may cherish their horizontal acrobatics. Sure enough, it does wonders for body-building, toning and stretching. Yet too clinical – let alone exhausting – for most Hungarians.

The French cultivate and mythologize quite out of proportion the mystique of their boudoir ecstasy. Not bad by any standard. However, a soupçon too stuffy and stifling. And definitely overrated.

Naturally, Hungarians demonstrate their authentic European credentials in their style of lovemaking too – or so they believe. In their fully objective judgement, they happily combine the best of all sex-cultures: acrobatics, smouldering ecstasy and the rest. They will, though, grudgingly admit that they need to pull up their pants on the hot-water bottle front.

PSEUDO-GLAMOUR: MACHISMO

"If I am alone in a room, I am a person.
If a woman enters, I become a man.
And the more of a woman is the woman who enters,
the more of a man I become."

— Frigyes Karinthy

*"Ha egyedül vagyok a szobában, akkor ember vagyok.
Ha bejön egy nő, akkor férfi lettem.
És annyira vagyok férfi, amennyire nő az,
aki bejött a szobába.*

— Karinthy Frigyes

In Hungary, women who don't cry wolf at the 'ticklish delights' – feminists and PC advocates beware – of wolf-whistling will have a twinkle in their eye. These spontaneous expressions of male appreciation of the glorious female body make some Hungarian women feel their 'precious femininity' reconfirmed while perambulating.

Flirting is quite acceptable and practised by most, regardless of age, and especially vehemently by those who pretend to have objections. The implicit code of behaviour, if not the explicit consensus – a somewhat rare state of affairs in Hungary in any case – is that *flört* (flirting) is a fundamental and natural part of the female-male relationship.

Take a group of English women, enter a male; there will probably be no striking change in their behaviour. Some argue they will carry on acting just as genderless as amongst themselves. Take a party of French women, enter a male; you will notice no transformation in their style. They will tend to go on acting with the same self-conscious, stylized femininity with or without the benefit of a man being present. You may find on the other hand that Hungarian women, instinctive as ever, are likely to be triggered into a demonstrative, flirtatious gender role under the invigorating and inspiring eyes of men. Indeed, it may seem that both sexes labour under the misapprehension that not making a pass at the other sex would undoubtedly qualify as gender-bending.

Socializing in Hungary means tactile gestures; drawing boundaries is not a bit self-evident. In more inhibited cultures you can afford to luxuriate endlessly in the thrilling pleasures of creating an intimate sphere between the two (three, four or more …) of you (i.e. participatory flirting). This is not quite the case in Hungary.

Seduction Versus Flirting

With Hungarians, be on the ball and watch your classic armoury of flirting – don't overdo it. The witty repartee, the expressive gaze, the long, challenging look, the incidental touch of knees and arms without a boo, the demonstrative hair-picking off the coat on cue, pouring your prune and carrot juice over your flirtee by assiduously designed chance – these well-worn routines may work just too well. You may well end up in the snug (and often smug) clutches of the other sex rather sooner than you would have anticipated. For better or for worse, you may quite easily become the beneficiary of seduction of a serious sort rather than an active protagonist in flirting.

The game of flirting is used profusely in professional and other work contexts as well, rather like in France. Hungarians subscribe to the idea that personal chemistry facilitates work – and makes life almost bearable, even enjoyable at times. In Hungary, flirting is a full-blown art, all-pervasive and sometimes nearly subtle.

Unlike in France, though, Hungarian men often retain more clout in the process. Some of them have a particularly long way to go to be liberated from the burdensome role they are stuck in – by their own will as much as pushed and shoved there by the brazen will of some of their gentlewomen. Asserting their masculinity is the absolute minimum expected of men.

Having to act macho by any means in any context is many Hungarian men's delight and desperation. They like to come across as chivalrously macho but they can, and will, snappily change gear into hyper macho if need be.

THE FLOW OF INFORMATION

Keeping personal information to yourself would be an insult to the traditions of (almost) free information flow in a thoroughly democratic society such as Hungary.

Intricate Intimacies Shared Indiscriminately

Many Hungarians cherish friendship, intimacy and falling in love – perhaps even more, making love – but most of all, comparing notes about their love life. Comparing notes, yes; but not, you understand, in the rather limited fashion of other Europeans. Not to mention the English, whose pride and joy, that high-tech virtual lover, the hot-water bottle, is not overly talkative to start with.

Do not be surprised if you find that some Hungarians thrive on discussing the *act* accomplished, whatever that act might be. Discussing the ins and outs of the in-out – but not necessarily between the participating partners themselves – is as hot, if not more, as doing it.

Public, Private and Intimate Spheres

Hungarians like a good story. They love to share the ups and downs of an experience with all who have not had the good fortune to partake in a particular episode. For example, if they are recounting an operation they or someone they know have been through, you will learn about the angle of the knife and the colour of the doctor's eyes.

Learning how to crisscross the boundaries of the intimate, private and public spheres of life with ease seems to be part of the socialisation process. As a result, you may have your symbolic as well as physical privacy invaded at times and places you may not necessarily expect this to happen.

Being involved and informed creates mutual bonds. Indeed, it is a relief to learn that it more than suffices to confide in a single Hungarian the most intimate intricacies of your life – love or otherwise. Once you have done that, you can relax in the knowledge that the crossovers between the public, private and intimate spheres more or less guarantees that the often flamboyantly contorted information will be disseminated effortlessly, efficiently and quite indiscriminately to all and sundry.

HOLIDAYS

Holidays celebrated in some way or another include the following:

January 1: New Year's Day; a public holiday

March 15: Revolution Day, to honour the Revolution and War of Independence of 1848–49, and the beginning of modern parliamentary democracy, a national holiday

April: *Húsvét Hétfő* – Easter Monday; a public holiday

Whit Monday: a public holiday

May 1: *Május Elseje;* a public holiday

August 20: *Szent István napja* – Saint Stephen's Day (see details below); a national holiday

October 23: Republic Day, to commemorate both 1989 (Republic of Hungary proclaimed) and the 1956 Revolution; a national holiday

December 6: *Mikulás* – Father Xmas

December 25 –26: *Karácsony* – Christmas and Boxing Day; public holidays

A Daily Rite – Déli harangszó (The Angelus)

Hungarians take it for granted that their middays are marked clear and loud, every single day, with bells ringing all over the country, including on state radio. Hardly anyone thinks any more about the meaning of this old tradition, which quite defeats the original purpose of the exercise: to remind people of a certain momentous event.

This event is directly related to two major obsessions of the Hungarian psyche. Yes, you have probably guessed: Hungarian history and its inextricable bond with Europe. Although for many the origin of it is lost in historical fog, the midday-bell custom is a highly symbolic tradition linking Hungary with the rest of the world. Or, to be more precise, with those parts of the world which follow Catholic traditions. Er ... that is to say, where they have a church bell ... as well as a bell-ringer.

For it was Pope Calyxtus III who ordered the Angelus Bell – the noontime tolling of church bells – around the Christian world in the West. This he did for no other good reason than to perpetually mark the Battle of Nándorfehérvár (today Belgrade) on 21–22 July 1456: the resounding Hungarian victory of János Hunyadi (c.1407–56) and his army over Sultan Mehmet the Conqueror, who had been rather keen on gate-crashing Europe for some time. Incidentally, this did not prevent the Turkish empire from making a successful move later although on a somewhat more modest scale – thereby hangs another tale. In any case, the enchanting Turkish idea of 'persuading' Europe to become part and parcel of the Ottoman empire was successfully put off by Hungarians by a good part of a century.

An Annual Ritual – Endsummer Night's Dream

The pagan custom to structure life and mark time passing, such as the end of the summer season, is quite unashamedly called Bank Holiday in England! What else would you expect from, in Napoleon's words, 'a nation of shopkeepers'! Something this mundane, of course, just won't do for Hungarians.

Hungarians are into more imaginative holiday names and they also like to change them from time to time. The particular tradition and the name of the event picked can be informative about the respective politics of the time.

In any case, a high-powered celebration of some sort, geared to reinforce national identity, is de rigueur on the 20th of August, which has been variously labelled Saint Stephen's Day, Harvest Festival, New Bread and Constitution Day.

Presently the preferred name is Saint Stephen's Day. Generally speaking, it is to celebrate Hungary's birth as part of the Western hemisphere. In other words, it is a sort of tribute to the tenacious and powerful, i.e. dogged and harsh, rule of the first Hungarian king: *István Király* (King Stephen). He forcefully persuaded the migrating and pagan Hungarians that, were they to survive as a European culture, it was time to conform to the prevalent norms of the times. This agenda included opting for Christianity and abandoning their pagan beliefs, adopting a drastically more sedentary lifestyle, and serious job retraining: to pursue the agricultural mode of being rather than continuing hunting and marauding which Hungarians endearingly refer to as *Kalandozások* (adventures). Stephen's work must have been appreciated since he got his gong from the pope – sainthood and a day to celebrate it.

In reality, he did not initiate all that he is normally credited with. He actually continued the policy of his father, Prince Géza (*c.*940–997), whose sense of political reality thoroughly prepared the ground for him, and more. Although a nonbeliever, Géza realized that embracing Christianity was a caveat for Hungary to be accepted as part of Western culture. He approached this project with imagination and managed it on many different levels. To start with, he got baptized (under the same name as his son, i.e. Stephen), and brought up his son as a faithful Christian. Then he formalized a friendly relationship with Western Europe by signing a treaty with Holy Roman Emperor Otto I, and arranged a family bond, i.e. marriage between his son and Gizella, a Bavarian princess. He supported Christianity, and thus Western values could take root in Hungary. But, as we know, history and memory are rarely precise, let alone fair – a lot of Géza's work is now credited to his son, Stephen – hence Saint Stephen's Day. (See more in chapter one, *Image and Self-image*, under the headings *The Germans*, page 33, and *The Italians*, page 39.)

Harvest Festival, Constitution or Saint Steven's Day – whatever name it goes by, the idea is to have a ritualized final fling, complete with speeches galore, barbecues, boozing, fireworks and all, before autumn sneaks in, and most importantly, school begins.

— Chapter Three —

LANGUAGE AND COMMUNICATION

"Are you aware that there is a language that because of its constructive ability and the harmony of its rhythm I have placed on the same level as Greek and Latin? It is the Hungarian language!"

— Giuseppe Mezzofanti, 1855

LANGUAGE AND IDENTITY

Hungarians take it as an outlandish insult to their identity if you assume, as Diderot did in his famous *Encyclopedia*, that their language is just another Slav language like so many of those surrounding Hungary.

There are around a thousand Slav loan words in Hungarian. These include some basic terms like days of the week: *szerda* (the middle of the week, Wednesday), *csütörtök* (Thursday), *péntek* (Friday) and *szombat* (Saturday), the latter from Hebrew originally but arriving via the Slavs in Hungarian. Some Slav loan words you will hear all the time refer to relatives: *család* (family), *koma* (godfather), *dédunoka* (great-grandchild). Other very common Slav loan words have to do with food: *ebéd* (lunch), *vacsora* (dinner), *uzsonna* (mid-afternoon snack), *pecsenye* (roast joint), *kondér* (cauldron), *kolbász* (sausage), *káposzta* (cabbage), *szalonna* (bacon), *kalács* (egg-bread) … and the list goes on.

Then again, the number of German loan words, old and new, is also high. There was a time just a couple of hundred years ago when German was more widely used than Hungarian in Hungarian cities. Not to mention of course the other sources of loan words to Hungarian: Latin, Old Iranian, Old Turkish, Turkish, Byzantine Greek, Italian, French and so on. 'Magyarized' loan words from these various languages have enriched Hungarian and, once borrowed, they function as part and parcel of the Hungarian language.

Nonetheless, Hungarians take enormous satisfaction from the fact that, in spite of numerous lengthy invasions of their territory, in spite of being surrounded by a sea of Slav languages, they have managed to stay in splendid isolation with their own exotic tongue. They have made a virtue of the fact that being locked into Hungarian has meant uncompromising loneliness: loneliness, both in psychological and practical terms, since their language is inaccessible and (seemingly) unrelated to speakers of other languages, and perfectly foreign even to their very own neighbours with whom they have been sharing history for the past millennium.

You may not think of a group of languages, say, English, Italian and Russian, as relatives of each other. However, a look at some basic terms of kinship and numbers – always revealing when comparing languages – in these three languages contrasted with Hungarian demonstrates the point of Hungarian being fundamentally different. *Sister* is *sorella* in Italian and *sestrá* in Russian as opposed to *nővér* in Hungarian. Or take a set of numbers, from one to three: *one*, *two* and *three* correspond with *uno*, *due* and *tre* in Italian, *odin*, *dva* and *tri* in Russian – but *egy*, *kettő* and *három* in Hungarian? Even to the linguistically untrained eye, the correspondences are fairly regular between the first three languages, each representing a subfamily of the Indo-European linguistic group: English – Germanic, Italian – Romance, and Russian – Slavic. However, the Hungarian words clearly do not conform to such patterns of resemblance, even though Hungarian has been surrounded by, and has interacted with the cultures of various languages.

The elusive search for the 'real' origins of the Hungarian language has kept many academics busy for centuries and no doubt will continue to do so for aeons to come. It has been related to the most likely and unlikely of languages, including Sanskrit, Japanese, Turkish, Persian, Hebrew, Greek, Latin, Sumerian, … here you can safely throw in a few others of your own.

Hal and Kala

As to the theories of the origins of Hungarian, for some time now the Finno-Ugrian connection has been favoured, viz. the Uralic branch of the Ural-Altaic linguistic group. It is not as complicated as it first sounds: 'Uralic' simply refers to the European languages of this family such as Hungarian and Finnish. 'Altaic', on the other hand, are the Asiatic languages of the group such as the Turkic languages including those of the Avars, Huns, Ottomans, etc.

At first sight, this may come as a surprise since there is no way a Finn or an Estonian (Estonian being another member of the Finno-Ugric group) and a Hungarian can understand or even faintly recognize the other languages it is supposed to be related to. Furthermore, not many go to any effort to visit their long lost relatives' homeland either. Just as well, since according to this theory the Finns and Estonians are relatively distant relatives of the Hungarians in any case. To visit their 'close-knit family', Hungarians would have to peregrinate to the not-so-nearby neighbourhood of western Siberia. Were they to embark on this family visit, they would have the privilege of meeting up with (but not to understand, you understand) other speakers of the Ugrian kinship, the Vogul and the Ostyak, some ten thousand people in all living along the Ob river in the Ural Mountains. They would not recognize the relatives either since they would be quite hard pressed to discover any major physical similarities. This is not altogether surprising, considering it is reckoned that Ugrian anthropological characteristics account for a humungous five per cent or so in Hungarians.

Most Hungarians will be surprised to learn from you that the Finnish word for *hal* (fish) is *kala*. So there you have it. If that is not enough, you can always point out the contrast/similarity between *kéz* (hand) and the Finnish *käsi* or *szem* (eye) and the Finnish *silmä* or the Estonian *silm*. Or, if we go back to the basic contrastive comparison of numbers as before, *három* (three) is *kolme* in Finnish, and *kolm* in Estonian. This pattern of consistent dis/similarity, such as the disappearance of the final vowel in Hungarian, should clinch the argument – depending, of course, on what exactly you're intent on proving or disproving.

Diacritics: the Hungarian Heart's Delight
Another trick up your sleeve is to point out the perplexing array of diacritics spread generously on words in a decidedly random fashion in both Hungarian and Finnish.

Regardless of any supposed or actual connection between Hungarian and Finnish, Hungarians exult in the rich variety of diacritics in their own language. Apart from looking so pretty in writing and adding variety to texts that would in other languages bore the pants off readers, the dashing little dots for short vowels, and accents – in singles or pairs – indicating long vowels, carry fundamental meanings. Two words you will quickly pick up in Hungary are *bor* (wine) – not to be confused with *bór* (boron, the element) or *bőr* (skin) –

and *sör* (beer) which, if you want to avoid a *sor* (queue) on a hot summer's day, you will have to learn to distinguish clearly. So beware, accents are not just a question of tradition or aesthetics of baroque mayhem; they often do make a semantic difference as in the following minimal pairs:

alma (apple)	vs	*álma* (somebody's dream)
fut (to run)	vs	*fűt* (to heat)
hal (fish)	vs	*hál* (to sleep)
hó (snow)	vs	*hő* (heat)
keres (look for)	vs	*kérés* (request)
ló (horse)	vs	*lő* (to fire)
ól (kennel)	vs	*öl* (to kill)
szó (word)	vs	*sző* (to weave)
szór (to sprinkle)	vs	*szőr* (hair, fur)
szóló (solo)	vs	*szőlő* (grape, vine)
szúró (piercing)	vs	*szűrő* (filter)
út (road)	vs	*üt* (to beat)
vad (wild)	vs	*vád* (accusation), and so on ...

Diacritics are not just for the delectation of the eyes and to make crucial semantic differences, but to delightfully entice the ears as well. While drinking your *bor* in the *borozó* (wine bar) or your *sör* in the *söröző* (brasserie or beer garden), with each clinking of their glasses – carried on to a manic degree – Hungarians will nonchalantly toss a long word at you that will make you choke on your drink.

When you attempt to repeat their *Egészségedre* (Cheers!), they will roll about in convulsions of laughter unless you are particularly careful about getting the third 'e', which is in fact an 'é', right. After all, it makes a slight difference whether you extend your good wishes to your host's 'health and wholesomeness', as in *Egészségedre*, or to 'the whole of their arse', as in *Egészsegedre* – diacritic fans, note the missing accent on the antepenultimate *e* in this version.

The downside of indulging in diacritics, however, is that Hungarians spend the first half of their lives trying to master the ever so slightly complex system, and the second half uptight about whether they've got it right. But take heart: if a Hungarian keyboard is at hand, it will come complete with all the diacritics you could ever wish for. All you need to do is to configure your word processor for it, then toggle between the two systems. Oh, and don't forget to keep your dictionary nearby so that you don't get your toggles in a twist!

Tá ti (Tum Tee)

In some languages a specific part of a word is more stressed than in others – there is an 'accent' on certain syllables. This accent may be fixed in each word as in English or Russian; or there may be a consistent pattern used throughout the whole language as in Turkish where the main accent falls on the last syllable, or as in Polish where the penultimate syllables have the most prominence. In this context, be aware – and this is easy to remember – that the main stress in Hungarian always falls on the first syllable of the word. This is the case even if a word is a foreign or borrowed one. Therefore, an approximation of sounds nonchalantly lumped together will not do the trick as when, for example, the French speak English or vice versa! The consistency of first syllable stress in each word, and the distinction between short and long vowels are not peripheral options to making sure your message is understood, however impressive a vocabulary you may build up in an effort to master the language. You will not get anywhere at all unless you get the first syllable stress right, and observe the rhythms of the language.

The trick is not to confuse the accent marked on a vowel to indicate length, with the stress which is always on the first syllable – as in, for example, *fehér virág* (white flower). So, an accent on a word does not indicate stress. For example, do not be taken in by the accents in *fehér virág*: the accent shows vowel length on the second syllable, but the stress is still on the first syllable. Listening to Hungarian folk songs and the music of Bartók and Kodály is one way of getting a better grip on the language itself. You may soon find that the same sort of *tá ti* (tum tee) rhythm transpires in the music as in the language.

The useful parallel between Hungarian language and music does not stop there. If you listen to Hungarians speaking as if you were listening to a piece of music, you will soon notice that the general intonation pattern of utterances falls at the end. The majority of the sentences, and therefore the general pattern of Hungarian speech, is the ascending-descending arch. So we are back to traditional Hungarian folk songs again – since Bartók and Kodály pointed out that this rise-fall is in fact the melodic pattern of traditional Hungarian folk songs. Listen to folk songs to remind yourself to keep the intonation of sentence endings falling rather than rising most of the time.

Mami, Mamika, Mamucika, Mamus, Mamuska, Mamicsek, Anyu, Anyus, Anyuci, Anyóca, Anyucika, Anyuka, Anyuska, Nyanya, Nyanyuci vs Mummy, Ma, Mum and Mom

Since Hungarian is an agglutinative language, you endlessly glue bits and pieces to word stems – in the one and only correct order to boot. Sometimes you add affixes to the front of the word, mostly to the back, or occasionally to both ends. You do this to specify what you mean exactly. The semantic and stylistic subtleties at your disposal are endless. For example, if you go by the number of diminutive suffixes, such as used in baby talk and love talk, Hungarian is a particularly endearing language, and, by implication, Hungarians loving souls. What would the linguistic relativism of Sapir and Whorf make of the hundred or so suffixes to express diminution in Hungarian? Just think, for example, of *anyu, anyus, anyuci, anyuka, anyuska, anyóca, anyucika* and so on, all of them meaning 'mummy', based on the word *anya* (mother). Or instead of the various versions of *anya*, you may prefer to endear her as *mami, mamika, mamácska, mamóca, mamucika, mamus, mamuska, mamicsek*, etc, all based on *mama*. Looking at the amazing choice of terms to lovingly clamour for your mother's attention in Hungarian, suddenly *mummy*, *ma* and *mum* sounds somewhat pedestrian and limiting.

Legeslegmegszentségteleníthetetlenebbeiteknek

Legeslegmegszentségteleníthetetlenebbeiteknek is just one example, hopefully for you to get the drift, of a perfectly possible construction with prefixes and suffixes. The most challenging part of this, of course, is just how to look up the word in the dictionary, should you be brave enough to have a go at it. Do you look under *leg* or *meg* or *szent*? Obviously, first you have to have a reasonably sophisticated overview of the language and its grammatical concepts and structures, before you can make any intelligent attempt at dissecting the word into its core. As a start, it is helpful to know that a Hungarian noun, for example *gyerek* (child), has five slots for inflectional suffixes. Think of a noun and its inflectional suffixes as the clever construction of the following schema:

gyerek (child)
gyerek-ek (child**ren**)
gyereke-i-m (**my** children)
gyerekeim-é (**that of** my children)
gyerekeimé-i (**those of** my children)
gyerekeiméi-ért (**for** those of my children)

The good news is that the order of inflections in the schema is always the same – once you have an inkling of it, it is pleasingly predictable. The stems normally also remain unchanged regardless of the suffixes that follow. And the best part is that there is no gender complication at all! Once you get the hang of it, you will discover how easy it is to build new words from old ones. For example, you can delight in creating adjectives from nouns: *gyerek – gyerekes* (child – child**ish**). And then why not recreate the adjective as an adverb: *gyerekesen* (**in a** childish **manner**). Or complicate it a wee bit by making it a comparative adjective turned adverb as in *gyerekesebben* (in a **more** childish manner); or even a superlative at that: ***leg**gyerekesebben* (in the **most** childish manner). So next time you look at a word like *legsikeresebben* (most successfully), you will see through what seems like a jungle of endings and quickly dissect the morphology of the word, until you get to its stem, in this case to *siker* (success).

Having successfully worked out the morphology of the word, should you still have the energy and inclination, you can look up the root in a dictionary with a reasonable expectation of finding it there. This leaves you with only the countless other bits and pieces at the front and the end of the word, the meaning of which you may, sadly, have less chance of tracking down quite so easily.

Well, when you hear that the core of *Legeslegmegszentségteleníthetetlenebbeiteknek* is *szent* (from the Latin *sanctus*, or saint), you will surely rush out to take up Hungarian lessons immediately! But before you do just that, you might like to know that this particularly agglutination construction means approximately the following: 'for your deeds of utmost ability to withstand desanctification'.

If you do take lessons, you will discover that some of the mind-boggling haze becomes clearer – there is method in the madness. You will be elated, no doubt, to suss out that whereas most case endings disappeared in the Indo-European languages, they survived in great abundance in Hungarian. Whereas English has none as such, German a mere four, and Latin six cases, Hungarian boasts a plethora of them: between seventeen and twenty-four, depending on the finer details of grammatical classification you are inclined to follow.

Now all these bits and bobs added onto words to express grammatical functions and spatial relationships may sound either incredibly complex, and thus inspiring, or else intimidating – take your pick. In fact, once you get the hang of it, you will enjoy guessing the right endings. These are on the whole fairly regular; it does not take a mastermind to guess them once you are aware of the system. So, to give you a rough idea of what you can expect:

kert is the nominative equivalent of *garden* as in '**this** is a garden'
kertet is the accusative as in '**she** bought the garden'

Then there is

kertben (in the garden)
kertbe (into the garden)
kerten (on the garden)
kertből (from the garden)
kertnél (by the garden)
kertnek (for the garden)
kertként (as a garden)
kertről (about the garden)
kertért (for the garden)

and so on and so forth ...

Joys of Harmony

You happily conclude that if *kertben* is 'in the garden', then *tó* being 'lake', *tóben* must be 'in the lake'. Wrong. This would be too easy! After all, this is Hungarian we are talking about! In principle, you have worked out the logical solution; but in practice, you have to add yet another dimension to the already pleasing complexity.

And this is an idiosyncratic phonetic feature of Hungarian, which cannot be underestimated: vowel harmony. You see, *kert* has a so-called front vowel '*e*' in it, therefore in the name of consistency – vowel harmony – it takes only front vowel suffixes: *be, ben, ből, nél, en, től*, etc. Whereas *tó*, sporting the back vowel *ó*, has exclusive preference for suffixes with back vowels: *ba, ban, ból, nál, on, tól*, etc. So it is not so difficult to figure out the somewhat delicate business of vowel harmony between word stems and their respective harmonic suffixes. For the sake of simplicity, all you have to bear in mind is a general distinction between words with *i, e, ö, ü,* and their respective long versions *í, é, ő, ű* (front vowels); and words with *a, o, u,* and their long versions, *á, ó* and *ú* (back vowels).

Indeed, one would be inclined to say it is quite simple. Almost elementary, were it not for the fact that of course you are bound to see words that may look less straightforward, like *házikó* (little house), *virág* (flower) and *palacsinta* (pancake). Both have front and back vowels – which means they always take the back vowel suffixes.

And there is the luxury of quite a few harmonic endings coming not in two but three versions, to accommodate yet a further level of sophistication. Some front vowel harmonic suffixes come in two versions: front rounded *ö* and front unrounded *e* vowels. (Front vowels, you see, come in two categories: rounded as *ö, ő, ü, ű*; and unrounded as *i, í, e, é*.) No need to panic: this simply further widens your choice of mix and match to keep your cerebral matter in fifth gear when you pick the appropriate harmonic suffix to the word stem: *kerthez* (to the garden), *tóhoz* (to the lake) but *kőhöz* (to the stone).

Well, the indisputable elegance and inner logic of vowel harmony may seem to you like a minor issue. It is not. Your Hungarian may be perfect in all other aspects – you may get the stress, the rhythm, the prefixes and suffixes and so on right – but if you mess around with vowel harmony, it will not only sound a tad odd but may not be accessible either. Try saying *tóhez* or *tóhöz* instead of *tóhoz*, and Hungarians will stare at you in quizzed amazement, unless the context is eminently clear, like you are actually swimming *tóban* (in the lake).

LANGUAGE GAMES

You will impress your Hungarian friends if you demonstrate a rare degree of intimacy with their cherished language by nonchalantly dropping palindromes at the right moment. Palindromes can be fun to create. The idea is to stretch your imagination by rustling up sentences that have the same sounds, and mean the same thing, whether you hear them front to back or back to front, as in this classic example: *Indul a kutya, a tyúk aludni.* (The dog, the hen are going to sleep.)

Once you start building up your Hungarian vocabulary, you will be amazed to find quite a few words which are palindromes in themselves and therefore lend themselves to the game easily. These words include *lepel* (shroud), *kerek* (round) *sebes* (rapid, also meaning wounded), *soros* (next), *sörös* (beery), etc.

The observant reader must have also noticed the astounding number of *e*'s (the same vowel sound as in 'red') in these words, as well as in the very commonly used *Egészségedre*.

As a novice to the Hungarian language, you will most likely see the great propensity of this one vowel in Hungarian as monotonous at best, deadly boring at worst. Not so Hungarians. They cheerfully, and with the greatest conviction, boast about this wonderfully unique feature of their dearly loved tongue. And indeed, there are not many languages in which inventive users can entertain one another by talking in *Eszperente* – not to be confused with Esperanto! – a playful and often very funny language of Hungarian words where the vowels are exclusively *e*.

First it seems deceptively easy, since you can confess your love in Hungarian in a exquisite string of *e*'s:

"Ne feledd kegyetlen kedvesem: eszeveszetten szeretlek. Egyetlen felejhetetlen szerelmem, merengve, hevesen szenvedve epekedem esztelen estelente, s reggelente. Rebegve s remegve, de szemtelen kerge, reszketeg kezemmel kezed keresem – sebesen meglelem e kecsest. Egyetlen egy percet sem vesztegetve, neveletlen kezem nevetve szende s megszeppent testedre teszem. Esdekelve szentelem eszem, s teljes testem-lelkem-velejem e megfejthetetlen s delejes szemeknek."

"Do not forget my cruel darling: I'm crazy for you. My one and only unforgettable love, I am sick with passionate desire for you and daydream about you night and day like a fool. Mumbling and shaking but naughty and crazy, my trembling hands look for and hastily find your delicate ones. Without wasting a single minute, I put my mischievous hands laughing on your coy and alarmed body. Begging you, I devote my mind, body and soul, my whole essence, to these impenetrable and enchanting eyes."

And so on and so forth ... You can further enhance intimacy by cutting right to the heart of the matter: *Megeszlek kedvesem* (I eat you my darling). But then, as you proceed to express more passionate desires, the perfect harmony of *e*'s gets slightly more difficult to maintain in useful words like *Imádlak* (I adore you) and *Csókollak* (I kiss you) – not to mention even more intimate exchanges.

A note of warning: Hungarians naturally take great exception to anyone confusing *Eszperente* with Esperanto. *Eszperente* was created by Frigyes Karinthy, a wonderfully creative, often hilarious Hungarian writer, and is continually reinvented as a national pastime. Naturally, there is no dearth of *Eszperente webhely* (*Eszperente* websites) on the worldwide web. *Eszperente* is innovative, intellectually challenging, and above all Hungarian. Obviously, Esperanto being just another foreign language, and an artificial one at that, stands no chance of comparison.

S, SZ, Z, ZS, SS, ZZ, SSZ, ZZS AND THE HUNGARIAN ABC

But it's time to get back to basics. The Hungarian alphabet has 44 letters. The good news is that the general principle governing both vowels and consonants is a virtually constant letter-to-sound correspondence! It will help you a lot if you remember that basically you can take each consonant and vowel letter at face value. Thus a given letter will correspond to the same sound, and vice versa – a given sound is spelled with the same letter or letter combination. If you bear in mind this principle of letter-to-sound correspondence, it will make your dealings with the language around you relatively straightforward when it comes to spelling and pronunciation.

Furthermore, most of the sounds of Hungarian are as straightforward as can be for speakers of Indo-European languages such as English. Not even the digraphs, or pairs of consonant letters representing single sounds, offer any substantial challenge, as will be seen in the examples that follow, including *cs, zs, sz, ty, gy, ly*.

More good news is that there are no diphthongs, except in some dialects, to complicate your life. This means you have to pronounce each and every vowel as a separate syllable regardless of how many of them are adjacent to one another. Take, for example, *le-ány* (girl) – three syllables, *le-á-ny*; and *fiúéi* (things belonging to the boy) – four syllables, *fi-ú-é-i*! So, unless you set out to specialize in regional dialects, you can relax in the knowledge that there are no diphthongs in 'regular' Hungarian – an easy enough rule to remember.

To compensate for this phonological 'slackness', however, each consonant letter can be doubled to represent long consonant sounds. For example, there are *s* and *ss*, as in *hús* (meat) and *hússal* (with meat); *z* and *zz*, as in *méz* (honey) and *mézzel* (with honey).

The fun does not stop here, for even digraphs have long sounds, so that while we have *zs* as in *zsűri* (jury)' and *sz* in *szűri* (it filters), we can delight in *zzs* as in *rizzsel* (with rice) and *ssz* as in *szósszal* (with sauce)!

Pulling the threads of our language lesson together, in the section on diacritics (pages 91–93), we covered the different sounds. Thus the familiar vowels – a, e, i, o, u – will also appear decorated with accents – á, é, í, ö, ő, ü, ű – to cover certain sounds in Hungarian. Similarly, many consonants will look familiar, but many others will not, such as *cs, dzs, gy, ly, sz, zs*. To make this scenario a bit more challenging, if the consonant is phonetically long, you can expect an adding-on of the consonants: *cs* becomes *ccs*, *zs* becomes *zzs*.

Letter	Example	Pronounced
a	*a*d (gives)	*a* as in h*a*t
á	*á*lom (dream)	*a* as in c*a*r
e	sz*e*retlek (I love you)	*e* as in p*e*n
é	*é*n (I)	*a* as in h*a*y
i	*i*tt (here)	*i* as in k*i*t
í	v*í*z (water)	*ee* as in k*ee*p
o	s*o*r (queue)	*o* as in *o*ven
ó	l*ó* (horse)	*o* as in *o*ven, but longer
ö	s*ö*r (beer)	*i* as in sh*i*rt
ő	l*ő* (shoots)	*i* as in sh*i*rt, but longer
u	szor*u*l (tightens)	*u* as in p*u*t
ú	g*ú*ny (mockery	*oo* as in l*oo*t
ü	*ü*res (empty)	*u* as in the French t*u*
ű	*ű*r (space)	*u* as in the French t*u*, but longer

Those are the vowels. For English speakers the following Hungarian consonants may cause some difficulty; the others are pronounced pretty much as in English:

Letter	Example	Pronounced
c	*c*iki (naff)	*ts* as in ha*ts*
cs	*cs*ók (kiss)	*ch* as in *ch*ops
dzs	*dzs*essz (jazz)	*j* as in *j*azz
gy	e*gy* (one)	*d* as in British English *d*ue
j	*j*ó (good)	*y* as in *y*es
ly	hü*ly*e (stupid)	*y* as in *y*es
ny	*ny*ughass (cool it)	*ni* as in opi*ni*on
s	*s*ajnálom (sorry)	*sh* as in *sh*oe
sz	*sz*eretlek (I love you)	*s* as in *s*orry
ty	*ty*úk (hen)	*t* as in British English *t*ube
zs	Z*s*u*zs*anna (Susanna)	*s* as in plea*s*ure

Getting Your Focus Right

Hungarians expect you to articulate your words clearly, with the main stress on the first syllable – remember? Consequently, they are not particularly adept at interpreting approximations, however creative, of Hungarian words.

On the brighter side, you can be as free as you like with word order (well, almost), to emphasize different meanings possible in a sentence. Here, you cannot really go wrong, unlike, for example, in English where it can make a slight difference whether you say "The dog bit the man" or "The man bit the dog."

You are perfectly free to choose any of the following patterns of word order for the same sentence in English. Each of them shows a different emphasis (in bold):

Én szeretném megvenni most ezt a könyvet neked ajándékba.
I would like to buy you this book now as a present.

Megvenni szeretném most ezt a könyvet neked ajándékba.
I would like to **buy** you this book now as a present.

Ezt a könyvet szeretném most megvenni neked ajándékba.
I would like to buy you **this book** now as a present.

Neked szeretném most megvenni ezt a könyvet ajándékba.
I would like to buy **you** this book now as a present.

Most szeretném megvenni neked ezt a könyvet ajándékba.
I would like to buy you this book **now** as a present.

Ajándékba szeretném megvenni most neked ezt a könyvet.
I would like to buy you this book now **as a present**.

The choice is dazzling. So, *which* word order to favour, if any? I hear you say. Well, remember the stress is always on the first syllable in Hungarian words; similarly, the part of the sentence you want to stress also goes right to the front. More specifically, if you look at the

103

sentences above, you will notice that in all of them, it is the part of the sentence that is in focus, i.e. emphasized (in bold), which directly precedes the conjugated verb *szeretném* (I would like) of the sentence. There is, you see, system in the madness.

The Language that Reaches the Parts Other Languages Cannot Reach

The number of people who feel they need the challenge of a lifetime, or, to put it more subtly, are daft enough to attempt to learn this fascinating language is few and far between. With good reason too. You may well be a polyglot, yet you can safely assume that none of your linguistic knowledge will help you master Hungarian. Cheer up, though: your prospects will be distinctly rosier if your linguistic repertoire includes another Finno-Ugrian language such as Finnish.

Nonetheless, if you do make the effort, you will be no doubt overwhelmed by the warm encouragement and personal attention you receive from Hungarians. A Hungarian linguistic encounter will be nothing like you have experienced before. It will also be quite unlike what you may recall about some French people, for example, who passionately despise you for the most insignificant slips in your French. It will certainly be unlike your frustration with English people who dispassionately tolerate imperfections with a fatigued condescension, steadfastly refusing to correct your mistakes, however you beg them to. And it will definitely be different from the sense you get from Germans who mightily patronise you for not yet having recognized that the language of Goethe never really ceased to be the number one language.

Quite the contrary to all of this, as model Europeans, Hungarians display the much-needed spirit of goodwill and cooperation by being totally enchanted with your most humble efforts to communicate in their cherished, albeit somewhat perplexing, tongue. They will find your repeated attempts at Hungarian pronunciation simply hilarious, and at the same time find your accent irresistibly cute, however it may impede communication.

Be prepared to receive spontaneous, loving and apparently endless tutorials triggered off by a word you mispronounced or misused. In short, if you can bear the intensive goodwill of Hungarians as they focus with missionary zeal on your modest efforts, the most rudimentary linguistic skills in Hungarian will go a long way and reach the parts that other languages cannot reach.

Hunglish

Recently Hungarian-English words – Hunglish – have been enriching the Hungarian vocabulary at the most rapid pace. This is happening mostly in the field of entertainment, business, and science and technology. At times Hunglish could not be an easier ride for English speakers since the original English spelling is preserved intact. Here is a selection to get you going in Hunglish:

all right
baby-sitter, bar, barbecue, body building, boyfriend, briefing
CD, cinema
DAT, disc jockey, drink
film, fitness
golf, grill
hamburger, happening, hifi, hostess, hot dog
image
jazz, jeans, jogging
ketchup, knowhow
lift, love
marketing, mega, mix, monitor, mono, music centre, musical
nightclub
OK, ombudsman
partner, playboy, producer, profit, pub, punk, puzzle
record, robot
sorry, sport, sprint, standard, start, stop,
talk show, team, tender, thriller, top, trend
VIP, western
yacht, yuppie

At other times, recognizing the English words gets your brain cells working since the words borrowed from English take on a Magyarized spelling, or two spelling versions coexist, at least for a while:

baby *bébi*, bar *bár*, blazer *blézer*, bluff *blöff*, boycott *bojkott*, box *boksz*, broker *bróker*, bungalow *bungaló*

camera *kamera*, camping *kemping*, caravan *karaván*, cardigan *kardigán*, cheque *csekk*, clan *klán*, club *klub*, cocktail *koktél*, computer *komputer*, cricket *krikett*

dandy *dendi*, design *dizájn*, director *direktor*, disc *diszk*, disco *diszkó*, distributor *disztributor*

fifty-fifty *fifti-fifti*, file *fájl*, flirt *flört*, football *futball*

goal *gól*

hardware *hardver*, hello *helló*, hippy *hippi*, hobby *hobbi*, hooligan *huligán*, humour *humor*, hurrah *hurrá*

jeep *dzsipp*, jelly *dzseli*, jet *dzset*

lady *lédi*, laser *lézer*, leasing *lízing*, lobby *lobbi*, lunch *löncs,* lynch *lincs*

manager *menedzser*, match *meccs*, morse *morze*

party *parti*, picnic *piknik*, pullover *pulóver*

quiz *kvíz*

residence *rezidencia*

safari *szafari*, sandwich *szendvics*, sex *szex*, sex appeal *sexepil*, sexism *szexizmus*, sexist *szexista*, sexy *szekszi*, slang *szleng*, snob *sznob*, software *szoftver*, solarium *szolárium*, sponsor *szponzor*, star *sztár*, status *státusz*, stereo *sztereo*, story *sztori*, stress *stressz*, striptease *sztriptíz*, supermarket *szupermarket*

teenager *tinédzser*, tennis *tenisz*, test *teszt*, trainer *tréner*, transit *tranzit* unisex *uniszex*

visa *vízum*

weekend *víkend*

yankee *jenki*

Sometimes you will have to have a double or treble take at Hunglish words to make out their English version. This is often the case because English words will happily mix and match with Hungarian suffixes. For example, to express the idea of being engaged in the following activities, Hungarians conjugate the Hunglish word as they would Hungarian words:

flörtöl, kempingel, lincsel, lízingel, lobbizik, löncsöl, morzézik, shoppingol, szexel, szörföl, etc

... or take Hunglish nouns decorated with Hungarian suffixes to express the spatial relationship of being 'in' or 'at' a place:

bankban, bárban, kempingben, klubban, lobbiban, partin, pikniken, postán, szupermarketben, etc

... or to create plurals of Hunglish words as in:

autók, bankok, buszok, filmek, jenkik, klubbok, lobbik, monitorok, partik, sztorik, etc

Whoever says Hungarian is difficult? Once you have grasped the pattern, it does not take a mastermind to decode these words. Then, feeling more enterprising, you can start combining the plural with the spatial suffix, and come up with satisfyingly complex Hungarian words as in:

autókban, buszokon, dokumentumokban, filmekben, lobbikban, klubbokban, partikon, víkendeken, etc

So, is it really worth being turned off by the omnipresent, traditionally prevailing claim propounded in books, and generally confirmed by Hungarians and foreigners alike, i.e. that Hungarian is a diabolical language to master? Surely this chapter demonstrates that this is not the case, and will inspire you to get further exciting insights into this language, and, in turn, its culture.

Indeed, if you keep your wits about you and heed the rules of stress, sentence melody, the endless lists of suffixes and other points of reference about Hungarian, you may start figuring out sentences like this without even having to consult your dictionary:

"Kati elfaxolta a dokumentumokat a bankba, telefonált a postára, postázta a csekket, majd az autóját leparkolta az operánál, elbiciklizett a múzeumba, aztán a jazz klubba, majd a bárba."

"Kate faxed the documents to the bank, telephoned the post office, posted the cheque, then she parked her car at the opera, cycled to the museum, later to the jazz club and then the bar."

Words from the World

If you keep an open mind, you will find Hungarian words familiar from languages other than English. How about *rúzs* (rouge), *parfüm* (perfume), *bross* (brooch), *bizsu* (bijoux) from French; or *makaróni* (macaroni), *spagetti* (spaghetti), *frittata*, *piac* (piazza), *gondola*, *trombita* (trumpet) from Italian; or *szputnyik* (sputnik), *glasztnoszty* (glasnost), *pereisztrojka* (perestroika) from Russian.

Like in many other languages, in Hungarian you can also fall back at times on Latin, and use some of the following:

a priori, ad hoc, Alma Mater, alter ego
casus belli, coitus interruptus, curriculum vitae
de facto, de jure, deus ex machina, divide et impera
ex-libris

genius loci
in vino veritas, ipso facto
modus vivendi, mutatis mutandis
non plus ultra
post mortem, primus inter pares, pro bono
quid pro quo
status quo
vox populi

When you feel adventurous, you can also try communicating using English words of Latin origin, many of which are also widely used in Hungarian. Here are just a few to get you going:

calendar	*kalendárium*
cell	*cella*
ceremony	*ceremónia*
chanter	*kántor*
diet	*diéta*
etc	*et cetera*
organ	*orgona*
paper	*papír*
pharmacy	*patika*
professor	*professzor*
rector	*rektor*
temple	*templom*
school	*iskola*

All That Jazz

Slang is very commonly used indeed, in Hungarian both in writing and in speech; so it makes sense to be aware of its widespread use and of some of the most commonly used words you will encounter.

Hungarian jazz-talk, or *argot*, is imaginative and expressive, and it grows on you irresistibly. It is mostly based on words of Romany (Gypsy), Hebrew, Yiddish and German origin.

Romany words that have become part and parcel of Hungarian slang include:

babe, bird, broad	*csaj, spinét*
barmy, goofy, have a screw loose	*dilis*
bloke, dude, guy	*csávó*
booze	*pia*
dosh, bread, dough	*lóvé*
fell off the back of the lorry, stolen goods, loot	*szajré*
talk double Dutch, spin a yarn	*dumál*

Around one third of Hungarian slang is of Hebrew or Yiddish origin, used mostly in cities and especially in Budapest.

big shot, top dog	*baldóver*
buddy, mate	*haver*
cool, groovy	*kóser, kassa*
daredevil	*brachista*
dish the dirt, bad-mouth somebody	*mószerol*
fluke, hitting the jackpot	*mázli*
graft, grind, slog, hard work	*meló*
humungous, hefty	*behemót*
jam, mess, hassle	*balhé*
junk, rubbish	*bóvli, tréfli*
kid, bloke	*srác*
playing Twenty Questions	*barkochbázás*
stony broke, penny-pincher	*sóher*
stubborn, bloody-minded	*dafke*
sweetener, slush fund	*jatt*

Bocsánat, Kösz, Na jó and Segítség! – *Words to Get You By*

Segítség!	Help!
Vigyázz!	Watch out!

Doktor, Orvos	Doctor
Kórház	Hospital
Patika, Gyógyszertár	Pharmacy
Rendőrség	Police
Tűzoltók.	Fire brigade
Taxi	Taxi
Kijárat	Exit, Way out
Bejárat	Entrance, Way in
Nyitva	Open
Zárva	Closed
Ki?	Who?
Kit?	Whom?
Mi?	What?
Mit?	What? (accusative, as in What do you want?)
Mikor?	When?
Hánykor?	At what time?
Miért?	Why?
Hogyan?	How?
Hány? Mennyi?	How many? How much?
Túl kevés	Too few
Túl kicsi	Too little
Túl sok	Too many, Too much
Milyen?	What is it like?
Jó	Good
Nem jó	Not good
Pont jó	Just right
Szörnyű!	Terrrible!
Szuper!	Super!
Fantasztikus!	Fantastic!
Klassz!	Cool!

Kösz, Köszi	Thanks (informal)
Köszönöm, Köszönöm szépen, Nagyon köszönöm	Thank you, Thanks a lot, Many thanks
Szívesen	You are welcome
Nagyon szívesen!	My pleasure!
Tessék	Here you are
Tessék?	Excuse me?
Bocs	Sorry (informal)
Bocsánat	Excuse me, I am sorry
Ezer bocsánat!	Terribly sorry!
Igen	Yes
Nem	No
Talán	Perhaps
Persze	Sure
OK, Oké, Nagyszerű	OK, Great
De még mennyire!	Very much so!
Egyáltalán nem!	Not at all!
Hogyne.	Yes indeed, But of course, By all means.
Hogyisne!	Not a bit! Nothing of the sort!
Na jó!	OK, it's decided then
Na ne ...	You don't say ... Come off it!
Naná!	You bet! You betcha!
Na és?	So what?
Na lám!	There you are!
Na ugye!	I've told you so ...
Na mi van?	What's up?
Na na!	Come now! You'd better be careful!
Tényleg?	Really?
Ejha!	Gosh!

Hogyan? Hogyhogy?	How come?
Ezt vegyük át újra?!	Come again?!
	(to request to repeat something
	we did not hear well)
Szia!	Hi!
Szevasz!	Hello! Also, Bye-bye! (informal)
Heló! (singular)	Hi! Also, See you! (informal)
Helósztok! (plural)	
Halihó!	Hi! (informal)
Viszlát!	See you!
Viszontlátásra!	Goodbye!
Jó napot!	Good day!
Jó estét!	Good evening!
Jó éjt!	Goodnight!
Jóccakát!	Nighty-nighty!
Szép álmokat!	Sweet dreams!
Szeretlek!	I love you!
Hogy vagy?	How are you? (informal)
Hogy van?	How are you?
Hát, megvagyok ...	Well, not so bad ... So-so ...
Remekül érzem magam	I'm perfectly all right
Hát, vigyázz magadra!	Well, take care!
Kellemes Ünnepeket!	Happy Holidays!
Boldog szülinapot!	Happy birthday! (informal)
Boldog születésnapot!	Happy birthday!
Boldog névnapot!	Happy name day!
Minden jót!	Good luck!
Sok sikert!	Wish you success!
Egészségedre!	Cheers! (informal)
Egészségére!	Cheers!
Fenékig! Le vele!	Bottoms up! Down the hatch!
Nyugi-nyugi!	Take it easy!

113

Winning Words Worldwide

Learning Hungarian offers a terrific deal. For the price of one, you get two languages: Hungarian, which for most people is sufficiently challenging in itself, and its mind-boggling version, *Eszperente*, for those extra special occasions when you feel intellectually fit.

Perhaps the most enticing part of this irresistible offer, though, is that you will be able to use Hungarian in countries other than Hungary. Apart from the 10.5 million or so in Hungary, there are another 4.5 million or so Hungarian speakers outside the country – for example, in parts of former Hungary, Austria (in Burgenland), Croatia, Romania (especially in Transylvania), Serbia, Slovakia, Slovenia and the Ukraine. You can also practise your Hungarian with speakers of the relatively extensive Hungarian diaspora all over the world, including New York City, Los Angeles, Cleveland, etc.

Hungarians think big. Having given the world two fascinating languages (counting *Eszperente*), they are not particularly interested in giving small treats to the rest of the world in loan words. And yet illustrious Hungarian words like *paprika, puszta, gulyás* and *Tokaji* are easily recognizable Hungarian trademarks in the universal consciousness.

Paprika, the Hungarian answer to chilli, has made its name mostly in its versions from Kalocsa and Szeged. Beware and treble-check if you are faced with its *csípős* (hot) or *édes* (sweet) version. (See more about *paprika*, *gulyás* and *Tokaji* in the chapter on *Food and Wine*.)

Puszta has a vaguely romantic connotation. This is partly due to the *betyár* ballads recounting the tragic life of Sándor Rózsa, Jóska Sobri, Bandi Angyal and other Robin Hood-like highwaymen living, or rather hiding, in the *Puszta* in the late 18th and 19th centuries. What used to be the stomping ground of the *betyárs* is the Hungarian-style prairie, the grassy lowland in the *Alföld*, the Great Plains in Hungary. This extensive breeding ground of horses and cattle is exactly where *Gulyás* comes from, the thick soup traditionally cooked by the *gulyás*, the cattle herders of the *puszta*, over open fire (see more about this in the chapter on food).

Huszár (hussar) is another word that made its way from Hungarian into many other languages. It is rooted in the word *húsz* (twenty), since every twentieth man in a village was expected to enlist when the light cavalry was raised in 1458. The hussars' famous *csákó* (shako) – a high, stiff military hat usually with a plume on top – also made it into the English vocabulary.

Most people have also heard about the *csárdás*, the fiery Hungarian dance. It normally starts deceptively slow and brooding but soon turns into boisterous turns and leaps until it reaches its stormy finish. *Csárdás* is also the name of the music which developed from *verbunkos* (recruiting dances) of the 18th century and various pair dances of the Renaissance. Indeed, *csárdás* is used now as the name of any music written for or in the style of this dance. *Csárdás* is undoubtedly the most famous Hungarian dance and seen as the old, traditional Hungarian dance per se. Yet it is not a particularly old one. It is first mentioned in writing as recently as 1835 by the composer Rózsavölgyi, when he used *Lassú csárdás* (Slow Csárdás) as the title for one of his pieces. The *csárdás*, along with the language revival at the time, expressed a cultural political statement of the national romantic identity in the face of Habsburg oppression in general, and against *palotás* (*palotache*, dance of the palace) in particular. It spread like wildfire, and soon became the most fashionable dance, replacing other Hungarian and most Western dances.

If you see a *csárda* while peregrinating in Hungary, the thing to expect is not necessarily dance or music but rather a Hungarian-style village inn, its décor usually in the vein of *puszta* romanticism due to its mythologized regulars, the *betyárs*. The expected paraphernalia includes thatched roof and veranda, candles, folksy objects and peasant tools and harness. Ceiling lights made of carriage wheels and a *cimbalom* player are also de rigueur in an aspiring *csárda*.

One word that is extremely common in several European languages – and not generally recognized as of Hungarian etymology – is 'coach' (Hungarian *kocsi* meaning *kocs*-i, something coming from

115

Kocs). Again, it is particularly appropriate, and adds to Hungarians' European credentials that this should be so since this light, early means of rapid transportation facilitated mobility and international communication, thus acting as an important catalyst to European integration.

Keeping up this tradition, Hungarian *Ikarus* buses – named after the more aspiring than fortunate mythical figure and operating in the most likely and unlikely parts of the world – have their ancestry in these light, rapid carriages first produced in the Transdanubian village of Kocs (midway between Budapest and Vienna), doomed any moment now to international fame.

In the 15th century, such a spectacularly fast carriage, that is, one that covered 45 miles (75 km in Euro-Hungarian) per day, made an excellent royal present for Charles VII of France when, in 1457, Lesley V of Hungary and Bohemia proposed to Charles's daughter, Madeleine.

This, of course, is another clear piece of evidence for the Hungarian historical-cultural argument for the unequivocal, well-established place of Hungarians in the heart of Europe where, remember, they have always belonged ...

WHY LEARN MAGYARUL (HUNGARIAN)?

Do not be taken in by the myth. Whatever many Hungarians and most foreigners and guidebooks say, learning Hungarian is perfectly feasible – even exhilarating. Take the plunge and put some of your time, money and energy into studying it and you will be rewarded on many levels. You will get a more profound insight into the culture, establish trust with its people much more readily, and ultimately will be likely to have more control over what is going on around you. Although these may be considered truisms that hold for all cultures and languages, if they fail to get you going, consider the following.

To start with, there is the psychological argument to ponder. As you may have gathered by now, for various reasons Hungarians have a rather special relationship with their mother tongue. Many Hungarians would argue that it is a significantly more intimate affair than you can possibly imagine – ever. Therefore, your attempt to learn Hungarian will be appreciated accordingly. In fact, your gesture will have momentous social-symbolic significance.

Should you not care much for the intangibles of soft sciences such as psychology and the like, there are also the hard facts – that is, if you accept statistics as a relatively trustworthy indication of reality. Either way, the following is well worth a thought. In Hungary, a mere 6.1 per cent of the post-18 adult population speaks reasonable German, 5.1 per cent English, 2 per cent Russian, 0.9 per cent French, 0.5 Italian and 0.9 per cent some other language. (Terestyényi, 1997). Well, you may ask yourself, what is the likelihood of me striking lucky and interacting consistently with this tiny proportion of the population?

The good news is that the data according to age groups makes it clear that your chances for meaningful communication are decidedly brighter if you limit your discourse activities exclusively to teenagers. You see, 12 per cent of those aged 14–17 speak English and German, 1 per cent French and Italian, 0 per cent Russian. Whereas if you were to interact with people in, say, the 31–40 age group, you would find that only 5 per cent and 6 per cent of them speak German and English respectively. It may be of some consolation to hear that 3 per cent of this age bracket will converse with you in Russian – should that be your heart's desire.

Mind you, the situation may be rosier, considering that the data is based on the subjective self-assessment of the survey's respondents. On the other hand, it may also be worse. After all, one man's 'reasonable fluency' is another man's 'shocking incompetence', so to speak. In any case, the approximately 16 per cent of Hungarians speaking some foreign language do not compare too favourably with, say, the 50 per cent of Austrians armed with some foreign language competence. The reasons for this impressive discrepancy are diverse, including four decades of mandatory, and generally atrociously

117

taught, Russian at all levels of the education system, with first total, then relative lack of freedom to travel abroad to boot. It is hardly surprising then that foreign language learning was not necessarily the top priority of the vast majority of the population for a good while.

The current trends are auspicious – more and more professional people may well be able to accommodate you in English or German, especially in Budapest and urban, educated areas. English is the favourite with the young, the university-educated and women in general; whereas German tends to be preferred primarily in less urbanized areas.

Present trends notwithstanding, the fact of the matter is that some investment in acquiring Hungarian is bound to bring significant benefits to your personal, social and business relationships. Even if your Hungarian discourse partners can communicate, say, in English at some level, the possibilities for mutual misunderstanding are endless, be it a transactional or a phatic exchange. There is understanding, and there is understanding. Your Hungarian language skills will reduce your discourse vulnerability, and provide you with a control mechanism for the level of understanding achieved.

The fundamentals of the framework of the *Magyar nyelv* (Hungarian tongue) in this chapter are meant to give you a general orientation towards Hungarian. It is to prepare you to know what to expect and thus, no doubt, to experience a more satisfying encounter with the language. The paradigm shift in your language expectation is imperative but not altogether that grinding, once you are aware of the need to switch.

The choice of readily available Hungarian language textbooks and tapes has some catching up to do, compared with the deluge of learning materials in some other languages. The trickiest part of learning this language is, arguably, grammar. Nonetheless, far from tedious, it will please you with a plethora of revelations about language and what it can do in ways you would never have expected. It may be beneficial to visualise your encounters with the Hungarian language as ones of experiencing the culture and a different way of thinking rather than just using it as a pragmatic, communicative instrument. You will be amazed by the insightful reflections you can make about how reality is recreated in a different language.

Where to Learn Magyarul (Hungarian)

Teaching Hungarian to speakers of other languages is a relatively young industry. It exists nonetheless both in and outside Hungary. Prices tend to be reasonable but, as with most things, it makes sense to shop around. Your choice will also depend on the type of language learner you are – so it is vital to explore your own preferences first. Do you like the intimacy of one-to-one tutorials or perhaps thrive on group dynamics? Is the location or the teacher's personality of prime importance? What is your timeframe and the degree of fluency you are aiming for?

Rather than drifting into the first Hungarian course you come across, as many people do, first reflect on and prioritise what you really need. Then make your expectations absolutely clear to the teachers, and sign up for the course only if it clearly matches your specific needs. Pinpoint the reasons why you are committing yourself to this intellectual expedition. Is it surviving in everyday life, negotiating in business or socialising; watching Hungarian films, getting the drift of local papers or delighting in Karinthy's novels; analysing Bartók's 'Dance Suite' or perhaps understanding or even cracking jokes? Similarly, which skill do you crave the most – writing, reading, listening or speaking? Does the rational and analytical approach turn you on or, on the contrary, does the more relaxed, spontaneous process seem to work for you? And so on …

Why not take an intensive course first, then refine and keep up your knowledge with regular classes, preferably several times a week? If you are a relative novice to language learning, or even worse, carry the psychological baggage of earlier frustrating experiences, try to focus on the characteristics of a 'good language learner'. Being inquisitive, risk-taking, tolerant, experimental, reflective, outgoing, organized and persistent are some of the qualities you want to aim for to meet this challenge – a list not unlike those for successful project management. A good sense of humour will come in handy as well.

Learning to Learn English by Gail Ellis and Barbara Sinclair (Cambridge University Press, Cambridge: 1989), although a training book geared for learners of English, will help you just the same to locate the most effective strategies for you as a learner of Hungarian.

Having embarked on the expedition to learn Hungarian, you will find your fellow Hungarians, their everyday rituals, otherwise meaningless signs, and indeed all aspects of life around you, will suddenly metamorphose into your very own, enticing learning resources. Who could ask for anything more?

Some of the places to learn Hungarian in Budapest include:

Hungarian Language School (HLS)
Year-round Hungarian courses and intensive 2–6 week summer workshops.
1068 Budapest
Rippl Rónai u. 4
Fax: 351 11 93

InterClub Hungarian Language School (HLS)
Company as well as one-to-one courses; 10 per cent discount for students.
1111 Budapest
Bertalan L. utca 17
Tel/Fax: 365 25 35
E-mail: interclub@hpconline.com
Website: www.hpconline.com/interclub

Inside Word Hungarian Language Centre (HLC)
Occasional 10 per cent discount on all courses.
1123 Budapest
Nagyenyed utca 11 I/1
Tel/Fax: 212 62 28

Eötvös Lóránd University (ELTE) Faculty of Humanities
Summer courses and intensive Hungarian courses for foreigners.
Budapest, V. Pesti Barnabás utca 1
Tel: 267 09 66 Fax: 266 35 21
Postal address: 1364 Budapest Pf 107

Arany János Nyelviskola (János Arany Language School)
With many local branches teaching several different languages,
including Hungarian. 10 per cent discount for students.
Budapest VI
Csengery utca 68

Magyar Nyelvi Intézet Nyelviskola
(Hungarian Language Institute, HLI)
Intensive courses and preparation in Hungarian for university in
Hungary and language exams.
1113 Budapest
Zsombolyai u. 3. 2nd Floor
Tel/Fax: 385 2
Fax: 319 32 18
E-mail: hlinst@mail.matav.hu

Magyar-British International School (MBIS)
Children aged 3–18 can prepare for the Hungarian GCSE (General
Certificate of Secondary Education) exam validated by the GCSE
University of London Examinations.
MBIS Main Office:
1026 Budapest
Pasaréti út 82-84
Tel: 200 75 72
Fax: 200 75 73
E-mail: mbis@pronet.hu

MBIS Nursery
1126 Budapest
Beethoven u. 1/c
Tel: 213 87 75

121

IN SZÉKESFEHÉRVÁR

Magyar-British International School (MBIS)
8002 Székesfehérvár
Lomnici út 82
Tel/Fax: (22) 300 119

IN DEBRECEN

Debreceni Nyári Egyetem (Debrecen Summer School)
The Debrecen Summer School is part of Kossuth Lajos University.
It offers a variety of courses in Hungarian language and also in
Hungarian Studies. Returnees get a 10 per cent discount.
Debrecen 4032
Egyetem tér 1
Postal address: Debrecen Pf35, 4010, Hungary
website: http://summer06.sum.klte.hu

— *Chapter Four* —

SOCIALIZING WITH HUNGARIANS

"A HUNGARIAN SHALL NOT SPEAK ..."

From the boisterous and chaotic arguments amongst Hungarians, it will not be totally self-evident that they traditionally have an image of themselves as the strong, silent type. Taciturn behaviour is seen as a deliberate strategy to pre-empt or sidestep any trouble, as in the popular saying, *nem szól szám, nem fáj fejem* (if I keep my mouth shut, I won't get a headache). Hungarian wisdom, encapsulated in sayings about successful life strategies, also holds that *sok beszéd szegénység* (a lot of talking leads to poverty – the wiser, the more reticent).

Paradoxically, silence is not particularly well tolerated. It tends to be viewed as suspicious and destructive in the long run; people wrapped in silence are often referred to as *csendes víz partot mos* (still waters wash away the riverbanks), rather than 'running deep'.

Then again, Hungarians are not easy to please, since, should you be perceived as overly talkative, you will be told in no uncertain terms that *sok beszédnek sok az alja* (a lot of talk is watery speech). Mealtimes are supposed to be particularly sacred. The oft-repeated saying, *Magyar ember evés közben nem beszél* (a Hungarian shall not speak while eating), encapsulates this notion. Since the taboo of speech during mealtimes is ingrained in children's minds, they have some adjusting to do when they become adults and realize mealtimes are in fact a very important part of socializing and therefore prime time for discussion. Hungarians, in spite of this popular saying, do in fact often talk profusely while eating. Some say it is only when they prefer others not to, that this saying comes in so handy.

However, talking is not always de rigueur at the table: after a heavy Hungarian meal, people are more likely to fall into a state of stupefied silence than launch into loquacious argument.

Argumentative – or Simply Assertive?

Hungarians may often appear to act in an arrogant rather than an assertive way, a flaunting of national pride. This may seem a bit odd in the light of popular perceptions of their performance in history: they have hardly been the best goal scorers, right? Well, wrong … actually.

First of all there have been times, as in the period of King Lewis the Great or the renaissance court of King Matthias Corvinus, when Vienna, for example, was part of the Hungary which they still feel they can take pride in by any standard.

Secondly, as suggested before, their mannerisms may be a kind of sublimation of their sense of self-pity; self-pity, at having been so misperceived by the rest of the world for the most part of their history.

Verbal Warfare

One Hungarian will suffice abundantly to pick an argument; with no one else in sight, he will be happy to do a round with himself. Take two Hungarians, and the argument will really go wild. Get a group of them together, and all you have is chaotic interruptions parading as discussion. They will enjoy it since the aim is not really to engage the content of the conversation, but simply to make sure their own theories and obsessions are properly aired.

Verbal exchanges are often highly competitive and intense. Repartees and unsolicited advice to all and sundry abound. 'Everything you can do, I can do better' is a favourite assumption, be it telling a joke, reading between the lines or decoding a cult movie.

Jostling to have the last word in a debate is a common pursuit. The much-heard admonition *Azt hiszed tied az utolsó szó?* (You think you can have the last word?) is to deny children the last word and thus put them in their proper place. The 'last word' trick is also customary between adults engaged in playing the debate game as children, relentlessly vying to be one up in the hierarchy.

Their style of argument will lead you to believe that they are on the verge of slitting each other's throats; but relax – mostly it is verbal warfare with Hungarian flair. Direct, awe-inspiringly confrontational discourse, with stormy, overlapping turn-taking. Stimulating stuff, really, once you know what to expect …

Ami szívemen a számon … (Whatever is in my heart …)

Hungarians are mostly of the coherent, integrated type: one person may quite happily hold amazingly incompatible views, and argue each with the same passion and conviction. Whatever the view expressed, it will be clean-cut, black or white. The wishy-washy, dilly-dallying of the English with their surfeit of expressions such as 'That could well be so but …' and 'I shouldn't necessarily think so …' is greatly mistrusted. Hedging is not a native Hungarian art form, however brilliant they may be at sitting on the fence when they want to. As Hungarians say, often with modest pride in their eyes: *Ami szívemen, a számon.* (Whatever is in my heart is on my lips!) As far as common sayings reveal aspects of a culture, Hungarians seem to value wearing one's heart on one's sleeve, preferably in a vivid and vivacious manner that will either impress or shock you with its muscularity.

They may, of course, deviate from their ideal of saying what they mean if they deem it instrumental, but would still get annoyed by others doing the same.

Szemembe nézz, ha hozzád beszélek!
(Now, look me in the eye when I'm speaking to you)

Ongoing eye contact, gazing openly and honestly into the other's eyes, is considered imperative, especially for the more manipulative discourses and transactions. For Hungarians, displays of direct eye contact are important for signalling an honest exchange between equals; shifting eyes are seen as suggesting a shifty character. Children are brought up with the exhortation of 'now, look me in the eye when I'm speaking to you', the implication being 'tell me the truth and nothing but the truth'.

The adult-to-adult version of this runs like this: *Na, mered a szemembe mondani?* (Now, dare you tell me that into my eye?) The illocutionary force of this verbal threat disguised as a question is serious. Rather than calling the other person an outright liar, this lightly veiled accusation is a relative face-saver for both parties concerned, allowing them to retreat from the conflict with a degree of self-respect. The tacit understanding of this verbal play is that whatever falsehoods there may or may not be, they would simply crumble by the magic power of direct gaze.

Eye contact has a role to play in situations where you would not expect it. If you go out on a relaxing stroll, for example, with Hungarian companions, be prepared to talk rather more and stroll rather less. Since side-glances will not satisfy their need for eye contact, your perambulatory partners will repeatedly stop and turn towards you to fully engage your gaze as and when the rhythm of the conversation requires – which will be frequently.

Ugyan, vegyél még... (Do have some more...)

Hungarians take great pride in their legendary hospitality. Adventurous guests must be prepared to endure substantial and exhausting bouts of eating, then feasting, then some more eating, and so it goes on; with boozing before, during and after these blowouts.

They will expect you to have at least second and third helpings: otherwise they take it as a negative comment on the lovingly prepared food, not to mention a personal insult. You can rest assured that they will not take no, however firmly put, for an answer. Your Hungarian hosts will simply be enchanted by your charming modesty. They are bound to take it on themselves to make sure you are 'properly' fed. *Ugyan, vegyél még!* (Do have some more ...) is persistently imposed on guests, with the frequency of 'pass the salt, please' in England.

First Names Second, Second Names First – Where Else?

As in the Chinese tradition, Hungarian surnames always precede first names. To make life more interesting, a first name can also be a surname. What is more, a male first name can be either a male or female surname; and you will also find men with either female or male first names as their surnames. To make it a bit less straightforward, Hungarians, being exemplary Europeans, and thus conscious of the difference in name sequences abroad, can (but not necessarily do) change the order of their names to accommodate foreigners.

Let us illustrate the puzzle you may be confronted with. The combination of Dávid (David) and Eszter (Esther) could indicate either the name of a woman, as in Dávid Eszter; or a man, as in Eszter Dávid. It all depends on the order of the names and whether the names are given in the Hungarian sequence or not. So, there you have it. But who said it would be easy?

127

Getting Time and Space Sequences Right

Just as names are presented in the reverse order of what you may be used to, so are sequences of space and time. The concept to remember is simple: the process is deductive rather than inductive. The more general information takes precedence over more specific details. Thus in the case of names, the family name precedes the first name – the family unit being larger than the individual belonging to it.

Likewise, context is fronted in addresses, with details relegated to follow suit. Whereas in English you start with the most specific detail of the address, such as the flat number, and build up the whole from the part, in Hungarian it is the other way round. The overall context, such as the name of the city, takes priority over more particular parameters. Having established the wider context, you then break it down in descending order to the smallest and the most specific: *kerület* (district, given in Roman numerals), *út* or *utca* (street), *házszám* (house number), *emelet* (floor) and *lakás* (flat number).

As opposed to a mixture of letters and numbers in some other cultures, Hungarian postcodes are eminently straightforward, what with sporting only four numbers, this time in Arabic numerals. For example, number 1 as the first digit indicates Budapest; the next two, the respective district of Budapest, with the fourth digit identifying the sorting office. So, should you be house hunting, and would like to figure out the location corresponding to the address in the advertisement, you can do so by glancing at the postcode. If, say, the postcode is 1124, then the house must be in the 12th district of Budapest.

The way of thinking about space corresponds to that of time, such as dates. In British English, dates are sequenced from the specific to the more general, the usual order being day-month-year; in American English this shifts to month-day-year. In Hungarian, however, you have to reorder this sequence to conform to the idea of presenting the whole first, and only then the parts – year-month-day.

Greetings and Bodily Contact

Csókolom! is a Hungarian greeting that will truly entertain the uninitiated. It literally means 'I kiss you', although its original meaning – from the full expression *Csókolom a kezét!* – is 'I kiss your hand'. This greeting demonstrates, yet again, how Hungarians conform to vital European traditions: *Csókolom* was adopted by Hungarians from Spanish etiquette via the Viennese court.

You must be prepared for this verbal assault on your privacy from two unlikely sections of the population. Children are expected to verbally 'kiss' all adults: *csókolom* is what you hear when children greet adults. Men, gents with grey, receding hair in particular, and courteous men in general, will greet you with *csókolom* if you are a 'lady'. Having more or less successfully divested itself from its original meaning, *csókolom* has metamorphosed into a respectful greeting by children to adults, men to women and women to the elderly, with the actual kiss as optional extra.

Should you be distracted, or not sufficiently focused, the more earnest may still actually grab your hand and plant a kiss of sorts on it. You see, you do not have to be a monarch to have your hand kissed in Hungary, which itself demonstrates the strong democratic traditions of Hungarians …

This hand-kissing business may sound elegantly alluring in theory, but is not necessarily so in practice. You had better make up your mind about this one well in advance: it is definitely not gracious to hastily withdraw your hand once it is just about to receive the heavenly kiss. Apart from the awkwardness of it all for both parties involved, the Hungarian gentleman affecting this debonair gesture is bound to feel spurned.

Should you be determined not to be graced in this charming way, the trick is to retract from the handshake, immediately and assertively. It is really a question of being forewarned and then, as with many things when dealing with Hungarians, the rest is simply a matter of improving your reflexes.

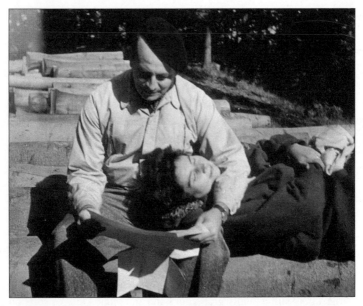

Tactile gestures of intimacy, publicly confirming tight bonds between people, are common – regardless of age or gender.

Plenty of Puszi (Kisses on the Cheek)

In reality, rather than wasting kisses on hands, Hungarians are much more inclined to plant kisses on, or in the direction of, the cheeks. This exuberant and boisterous greeting is practised mostly, but not only, by women.

Much sooner than you would expect in your wildest dreams, you may become the hapless recipient of euphoric kisses and bear hugs that render you immobile since they go on forever. Hungarian culture has its Mediterranean streaks, remember. The tactile ritual of 'kiss and hello' may take a bit of getting used to, should you come from a more reserved culture – then again, you just might enjoy it once you have got over the initial shock.

Even More Kézfogás (Handshakes)

Most women nowadays extend their hand not to be kissed but to exchange handshakes in a vigorous fashion, quite like men. Not unlike in other cultures, here too people are often inclined to make well-considered judgements on your character based on the nature, length and vitality of the shake, together with the temperature and moistness of your hand.

However, unlike in many other cultures, in Hungary a one-off effort to make the right impression will not do. Be warned: you must be able to persistently repeat the image you wish to convey via your handshake. Hungarians will 'handshake test' you as a matter of course at the opening and closing of each and every encounter – several times a day if need be.

Hungarian culture is definitely a tactile culture, where a stranger doesn't think twice about touching you while giving you directions in the street. The English habit of apologising profusely if, god forbid, someone happens to violate the two-mile intimacy zone of another person, is perceived by Hungarians as more pretentious than polite.

Szia! and Viszlát! (Hi! and See You!)

You can tell who is on *tu* terms with whom by the choice of their greeting. *Szervusz* or *Szerbusz*, the more informal *Szevasz*, the even more confidential *Szia*, the quite intimate *Szió* with its diminutive *Szióka* can all be used as *tu* greetings. They are used between just about anybody, regardless of gender, age or context on the condition that the degree of intimacy in the relationship warrants their use. They all translate roughly as 'hi' or 'hello', and indeed 'see you' since you can say both hello and goodbye with them.

All the variations on the *Szervusz* theme have of course their plural version for the occasions when you are faced with more than one individual. No need to panic. In such cases you simply add the suffix *tok* or *sztok* to your favourite version of Hungarian 'hi', and you will get *Szervusztok, Szerbusztok, Szevasztok, Sziasztok* and *Sziótok*.

131

These greetings are commonly used between people to reduce social hierarchy and psychological distance. During the four decades of Hungarian socialism, equality ruled supreme – if not in real terms, at least in greetings. Greetings and terms of address rooted in feudal, intricate hierarchies were replaced by *Szervusz* terms with almost everybody and anybody. However, treating all and sundry in this personal way has a tendency to achieve the opposite of the desired effect: it rapidly depersonalises personal relationships. But life finds a way ... a plethora of *Szervusz* permutations were engineered. These, far from being redundant, offered a loophole to escape from the surface equality by their multifarious shades of formality within the uniform informality of *Szervusz*.

In the light of its pseudo-democratic usage, it is paradoxical that the Latin original of *Szervusz* – *Servus humillimus* – means 'your humble servant'. Hungarians adopted *Szervusz* from both Latin and German, and then cleverly created countless new Hungarian versions of it. Similarly, *Csáó*, the Hungarian version of *ciao* or *chow*, originally also means 'slave', i.e. 'I am your slave.'

Now *Csáó* may be a bit old-fashioned, but not to worry; there are a good number of other glorious greetings to sustain symbolic intimacy with. There is *Heló!* and *Helósztok!* (plural), the Hunglish version of 'Hello!', and *Heló-beló!*, *Hali!* and *Halihó!* for the times you feel sufficiently playful and/or young. Beware: *Heló!* is a false friend of sorts since it often usurps the function of *Viszlát!* (See you!) when it is used as an informal term of parting rather than greeting as is customary in English.

It may sound at first that almost everybody is on *Szervusz* terms in Hungary; but this is not the case. Indeed, nowadays it makes sense to be cautious about its use. In English, for example, it is relatively common to say 'Hi!' to a stranger. However, this is not at all acceptable between adults in Hungarian. To be able to use *Szervusz* and its many varieties, first you have to be *pertu* (on *tu* terms) with the other person. (See more below, under *Tu, Vous – and More*.)

Now *Jó napot!* (Good day!) or *Jó napot kívánok!* (I wish you a good day!) – as a formal sort of Hello! – are safe when you meet strangers and relative strangers, such as when you are doing your shopping, talking to professionals like your doctor, or tradespeople like your plumber. Your neighbours and colleagues will also expect to be greeted like this unless you have established an informal relationship.

Viszontlátásra – literally, 'I'll see you again' – is used to say goodbye in such situations. *Jó reggelt!* and *Jó estét!* (Good morning! and Good evening! respectively) also express the degree of respect and distance that is due in formal exchanges.

Tu, Vous – and More

The Hungarian system of status markers in social relations may not look elaborate, compared with some Asian languages such as Korean, Thai or Japanese. Nonetheless, in the European context, Hungarians have a rather sophisticated system for keeping and reducing psychological distance, imposing and refusing hierarchy or intimacy. The French may have their *vous*, and the Germans their *Sie* for keeping people at a distance, while the English have to do with only one form of second person. Hungarians, however, have several language forms to indicate the relative status between speaker and listener.

First of all, there is *Te*, the familiar second person singular like *tu* in French, complemented by two formal *vous* forms: the somewhat brusque-sounding *Maga*; and the much more polite *Ön*. Not to mention the plural versions, of course: *Ti, Maguk* and *Önök* respectively. Then there is the most courteous, and a pinch convoluted, *Tetszik* or even *Tetszene* option, normally used nowadays to address the elderly, as in *Tetszik/Tetszene jönni a telefonhoz?* (Does/Would it please you to take this phone call?)

Unlike in English, in written communication terms of references such as *Te, Maga* and *Ön* (singular) and *Ti, Maguk* and *Önök* (plural) are usually capitalised as a gesture of politeness. In spite of this and

other relatively formal features of written Hungarian, you may find that both written and oral communication abounds in more anecdotes, jokes, metaphors, quotes, proverbs and sayings than you are used to.

So there are various honorific forms to choose from, and thus many ways to go wrong ... Paradoxically, you can also omit *Te*, *Maga* and *Ön* at times since a conjugated verb can actually express subject, verb and object all by itself, as in the classic example, *Szeretlek* or *Szeretem*. It takes three words to translate both of these single-word sentences into English – 'I love you.' Although less compact, the English version still fails to convey the substantial difference in the interpersonal relationship between the subject and the object in the two Hungarian sentences. *Szeretlek* implies an intimate relationship, whereas the relationship in *Szeretem* is either very formal or else it refers to a third person: him or her, or even it ... depending on the context.

Another layer of subtlety to this somewhat complex arrangement is the fact that being on first-name terms with somebody may or may not imply *te*-ing. Colleagues, for example, will happily address each other by their respective first names and yet keep the formal *vous* language forms otherwise. So the permission that, for example, 'You can call me Paul!' does not really lead to *te*-ing. It reduces some of the social hierarchy but not all. It is more informal than the term of address prefixed with Mr, let alone Dr, but not as informal as it could be. Therefore, the term of address is a necessary but not sufficient condition to be on *te* terms.

The thorny issue of whose right and responsibility it is to initiate the use of *Te* (French *tu*, German *du*) in conversations is a delicate business – it preoccupies and befuddles Hungarians themselves. It is wise not to consider *te*-ing anyone unless you are obviously older and/or of a higher status; or you happen to be a woman.

Normally this gesture is volunteered by the senior or the female participant in the discourse by saying something like *Tegeződjünk, jó?* (Let's be on *te* terms, shall we?) or the somewhat imperious *Nyugodtan tegezz!* (Do call me *te*!) If this permission is not forthcoming, it is possible to ask for it if you feel it is appropriate by making the request explicit: *Tegeződhetnénk?* (Could we call each other *te*?) Beware: if the *te*-ing is not mutual, it is called *csendőrpertu* (gendarme pertu). The name implies seriously feudal social relations – as, for example, used to be the case when gendarmes or other authoritarian figures (parents, teachers, clergy, employers) *te*-ed others unilaterally.

If the context is a party or something similar, people sometimes mark this momentous decision by saying: *Igyunk pertut!* (Let's drink a *pertu.*) This old ritual is a bonding experience, much like blood treaties must have been. It signals the desire for friendship between the participants and formalizes the decision to shift towards being on intimate terms with each other. The ritual itself can be quite fun since it involves sipping your wine while being intertwined, arm in arm, with the other person. This celebration of informality is an ingenious excuse for extended and intimate physical contact, which culminates in smacking kisses on each other's cheeks.

All of this should give you an idea of the subtleties of Hungarian thinking and intricacies of social hierarchy. It may sound a bit pointless unless one looks at the bottom line of the whole *te*-ing business. Similar to the shift to being on first name terms, except more so, offering *pertu*, or asking for it, acts as a social symbolic leveller. Explicitly, it provides informality. Implicitly, though, there is more at stake: a degree of social equality is granted. Symbolic though it may be, once social hierarchy is reduced, it is tricky to re-establish it – although not unheard of. Couples, for example, sometimes switch back and forth between *tu*-ing and *vous*-ing to play with levels of intimacy in their language behaviour.

KEEPING IN TOUCH

Erre jártunk, hát beugrottunk …
(We've been in the area so just popped in …)

Hungarians are very much into phones, mobile or otherwise. Spending what may seem incredibly long periods on the phone is a popular way of socializing and keeping in touch. Parents, especially mothers, excel in the art of educating, controlling and supporting their children over the phone. Partners likewise. Courtship and friendship flourish in the intimate company of the phone.

Having said that, you may actually find that some Hungarians quite happily ignore common facilities, such as mail and phone, taken for granted by others in communicating with friends. They can be quite uninhibited about descending on you, often with a posse of friends, without any warning or previous arrangement. They love to do this particularly on what you thought would be a quiet Sunday afternoon, or an evening engrossed in long overdue work. It is not an altogether odd phenomenon if you bear in mind, for example, the scarcity of phones in the past.

Unless you don't mind hurting your Hungarian friends' extremely delicate feelings, you are supposed to grin and bear, gracefully and without resentment, these unprovoked gestures of friendship and forced intimacy demonstrated at the worst possible times.

Getting Invited

Although some Hungarians have indeed no inhibitions in descending on you without a word of warning, in this case it is not really advisable to model yourself on the native behaviour. To start with, a degree of intimacy has to be created first. Yes, but how? You are hardly under the skin of the culture you live in, unless you have been to the homes of the natives of that culture. How do you get invited?

Well, it is not that easy but not that difficult either. Not easy, because quite a few Hungarians have more than one job to hold down, more than one family to support and probably an extensive network of friends to boot. So you can be up against impressively intricate schedules and tangled webs of social and professional commitments. As a result, finding a niche for you to fill in their oversubscribed life may prove a challenge.

A challenge, certainly. But a serious hurdle it is certainly not. Hungarians tend to think of themselves as gregarious and outgoing people who thrive on extending and receiving hospitality. Therefore, one way of getting invited is inviting those whom you want to get invited by. Encouraging them to bring their family and/or some of their best friends may increase your chances of success: double or treble 'dating' offers them the opportunity to make excellent use of their time. And it works for you too. You can slot yourself into their lives; you can extend your own circle of Hungarian friends by inviting their friends as well; and, most importantly, you can learn a lot about Hungarian discourse styles watching your guests interact with each other. There is an invaluable extra bonus in this arrangement: you are likely to get a more varied and balanced view of matters discussed, for your various Hungarian guests would virtually violate their own self-imposed code of behaviour were they to concur on any single issue.

Favours are generally taken seriously: reciprocity is implicit but imperative. Once you have established your system of social credits, you can draw on your credit from people, just as from banks. Overdrawing is not welcome in either system. Most cultures operate a form of invisible credit in their social networks – in Hungary it is nothing short of vital in many aspects of life. Neglect or ignore it at your own peril.

Oh, Those First Moments of That First Meeting!

Now this looks like a daunting affair at first. When meeting Hungarians for the first time, you may find them relatively formal, compared with, say, North Americans. You cannot get away without shaking everybody's hand thoroughly while exchanging full names – just first names will not normally do in this sort of situation.

Should it be a meeting or a party, whoever arrives later is likely to have the pleasure of going through the same process with the rest of the group. If half a dozen guests arrive at staggered intervals, then the ritual is carried out six times; if ten, then ten times. The initial contact is likely to be quite formal, physical and ritualistic.

FORMAL NO MORE ... GETTING TO KNOW YOU

Once the first, ritualistic handshake has been consciously and extensively carried out, the ice is broken: the initial formality then tends to evaporate.

When interacting with Hungarians, it is helpful to keep in mind that it is for them a question of profound principle – not to say second nature – to share whatever public, private and, above all, intimate information you have about yourself. Better still, about others.

To illustrate how this principle works in practice, pure and simple, take the case of an innocent (just wait and see ...) telephone call you decide to make using the Yellow Pages. What you naively thought would be a quick inquiry about some trivial business matter may, with a Hungarian at the other end of the line, be turned into an in-depth Freudian session on the phone-turned-couch about the complex relationship between love, ego and id. Granted, whatever the information you are after, you are not terribly likely to get; then again, you should count yourself lucky and be grateful for the insights you do get into your own and others' lives, gratis. Courtesy of the probing questions of a convivial armchair shrink, you will be granted a chance for forced self-reflection in the form of mutual self-revelation.

Armed with this sort of valuable cultural awareness, you will not find it entirely overwhelming to cope with the slight culture shock when you join the company of a group of unknown Hungarians. Having got through the handshake-cum-full-name ritual, you may find yourself in the firing line without any further ado. Now this Hungarian ritual – the creative cross-examination of a stranger – is otherwise known as the 'friendly getting-to-know-you the Hungarian way'. Grilling it is not, simply an eternal longing to hack into others' innermost code of being by deconstruction, thereby constructing a semblance of intimacy. This may involve the routine rap of greetings and introduction tagged with rapid queries about marital status, love life and all that jazz.

Now bearing this in mind, if or when this happens, you will not curl over with embarrassment, but will be positively peeved, if the predictable 'how do you do' fails to come in its Hungarian version.

Explorations and Extrapolations
Now, this is a likely scenario only if the whole of your personality and personal history can be construed in a straightforward fashion, and to their satisfaction, on the nifty interpretation of your name, aura and the size of your pet newt's left earlobe. To give credit where credit is due, some Hungarians may also include, as a variable in their scientific analysis, other socially significant prototype markers such as the colour and symbolic meaning of your neighbourhood neurologist's nightcap – to pre-empt illusions of single vision.

Should the ritual sequence of instant name etymologising and the well-rehearsed vivisection of its mandatory paraphernalia leave any nagging doubt as to how exactly to map you out and pigeonhole your family tree, that must, in all fairness, be clarified first and foremost. To successfully preserve confidence in their category system, they apply snappy strategies to deal with ambiguities. These include sophisticated elicitation processes such as 'Hmm, interesting name …', coupled with the penetrating look of an inquisitor, and 'What sort of name is that?' or 'Is your name originally … (fill in as applicable)?' with the detached professional interest of a linguist. These explorations and extrapolations are rather popular activities, practised on fellow Hungarians and foreigners alike.

Amo Ergo Sum: The Happy Merger of Public, Private and Intimate Blues

Evidently, Hungarians know their priorities. Understandably, when, and only when, such vital issues have been adequately investigated will they engage in such other obviously public matters as the gregarious discussion of the hurly-burly of others' endorphin pursuits and their own luscious libido. With close friends you may have to brace yourself for all the conceivable 'wh' questions followed through conscientiously – 'who, with who, what, when, where, what time, why and why not', let alone 'how frequently'! Glamorous or exotic it may not necessarily be, but, if done with Hungarian flair, this process will generate blues enough to jazz up all concerned.

Hungarians pride themselves on being genuine and generous European democrats with a particular penchant for taking a lively interest in all aspects of the individual's wellbeing … well, almost all. Failing that tall order, what they by no means can afford pussyfooting around is looking after – or rather into – such clearly public matters as the rhapsodies of each other's private passions … Not for them the orthodoxy of droll distinctions between the public, private and intimate spheres of individuals. Arguably, the preferred Hungarian version of *cogito, ergo sum* is *amo, ergo sum*. Hungary is, after all, a country of tortured intellectuals cum emotional contortionists who out-Euro the best of European traditions …

LATECOMERS' GRACE

Theatrical, musical and most other public events do not start on time as a rule; if they do, there must be something seriously wrong.

Hungarians are generally empathic enough to give a maximum of ten minutes' grace for latecomers – the vast majority of the audience. The absolute minimum expected is five minutes, which is taken for granted by Hungarians and is part of their sense of timing.

As opposed to Germans, for example, who are often regarded as phobic about being on the dot, or Spanish who seem (enviably) overly relaxed, the Hungarian solution is outstandingly sensible: the perfect balance of exercising tolerance and good timekeeping at the same time.

BOLDOG NÉVNAPOT! (HAPPY NAME DAY!)

If you think birthday celebrations are the annual highlights of reconfirming the existence of an individual, think again. As with many ideas, this too comes in – at least – a double whammy version in Hungary. Birthday get-togethers are important but then so are Name Day celebrations. Birthday parties are generally more intimate, family affairs, often culminating in the eloquent performance of that well-known choral piece, *Happy Birthday*, sung in English. This community effort to produce music leads up to the climax of the ritual blowing out of candles by the birthday person. Ideally, all the candles are supposed to be blown out in one go, while the celebrated person concentrates on making a wish. The rest of the happy tribe lends its support to the hero or heroine of the ritual by withholding their breath and eagerly following the fate of the candles.

Now Name Day celebrations are no small matter either, but they tend to be more of a public event, providing major excuses to socialize. Most first names are allocated several different dates of the year when the bearer of the name can be celebrated, thus giving all involved a veritable feast of a choice. Pocket and desk diaries often include the names matched with each day. Some of the national papers take it upon themselves – even on their website – to send the public at large on a regular guilt-trip by reminding them which names should be celebrated on any given day. Since you are bound to know

at least one person of that particular name, this raises the tr
question whether you should be 're-bonding' with them by sendil
bouquet of flowers, a bottle of wine or at least a call.

This particular obsession is a real blessing for businesses deall
in flowers and plants, since quite a few women expect – or at least m
seem to think they do – to be showered by flowers on this occasio
A wee bit of drinking also plays its part in the ritual, be it in the offic
or at home.

If one feels an urgent need to spice up some dreary day, there is
always a Name Day at hand to provide the excuse to caress one
another's ego. Should the subculture of the office you find yourself in
sanction Name Day celebrations, you will not be able to extricate
yourself from it without becoming a relative outsider to the group.
Name Day rituals are as much about reaffirming the individual whose
name is being honoured as about tribal bonding.

Being labelled a wet blanket or missing out on vital office
information, a.k.a. gossip, may not be high on your list of anxieties.
However, a conspicuous lack of attendance may also be interpreted
symbolically as a challenge to the legitimacy of the ritual. It may also
be construed as a lack of respect for the person whose name is being
celebrated, and, more importantly, for the group itself – not altogether
insignificant issues if you wish to work as part of that group.

So what if Name Day celebrations do not set your heart aglow but
nonetheless co-membership is a prerequisite to the success of your
work? Well, a little gesture may have significant symbolic value: your
attendance, however fleeting, may still be a statement of solidarity.

CRACKING A JOKE CAN BE A RISKY BUSINESS

Anecdotes, storytelling and jokes in particular are serious matters for
Hungarians. The major criterion for Hungarians in deciding whether
a joke is good or bad is quite sophisticated: what is significant is not
so much what is being said, or how, but rather who is saying it. Unless
they approve of the person telling the joke, they will refuse to laugh

at it; indeed, they may take a lifelong antagonism, swearing revenge on the unwitting perpetrator of what they may (decide to) interpret as an offensive remark.

If they see you as a potentially malicious outsider who does not have the foggiest idea about the spectacular sorrows of the Hungarian soul, you had better not indulge yourself in hazardous activities such as cracking jokes. It may be all right for the British to ruthlessly make a fool of their Royal Family, but it is the privilege of insiders to poke fun at their own foibles – or so some Hungarians think. Others, who beg to differ, risk any claim to being an authentic Magyar.

Note that to be considered an outsider by some Hungarians, you do not necessarily have to be a foreigner. Indeed, a humble voice of dissent on one point or another by a fellow Hungarian is more than sufficient for some to take the sword of justice, flaming with indignation, and strive to excommunicate you, briskly and irrevocably, from the righteous Hungarian community. This may be the case even if the fool who is reckless enough to risk going against the grain could be nothing but Hungarian for want of any language other than their native Hungarian.

No Sense of Humour

You may think it spot-on to play a pun on the words Hungary and hungry. Most Hungarians will differ with you on this one. To start with, this particular pun – 'Hungarian' to mean hungry, beggarly and marauding – qualifies only as obsolete slang as evidenced in the Oxford English Dictionary. It is hardly any consolation that one of Shakespeare's characters abuses another fellow in the first act of the *Merry Wives of Windsor* by calling him 'hungarian': "O base hungarian wight: wilt y' the spigot wield?" Predictability is a criticism that may be hurdled at you: the joke is ever so slightly worn out, banal, boring and boorish. Apart from all that, Hungarians will just love it.

Now, whether they trust you, or care about you enough to scold you for what may appear to you an innocent joke, is another matter.

143

At best, you can expect to be vigorously enlightened about your astounding insensitivity. In the worst-case scenario, they will just write you off in seething silence. Humour can reduce distance dramatically between two people by creating a sense of community; it can also cause frustration by falling flat, or worse, be deeply alienating and damaging. Not altogether surprisingly, this particular faux pas belongs to the last category.

Other than this pun, as with almost everything, Hungarians are gloriously divided in their attitude to humour and what they regard as funny. Some may entertain you with jokes demonstrating their mercilessly critical self-awareness, such as the legendary one about the Hungarian who enters a revolving door behind you but, inexplicably, and refuting the laws of physics, exits in front of you. (Yes, this is a 'genuine' albeit hoary Hungarian joke!)

Other Hungarians will simply do you in for telling this joke, having pointed out the blatant absurdity of it in the light of Hungarian history: "Is it conceivable you don't recollect that Hungarian history has been a series of daringly heroic, but mostly losing battles? It was invariably others (Tartars, Turks, etc) who came out of the revolving doors of history first; certainly not Hungarians."

Philosophy: Humour Is Thy Name

Hungarian humour has been a primary outlet for varied and numerous political frustrations. Creative political thinking and philosophy often found its way into black humour and/or samizdat literature.

During difficult times, almost anything forbidden or risky could and was said via humour. Indeed, Hungarians used to exorcise their opposition to oppressive regimes through the cruellest jokes possible against the political system, the police, corruption and what have you. They still cherish a national passion for decoding the gravest political implications of quite innocuous remarks or innocent jokes. The intellectual excitement of joke-decoding was quadrupled by the adrenaline triggered by being forced to make on-the-spot decisions as to whether it was safe or expedient to tell a particular joke in a particular place in the presence of a particular group of people – or whether to risk laughing at someone else's.

Now that humour is no longer supposed to have the role of circumventing censorship and keeping the personal and national psyche reasonably healthy, all the delicious excitement of guessing the hidden layers of meaning has gone out of it. Instead, humour acts as one of the more obvious clues to people's political hue, and is thus used as a venomous weapon. What has not changed, though, is the Hungarians' ability (given the right context!) to roll in the aisles at the blackest imaginable satire about their misfortunes – no shortage of raw material here …

LANGUAGE LEARNING GALORE

When the tower of Babel fell
It caused a lot of unnecessary Hell.
Personal rapport
Became a complicated bore
And a lot more difficult than it had been before,
When the tower of Babel fell.

—Noel Coward

Socializing is predicated on language and communication skills. Either you will have to make an effort to master Hungarian, or Hungarians will have to grapple with a language you both understand. There is no denying that nowadays Hungarians do work at it. Indeed, foreign language learning is a marathon exercise for them. From toddlers to pensioners, many Hungarians now cultivate a lifelong involvement in learning a foreign language, preferably several simultaneously. More and more of them spend enormous amounts of money, time and energy on ever-changing fads in languages and language learning methods.

The results are not exactly spectacular so far and, as illustrated by the following popular Hungarian joke, you should not expect to converse with simply any passer-by in a language of your choice:

"A foreigner is trying to get some directions from two traffic wardens. She tries to communicate in English – no response. Neither German, nor French or Spanish moves the Hungarians to any utterance whatsoever. In a last-ditch effort, the tourist tries some Russian, also in vain. In desperation she leaves. The traffic wardens, relieved, look at each other. One of them remarks: 'Perhaps, after all, we should be able to speak a foreign language, don't you think?' 'What on earth for?' quips the other. 'This woman spoke five languages, and it didn't do her any good, did it?'"

Having said that, once they have the hang of it, Hungarians are often remarkably apt communicators in a foreign language. Although they retain some Hungarian accent and intonation – besides a powerful body language – their English or French, for example, is not half as much fun to interpret as that of a French person feigning English, or the other way round. The Beatles and the Internet have done their bit for the somewhat dented British Empire; and, indeed, English is the language you are most likely to have some success with in accosting young Hungarians on the street. (See more in chapter 3.)

In addition, now that German is no longer imposed on Hungarians, they invest formidable energy in learning it. Though they rather like to feel they are doing it voluntarily, in fact there is a different sort of imposition, more authoritative and efficient than any imperial order: the dictates of business.

The common assumption that Russian will get you by in Hungary is totally misplaced. Russian is not a compulsory language any more from the tender age of 12 through to one's PhD – not that it was a roaring success with Hungarians in any case. As with German, some people may now actually learn it, unlike before. Give it a few years and if you are trying to locate someone able to communicate in Russian, you may not be quite as hard-pressed as at present. In short, considering the hundreds of thousands of Hungarians supposedly learning Russian for forty years or so, the results are mightily impressive!

— Chapter Five —

FOOD AND WINE

Hungarian cuisine is a demonstrably powerful part of the Hungarian identity. Hungarians wouldn't dream of leaving their native soil without adequate supplies of Hungarian sausage and salami, whilst Hungarian emigrants around the world will plant a vineyard, start growing sorrel, marrow and cherry-paprika long before making any serious attempt to adjust to the eating habits of their adopted country. Whether in Hungary or abroad, the meticulous discussion of idio-syncratic variations on recipes is a major conversation maker for Hungarians, quite like for the French.

Eating, or better still, feasting, holds a tight control over the Hungarian psyche. Believe it or not, there is even a political party named after those who cultivate the land and feed the nation – the Smallholders' Party, whose members hold roughly 10 per cent of parliamentary seats.

Rites of passage and annual rituals that structure life are perfect excuses for feasting till all participants drop dead with overeating. Family occasions, or indeed, get-togethers of any sort, mean the mandatory stuffing of yourself to the brim. Before, during and after the extended and elaborate menu, Hungarians like to swig Hungarian wine in generous quantities – just as a common-sense health measure, you understand, to neutralize the richness of the food.

Hungarian cuisine has an outstanding international reputation notwithstanding that a lot of it defies prevailing dietary laws and prescriptions. Hungarians eat just about everything that you are not supposed to, prepared in the way it shouldn't be, and consumed in deadly quantities. Naturally, they enjoy it tremendously. And they want to make sure their visitors enjoy it too. As a guest, you must be prepared to endure substantial and exhausting events of feasting, punctuated by spontaneous singalongs and bawdy joke-cracking in true Mediterranean style. "But you *must* have some more ..." (*Dehát vegyen még* ...) will be persistently imposed on you.

Nowadays, obesity is seen as a health hazard in theory but, at the same time, a forgivable and charming indulgence in practice. Good-sized love handles on women and generously proportioned potbellies on men are quite a common sight. As Prince Philip remarked to a British tourist in Hungary, "You can't have a potbelly; you haven't been here long enough."

Meals of the Day

Since the 1930s when the Italian coffee fad took off with a vengeance in Hungary, the day kicks off with an espresso that makes anyone not used to it hyperventilate for the rest of the day. (See more under

Coffee Craze, page 160.) Hungarians drink this murderous brew, with or without milk, first thing in the morning – usually on an empty stomach. The dosage is repeated at regular intervals throughout the day, and for maximum effect, many combine this ritual with smoking a fag or two. In any case, Hungarians wouldn't contemplate leaving home without imbibing a mugful of this pitch-black substance.

Breakfast is considered a very important meal of the day and working Hungarians make up at work what they missed at home. Once at work, the first thing they do is to tuck into a proper breakfast of fresh rolls with cold cuts, cheese and yogurt – plus another espresso, of course.

This is a remarkably efficient custom, since Hungarians clearly save time by not having a proper breakfast at home and need no brunch to tide them over till lunch. Besides, they make very good use of their time by socializing with family and friends over the phone, and colleagues in the office, while enjoying a well-deserved picnic spread all over their desk.

Traditionally, the main meal of the day is a hot lunch, but it is not easy to keep it this way, what with the quality and quantity of canteen food these days. Hungarians complain if there is no cooked meal available at work, but even more so if there is. In any case, a piping hot espresso rounds off lunch, however ghastly it may be.

There is only one more espresso to survive, in the afternoon, with something to nibble on – possibly cake or biscuit. This 4 o'clock coffee version of the English 5 o'clock tea is designed to give you just enough energy to wrap up work and fight your way home through the traffic jams.

This strenuous process undoubtedly makes you famished enough to sit down to a relatively early cooked dinner, or meal consisting of cold cuts with bread and – surprise, surprise – no espresso this time! Unless, of course, it is a formal dinner, in which case you will be offered one even at 11 p.m.

Vegetarian Options

Although caffeine addicts are well advised to make haste to Hungary to have the time of their lives, for vegetarians and vegans the case is not quite so straightforward. They will certainly find it challenging, but not impossible, to locate a speciality of Hungarian cuisine conforming to their dietary principles.

Veggies often come disguised in a heavy roux (*rántás*) of flour and oil. Traditionally, and even today quite often, lard (*zsír*) is favoured to oil – lard being to orthodox Hungarian cooking what butter is to French or sesame oil to Oriental cuisine. Considering that pork did not originally feature in the diet of Hungarians before they settled around AD 895, pork in general, and lard in particular, has made an impressive career in the Hungarian stomach.

Many Hungarians, who may be otherwise health freaks, will tell you to keep some good old-fashioned lard, preferably pork lard, or else some duck-dripping, stashed carefully behind your fat-free yogurts, skimmed milk and semi-skimmed cream. A meal cooked with lard, as opposed to oil, just simply tastes more like a *real* Hungarian dish, or so they say.

Fruit Soups, Pastas and Pastries

A more enterprising idea is simply to start with soup (*leves*), for example sour cherry (*meggy*) or fragrant cinnamon apple (*fahéjas alma*), skip the main course, and finish with a choice of three strudels (*rétes*) – apple (*almás*), cottage cheese (*túrós*) or cabbage (*káposztás*) – or apple and walnut pie (*almás-diós pite*).

Now, if you're a cottage cheese fan, you may well get addicted to the famous cottage cheese noodles (*túrós csusza*). Beware of the mandatory greasy bacon bits piled on top and generous helpings of sour cream (*tejföl*), a traditional component of Hungarian cooking. Then there are the lovely dumplings (*gombóc*) which, besides cottage cheese, come filled with juicy blue plums (*szilva*) and golden apricots (*barack*). Hungarian versions of Austrian strudel, and dumplings from Czech cuisine, are evidence of the culinary legacy of the Habsburg monarchy.

If you have no qualms about ingesting opium, you can also have a go at the delicious poppy seed vermicelli (*mákos metélt*), which will leave ubiquitous stains on your teeth for days to come, but otherwise tastes delectable.

Lángos, Garlic and Beatrice

Another attractive option is to grab a steaming *lángos*, one of the most popular Hungarian answers to fast food with a difference. To start with, it is as fast as fast food can possibly be – customers normally eat it on the go. Whether this go-as-you-eat habit is some reflection on the Hungarian psyche (compulsively wandering even while enjoying food) or just rooted in lack of space or facilities is unclear, but you are most unlikely to find a cosy place to settle down and gobfest while you are gorging on your lovely *lángos*.

Make the most of *lángos*, while it is available. For some unfathomable reason, Hungarians treat their *lángos* as if it were some delicate fruit from the Orient: it is a seasonal food. As summer days get smouldering hot, more and more *lángos* addicts will be strolling about with their steaming hot treat. Somehow, the idea of a *lángos* parlour chain to tempt *lángos* fans with cheap-and-cheerful eating-meeting places all year round has not caught on – yet.

Perhaps there will be a time in the not-so-distant future when you will be able to meet friends to have a hearty *lángos* and a heart to heart, or even order a *lángos* home-delivery, as is customary in the case of pizza. But at present, having an 'eat as much as you can' *lángos* eatery next to the Opera House in Budapest, modelled after the successful pizza parlours right beside English National Opera in London seems somewhat unlikely. Indeed, such a merger of highbrow and popular culture is iconoclastic enough to send shock waves through Hungarian culture, however obsessed its intellectuals are with postmodernism.

The irresistible lángos, *which is one of the most popular Hungarian fast foods in summer, especially around markets, beaches and pool sides.*

The essence *lángos* culture is spontaneity at its best, albeit within carefully defined boundaries. You may be purposefully whizzing about or just perambulating along the street when you are struck by a sudden whiff of *lángos*-like quality in the air. Compulsively, you follow the smell. To your utter relief as a sleuth, your hunch is confirmed when you notice that at least every second person coming towards you is busy chewing on a huge *lángos*. These live, moving-eating signposts are bound to lead you to a tiny stand or pavilion dispensing the titillating treasure that you can't help buying. Then off you go, munching happily away, your hands and face glittering with *lángos* grease, your pace and stomach weighed down with hot and heavy leavened dough. Now you are finally free to do whatever you had been doing before this compulsive action distracted you to make the worthwhile detour.

But what is this *lángos* after all? Well, a sort of a mammoth savoury doughnut ironed flat into a medium-size pizza with many holes and a varied geographical surface of hills and valleys. Sometimes the dough is mixed and deep-fried with grated cabbage (*Káposztás lángos* – can be disarmingly delightful), and comes with huge dollops of grated cheese (*sajt*) and/or sour cream on top. You may or may not want to follow the Hungarian custom of sprinkling the beloved *lángos* with more than a generous pinch of salt. It will probably prove too tempting though to resist that other highlight of Hungarian cuisine, garlic (*fokhagyma*), also sprinkled or poured on the luscious *lángos*.

Again, Hungarians like to think of garlic as their very own, and yet garlic – along with red onion – was brought in and adopted in Hungary as late as the 15th century, thanks to a foreigner called Beatrice, the Italian wife of King Matthias (*Mátyás király*), one of the most mythologized Hungarian kings.

Thus nature's remedy is another example of Hungarians assimilating foreign influences so successfully that they become part and parcel of the Hungarian experience (and sense of taste). To the originally Turkish *lángos*, Hungarians added the garlic juice they adopted from Italy and the result is an addictive and authentic Hungarian snack, along the lines of many similar Mediterranean savoury dough specialities often made with olives and/or olive oil. The overall effect is quite, quite irresistible; and, at least as far as the garlic is concerned, it is even good for your health. It will, to boot, effectively keep any unwanted company away for some time.

Pogácsa

There is one thing all youngest sons in Hungarian folk tales take with them in their *tarisznya* (knapsack) when off they go on their rite of passage to kill a dragon with seven heads and seek their fortune. It is a dozen or so savoury scones baked in ashes (*hamuba sült pogácsa*) that normally sees them through their journey of initiation into manhood.

Like *lángos*, the name *Pogácsa* is of Turkish origin. Etymology suggests this humble savoury treat with almost symbolic status in Hungarian culture was one of the (few) gains of the 150 years of Turkish occupation.

The everyday reincarnation of *Pogácsa*'s literary tradition nowadays is the basketful of *Pogácsa* that often awaits the weary wanderer in restaurants. It comes in different sizes and styles, but tends to be savoury like Pork Crackling Scones (*Töpörtyűs pogácsa*). It is there to kill your pangs of hunger while you make your well-considered choice of main course. Beware: if it is fresh from the oven, it is much too easy to gobble up more than enough of them to end up virtually stuffed by the time the meal itself is served.

Drinking beer or dry white wine is traditionally also carried out in the comforting company of *Pogácsa* to keep your mind lucid and tongue quick for the endless repartee.

Körözött

Health-conscious visitors should be on the lookout particularly for spicy curd cheese (*Körözött*) spread on a fresh roll or stuffed in the local version of green pepper (which, confusingly, comes in a subtle yellowish colour and, needless to say, tastes like heaven).

Like most Hungarian culinary creations, *Körözött* also abounds in red pepper and garlic, and basically looks like some heavily sun-tanned cottage cheese pâté. Forget, then, any memories of boring old cottage cheese – this version is spicy enough to bring it alive and kicking. You will inevitably find yourself asking for the recipe. If the *Körözött* you are offered feels particularly creamy and tasty, it may well have been made with a dash of beer. Indeed, it is sometimes made during beer-drinking sessions and consumed on the spot to facilitate further drinking by mitigating the immediate effect of alcohol.

Lecsó – the Hungarian Ratatouille Par Excellence

The ultimate summer favourite with Hungarians, which they happily consume for brunch, lunch and supper, day in and day out, is *lecsó*, the darling of Hungarian gastronomy, and the Hungarian answer to vegetable stew.

Rustling up a *lecsó* is not a mind-boggling exercise; indeed, it needs no marinating, no preparation but simply lots of onions to golden-brown in lard (what else?), with red pepper, tons of tomatoes and Hungarian green pepper. Needless to say, most Hungarians carnivorize it by eating it with plenty of spicy, greasy Hungarian sausage (*kolbász*) or even bacon (*szalonna*), but if you are a vegan or vegetarian, you may enjoy it simply with rice and/or eggs.

In the light of such a wide choice of non-meat-based Hungarian specialities, who can say all Hungarian dishes are waiting for redemption from po-faced dieticians?

HOT NUMBERS IN HUNGARY

Indeed the carnivorous, and generally those who wish to sin profusely by violating the laws of supposedly healthy eating, should definitely head for Hungary, to treat themselves to the very rich variety of Hungarian dishes. Most specialities, as you ought to have guessed by now, feature generous amounts of meat, oil (if not lard) and burning hot spices, and are, happily, irresistible to adventurous palates.

Spanish Sailors, Turkish Occupation and Paprikás Csirke

Most visitors to Hungary immediately succumb to the mouthwatering delights of Chicken Paprika (*Paprikás Csirke*), the pride and joy of the Hungarian stomach. Copious amounts of ground paprika and sour cream – the piquant Hungarian alternative to fresh cream in French cuisine – are an absolute prerequisite for the authentic taste. The traditionally popular side dish is a generous helping of home-made gnocchi (*nokedli* or *galuska*) – a sort of instant pasta created from

Hungarian cuisine is mostly meat-based: beef and pork are used in many dishes, as are poultry, game and freshwater fish; spicy salami and sausages are among the traditional sandwich fillers. It is not uncommon for women to talk about 'their' butcher, and be on first-name terms with him.

flour, water, eggs and a pinch of salt, gently pushed into the pot of boiling water through a special kitchen utensil called *nokedli* or *galuska szaggató*.

Now, paprika is the single most important spice in Hungarian cuisine, and for some if not most Hungarians, as well as visitors, it is impossible to imagine an authentic Hungarian dish without it. And yet this typical Hungarian trademark simply did not exist in Hungary for many centuries. Indeed, the seeds of this Central American plant made its way into the Hungarian way of life – and consciousness – thanks to Spanish sailors (and, in particular to Dr Chanca, on board Columbus's ship, the *Santa Maria*, one of the three ships which sailed to America with Columbus in 1492) and then via the Turkish empire, to become truly widespread in Hungary only around the 19th century.

While Hungarians do not hold a monopoly on paprika in any way – in fact, it is a very popular spice in several other cultures and gastronomies, including Central American, Turkish and Bulgarian – ground paprika has been a major Hungarian contribution, given the obsessive way it is creatively used in so many widely different dishes. The illustrious history of paprika illustrates well how history, cultural adaptation, and the merging of many different Eastern and Western influences are present in something as mundane as eating in Hungary.

Fish Soup in the Cauldron

You should be wary though of Szeged Fish Soup (*Szegedi Halászlé*). This cultural trademark is made from a variety of fishes and named after Szeged, a town by the Tisza, the second largest Hungarian river after the Danube (*Duna*). Indeed, wherever you go in Hungary, you are likely to encounter *Halászlé* in some form or another. It will sometimes parade as *Dunai*, at other times as *Balatoni Halászlé*, depending on where the fish was caught before making its way into the soup. But whatever the name, it is consumed, unless it consumes you, piping hot and very spicy unless you specifically ask for a watered-down version for the uninitiated.

This traditional favourite is often served in flaming, 'personal-ized', miniature cauldrons (*bogrács*), the handy portable pot of the nomadic Hungarians of old. *Bogrács* is not just a museum piece, nor is it a mere symbolic gesture towards cultural heritage, be it on your table in a *csárda* (an inn with strong pretensions to a theatrical or rather operetta interior) or even a posh restaurant. It is possibly the oldest Hungarian kitchen utensil in existence, the favourite piece of cooking paraphernalia of present-day Hungarian nomads kayaking, rowing or canoeing on the Danube or the Tisza, and it often makes its appearance at barbecues, surrounded by countless, normally male 'chefs', demonstratively engaged in communal cooking.

Consuming the Macho Way

A vital piece of advice on how to survive enjoying your Szeged Fish Soup may come in handy, should you be daring and decide to go for the authentic rather than the watered-down version. The simple trick of stuffing yourself with huge chunks of fresh bread as you go along will seriously facilitate coping with the delicious sensation of flames burning right through your body.

Your daring performance will impress Hungarians since they think only they are macho (for *macho* read *Hungarian*) enough to enjoy an authentic Szeged Fish Soup without the flutter of an eyelid

or sharp intake of breath. By no means be distracted by their praise of your bravado – feigned or otherwise – and do not for a moment heed their friendly exhortation to add some more cherry-pepper seeds (Hungarian chilli) to your soup! Disaster is bound to follow, and you will end up 'swallowing the tears' triggered by the powerful Hungarian chilli.

Some would say, tongue-in-cheek, that the dramatic display of Hungarian empathy for your predicament will be pure pretence. Arguably, this is a plain ego-boosting exercise for them: the incident will fill them with surreptitious satisfaction, confirming their expectations and sense of superiority. They have proved beyond any reasonable doubt to you, and more importantly to themselves, that they are mightier in coping with the waves of ferocious attack on one's taste buds which they delight in calling 'culinary sensations'.

Gulyás vs Pörkölt

Hungarians resent the fact that – and who can blame them – their sacred goulash (*gulyás*) is bastardised around the world. It is not, repeat *not*, an ordinary sort of peasant stew as the uninitiated think.

Hungarians do boast, thank you very much, a stew of their very own called *Pörkölt*, which simply means 'lightly burnt'. And for good reason too, since *Pörkölt* acquires its unique smoky taste by the onion and garlic covered in generous amounts of ground red pepper, and the whole thing slightly burnt. It goes without saying that only Hungarians know just how much it should be burnt to achieve the ideal degree of smokiness without turning it bitter.

It is traditionally served with some peculiar Hungarian dried pasta, *tarhonya*, somewhat resembling rice or barley in appearance but not in taste – yet another culinary souvenir of ancient Hungarian ramblings in the East.

Now remember, *gulyás* – note the Hungarian spelling – is not a stew as is widely believed, but a soup rich enough to knock you out for the rest of the day. This is hardly surprising considering that *gulyás*

159

means 'cowboy' and the meal was traditionally cooked in huge cauldrons on open fires by herdsmen on the Great Hungarian Plain (*Puszta*). The basic ingredient of this Hungarian dish par excellence, beef, was originally 'imported' by the Magyars during their trekking expeditions in the East – along with the cattle domesticated around Hortobágy, to later become its cowboys' hallmark.

The Hungarian alter ego of Italy's Tiramisu: Somlói Galuska

A substantial meal in itself, *gulyás* is often followed only by a Hungarian dessert such as *Somló Gnocchi*, or *Somlói Galuska*, Somló being a volcanic mountain by Lake Balaton. And what a dessert it is! It parades as an unassuming gnocchi in name, but is deliriously delightful in nature.

Somlói Galuska is a gargantuan dream of chocaholics: chocolate sauce, walnut and vanilla cream, rum and raisins, in a depressingly irresistible pile of chocolate and vanilla cake. *Somlói Galuska* will give an instant energy boost and pick you up just as the name of its more refined Italian counterpart, Tiramisu, suggests. Throw yourself into this volcano of decadent delights, then book a visit to a doctor.

Since Hungarian cuisine is rumoured to be changing, those who yearn for old favourites like goose liver (*libamáj*) with fresh spring onions or garlic toast and duck dripping topped with red pepper and red onion should hurry. For Hungarians, hellbent as they are on proving their European credentials in almost everything, these will surely include their diet. Like it or not, the health food craze is bound to take off with the usual Hungarian gusto. In fact, it may not be long before visitors are offered spicy muesli instead of espresso five times a day.

THE COFFEE CRAZE

Drinking espresso (*Eszpresszó*) is a serious national addiction and all visitors must be forewarned about the acuteness of the disease.

Hungarians just love sipping their steaming coffee while catching up on news of each other and the world. The elegant Café Gerbeaud, founded in 1858, is one of the famous places to indulge in this ritual. Foreigners frequent this Cukrászda (pastry shop) as much, if not more, than the locals. It is easy to get to with the so-called Földalatti or 'Little Underground', the first underground in continental Europe, built in 1896.

Eszpresszó is to Hungarian culture what tea is to the Japanese and the Arabs, or indeed what 'having a cuppa' is for the English. On street corners in all parts of the country you'll find dedicated places called *Eszpresszó* where you can join Hungarians in their national ritual. These places are a cross between a pub, a coffeehouse, an ice-cream parlour, a cafeteria and a bar. Quite often *Eszpresszó*s display some terribly impressive name in glaring neon light, such as Little Post, Liverwurst and Ice Queen. Please note the vital difference between an *Eszpresszó* and a *Kávéház* (coffeehouse). Coffee is consumed in both places, granted; nonetheless the latter is an altogether different cup of coffee, so to speak.

161

A meeting in the neo-baroque Café New York, perhaps the most stunning coffeehouse in Budapest, in the New York Palace built by Alajos Hauszman in 1891–95.

Although it may look like it, rigid categorization of their activities is not for Hungarians. Wherever and whenever, regardless of the occasion, people or time, in private or public, for business or pleasure, Hungarians are bound to treat you with their favourite poison, some coffee (*kávé*), which they endearingly refer to as *fekete* (black). And remember, more often than not, the tinier the cup, the stronger the *fekete*. Indeed, they have separate sets of tiny china or glass cups dedicated to this single ritual. Newlyweds in Hungary can be expected to do without pots and pans in their household but certainly not without a couple of sets for their *fekete*.

Though they often serve it with a glass of cold water, this will most likely represent a choice for you. At best, it is simply an opportunity to wash down the bitter aftertaste of the *fekete*. Just like their hot spicy dishes, which supposedly only Hungarians themselves can handle with appropriate nonchalance, their espresso is made to kill and be consumed with a passion on every conceivable occasion.

SOMETHING MORE TO YOUR FANCY ...?

Your alertness should increase in inverse proportion to the size of what looks like a glass of water. The smaller the glass, the greater should be your caution before taking the tiniest sip. Unless of course you wish to be instantly knocked out to float in a hazy dream for hours.

The water-like substance you have to be wary of – or look forward to with eager anticipation, depending on your preferences and personal history in spirits – is the infamous *Magyar Barack Pálinka* (Hungarian apricot brandy). Should you wish to postpone this particular venture into the tantalising world of hard liqueur, a casual smelling of the glass will suffice to confirm your suspicions.

Something to remember is not to make any false assumptions based on the time of day it is served. Traditionally, particularly in the countryside and in working-class culture, there is nothing like launching into the day by fortifying yourself with a *kupica barack* (a snort of apricot brandy) – not unlike the quick glass of red wine to greet the morning for some traditional Frenchmen. For the health-conscious, you can have a different fruit from a different region of Hungary every day of the week: plum (*szilva*) from Szatmár on Monday, cherry (*cseresznye*) from Eger on Tuesday, pear (*körte*) on Wednesday, apricot *(barack)* from Kecskemét on Thursday, and so on …

Those who wish to poison themselves in a truly effective manner should go for a cocktail made of apricot brandy, Tokaj liqueur and Tokaj wine (*Tokaji Szamorodni*). This somewhat lethal concoction is called *Puszta-koktél* (Puszta cocktail) – which sounds as authentic as it is not: a tourist drink per se.

Although espresso is served in posher and/or pretentious places with a glass of water, spirits are not – unless you specifically ask for a *kísérő*, a 'chaperone', literally an accompanying drink. In this case, the Hungarian answer to tonic, a glass of soda water, will 'accompany' your glass of spirits. If your powers of logic do not let you down, you can easily deduce that when you ask for a vodka and soda on ice, or a gin and tonic, you will certainly get what you ordered in essence but not in style: the mixing job may be up to you.

Hungarians nowadays do not fancy being seen as predisposed to spirits, but when it comes to Hungarian brandy – especially the apricot (*barack*) variety – many still go weak at the knees. Patterns of hospitality are changing, so you may have to be satisfied with an espresso unless you can cajole your hosts into treating you to a *kupica magyar pálinka* (a thimbleful of Hungarian brandy) stashed away in the liqueur cabinet.

Hungarians will expect you to know all about their fabulous wines, especially one with a name that may turn off vegetarians and animal rights activists from wine for ever: *Egri Bikavér (*Bull's Blood from Eger). Another Hungarian wine you may have heard about, and certainly must experience if you haven't so far, is *Tokaji* (more of which later).

Table wines (euphemism for plonk), quality wines and special quality wines are categories specified by Hungarian legislation, and tested by the National Institute for Wine Qualifications set up more than a hundred years ago. As a rule of thumb, and as with most things, there is a direct correlation between the size and the quality: the smaller the bottle, the higher the quality of the wine inside. Most plonks, as you would probably expect, come in ordinary one litre bottles; quality wines come in elegantly slim 70 cl bottles; whereas *Aszú* wines and *Tokaji Szamorodni* you can pick out from a distance by their less generously sized, 50 cl containers.

In terms of best temperature for consumption, note that *Tokaji Aszú* wines side more with rosé and white wines: ideally, you want to enjoy your *Aszú* at around 10°C as opposed to the room temperature that red wines are supposed to be served at.

Apart from the state's seal which special quality wines must have by law, other information you should find on the bottles is the variety of the grape, where it was grown and bottled, and its vintage and sugar content (dry, semi-dry, semisweet, sweet).

Arguably, Hungary is not an overly huge country. Nonetheless it boasts at least a dozen separate wine regions which may well signal something about the traditional relationship between Hungarians and their wine. Wine-making for many is not just moneymaking but a hobby they are committed to. Crisscrossing the countryside, you should not find it too difficult to get yourself invited into vineyards and wine cellars. It may well prove a challenge to extricate yourself from the wine-tasting ritual. Once you have joined your hosts, you are expected to do the job at considerable length and with unending enthusiasm. There is, you will be reassured, music in Hungarian wine; therefore you will (have to) find yourself singing while drinking. White wines from the volcanic soil of the Balaton Highlands (*Balaton Felvidék*) boast centuries of history (… here we go again!) going back to the Romans who also favoured wine produced here.

It is just Hungarians' bad luck that, for example, Californian wine should compete with their own in the European market, when in fact many of those Californian vineyards were originally planted with the finest Hungarian wine-shoots, by Hungarians. Unlike most Hungarians, the Senate of the US Congress was well enough aware of Ágoston Haraszti's significance in creating the Californian wine industry to have commemorated the 100th anniversary of his death in 1969 with an exhibition.

Just What the Doctor Ordered:
The King of Wines, the Wine of Kings

If you are presented with a medieval looking pharmaceutical bottle to drink from, do not despair. On the contrary, on opening it, you will smell a deliciously intoxicating bouquet and aroma. Expect your taste buds to go wild from the smallest drop of it.

Tokaji Aszú is commonly referred to, and marketed, as 'medicine', but as a matter of fact, this magic potion with the golden glow is divine nectar. *Tokaji* wine is modestly referred to by Hungarians as 'the King of Wines, the Wine of Kings' (*A borok királya, a királyok bora*). Most Hungarians will tell you this, and expect admiring surprise/surprised admiration in return. It will be their turn though to be surprised if, on such occasions, you reply with a casual nod and your best French accent: "*C'est le roi des vins et le vin de rois.*" ("It is the king of wines and the wine of kings.") Finish off by dropping the name of Louis XV who is credited with having pronounced this profound judgement on offering some *Tokaji* to Madame Pompadour.

Indeed the list of *Tokaji* references is impressive. It includes such dignitaries as Popes Pious IV and Benedict XIV (who felt blessed to have received such a gift from Queen Maria Theresa) on the one hand, and Voltaire, who happily consumed *Tokaji* from the cellars of Frederick the Great on the other. Peter the Great, czar of Russia, was another royal *Tokaji* enthusiast, making sure his port was secured from Tokaj. He must have had reasonable taste since it was shared by the wine connoisseurs who gave a prize to one of these *Aszú*s at the International Exhibition in Paris in 1900.

When you learn that the Hungarian Diet made it its parliamentary business to deal with procedures of *Tokaji* production in the middle of the 17th century, and one of the most popular Hungarian poets, Petıfi, admired its 'golden flame' in the 19th century, then perhaps you will have some appreciation of the beloved *Aszú*'s role and significance in the Hungarian psyche. You will also have an inkling of just how something as primary to body and soul as the Tokaj vine stalks and their nectar can feature in the Hungarian National Hymn, to the tune of two full lines in the third verse. Where else? As a rule, national hymns do, of course, have ravishing references to the high quality of local grapes and their nectar.

Culture shock? Perhaps a bit. But less so if you consider the arguably manic Hungarian obsession with history, the role and status of tearful merrymaking in the national psyche, and last but not least, that local viticulture going back many a century. Indeed it was apparently started by the Celts and continued relentlessly by the Magyars acting on the advice of Italian and French wine experts to various Hungarian kings. Therefore, shocking as it may seem at first, it is in fact most appropriate that Tokaj and its aromatic juices should have a prime place in the National Hymn, a poetically and passionately rendered readers' digest survey of Hungarian history.

The famous *Tokaji Aszú* is *the* Hungarian port and it is normally referred to simply and lovingly as *Aszú*. It is a most delectable dessert wine from the sunny slopes of the Zemplén mountains in northeastern Hungary, at the confluence of two rivers, the Tisza and the Bodrog.

The French are extremely particular about just who exactly can and cannot call (and more importantly, market) their sparkling wine 'Champagne'; well, so are the two dozen or so Hungarian villages in the Tokaj-Hegyalja area of around 12,500 acres. Tokaj, Tolcsva, Tarcal, Tállya, to mention just a few of the villages, are blessed with volcanic soil and plenty of sunshine during the day and humidity at night due to the long Indian summer of the region, and are entitled to use the label *Tokaji* on their wine products. The role of nightly humidity may not strike you as immediately self-evident. It is, nonetheless, of paramount importance for the existence of a fungus which, in turn, is vital for the production of the bouquet and aroma of *Tokaji*. It is exactly these fungi that make all the difference between ordinary dried berries turned raisins and the Aszú grapes shrivelled naturally by the so-called noble rot.

When choosing a bottle of *Aszú*, look closely for two pieces of evidence of high quality: the year of vintage and the number of so-called *puttony* or hods (containers for grapes carried traditionally on the grape-pickers' backs). The choice you are faced with is bottles of 3 to 6 *puttonys*. The more *puttonys* – each containing approximately 20 kilograms of grapes – that have gone into one cask of base wine, the nobler the resulting nectar.

Another 'medicine' Hungarians will offer you to round off the trials of a meal is *Unicum* or *Zwack-Unicum*. Like *Aszú*, *Unicum* comes in a little medicine-like bottle, with a huge golden red cross on it to make its message absolutely clear. Without a doubt, *Unicum* 'outbitters' any bitter medicine and, perhaps for this reason, Hungarians swear by it as a panacea for all ills.

Maudlin Merrymaking
Traditionally, some fine Hungarian wine triggers off, rather sooner than later, the great Hungarian behavioural paradox epitomized in the

saying, 'Hungarian merrymaking is a tearful affair'. They even have a word for this unique Hungarian trait – *sírvavigadás*, which to outsiders seems just a wee bit weird. It means 'the dramatic shedding of tears in the midst of merrymaking'.

Sírvavigadás is, however, most appropriate and understandable in the light of behaviour mellowed by sacred spirits. The Hungarian id, in particular when fired up by Bull's Blood (see above), may be demonstratively woe-stricken and resentful. Nonetheless, the amazingly go-ahead ego, bubbling with irrepressible energy, is never too far away. Hungarians have a knack for surprising the world with yet another resurgence of vitality at the most unlikely times.

— Chapter Six —

DOING BUSINESS IN HUNGARY

Pharmaceuticals, chemicals, clothing, vehicle manufacturing and machinery production are some of the country's more developed industries, along with its long-standing tradition of producing and exporting agricultural products. Hungary's major export markets include Austria, Germany, Italy and the United States. Most of the industrial production is based in the western part of Hungary called *Dunántúl* (Transdanubia) and also in *Pest Megye* (Pest County), Budapest in particular. Investment in real estate, for example in the construction and management of numerous large shopping centres and high-tech office complexes, has become another significant area of business activity in Hungary.

Around half of Hungary's GDP is based on import-export trade. Neither its size, natural resources nor development through the 20th century have provided Hungary with favourable economic potential. Its size was reduced as a result of the post-World War I treaty (1921, Trianon), which meant substantial loss of population, natural resources and markets. After World War II, the Hungarian economy found itself part and parcel of the introvert and highly controlled Russian economic system, including satellite markets and the hierarchical, rigid and centralized business structures that went with it.

1989 – Adieu to Forty Years of Economic Experiment ...

Even before the watershed of 1989, Hungary's economy, compared with other Central and Eastern European countries, had the most market elements and was the most decentralized and deregulated. In 1989, Hungary's political transformation took off – finally the experiments aimed at tinkering with the socialist model were given up. Hungary committed itself to a self-regulating market economy based on private ownership and reorientation to the West.

Economic and political transformation apart, many of the complex, multilayered and often radical changes were of a social, cultural and institutional nature. Although the transition may have seemed smooth, it involved significant and abrupt discontinuities. For example, various new systems and laws were introduced regarding parliament, political parties, finance, banking, trading, accountancy, taxation, companies, labour, land, privatization of industries and so on. The changes have had many implications, such as an impact on the social structure and identification of social roles, on status perception and the rhetoric of public discourse.

At the social symbolic level, red stars were knocked off the tops of buildings, including parliament, and street names were changed. Many public statues were physically removed and symbolically relegated to the past – they are now displayed in the open-air museum of socialist art, privately owned and operated for profit. Institutions were not only transformed but also often renamed as well. The Karl Marx University of Economics, for example, removed Karl Marx from its name as part of the transformation process, although not his imposing statue from its lobby.

The ideological changes were reflected in the use of honorifics: *elvtárs* (comrade) became a taboo title, just as *úr* (sir) and *hölgy* (madam) used to be for forty years. The threshold period suspended the previous perceptions of social rites and roles, norms and expectations, which had hinged on sociopolitical and economic situations that now became irrelevant.

... and Hello to Capitalism

The 1990s were busy years of gradual transition to capitalism with an extensive privatization programme of companies, en masse, through market sale. Private investors have bought most of the state-owned companies, and the greater part of the GDP is now created by the private sector. A plethora of joint ventures was also created to attract expertise and further investment; prices were liberalized, controls removed; and the liberalization of the economy was set in motion.

Direct foreign investment is around $20 billion, about one-third of which is US investment. Venture capital tends to support relatively large and well-established firms rather than start-up companies.

Investing companies have often at least doubled – if not tripled – their original investment. Some of the major American investors, for example, operating Hungarian subsidiaries include the following:

- Ameritech International Inc. (MagyarCom) – Matáv Rt. – telecommunications
- General Electric Co. – GE Lighting Tungsram Rt. – manufacturing (light sources)
- General Motors – Opel Hungary Kft. – manufacturing and sales (automobiles)
- MediaOne – Westel 900 Rt./Westel Rádiótelefon Kft – mobile telecom

- Alcoa Inc. – Alcoa-Köfém Kft
- The AES Corp. – AES-Tisza Power Plant Kft.
- Bristol-Myers Squibb Co. Pharmavit Rt.

The top foreign investors in Hungary include several companies from Europe as well, such as those listed below from Germany, France, the Netherlands and Belgium, along with a major investor from Asia (Japan) and one from Australia. Looking at the company names and their activities, you can get a good idea of the pattern of investment and economic development:

Energy Industry
- RWE Energie AG/Energie (Germany) – electricity generation and distribution
- Bayerwerk AG (Germany)
- Électricité de France (France)
- Tractebel S.A. (Belgium)

Food Industry
- Eridania Béghin-Say (France) – sugar and vegetable oil production)
- Coca-Cola Beverages (Australia) – nonalcoholic drinks

Financial Services
- Aegon (Netherlands) – insurance and pension funds
- Allianz AG (Germany) – insurance

Telecommunications
- KPN, Telenor Invest AS, Tele Denmark, Sonera (Netherlands. Norway, Finland, Denmark) – mobile telecom
- Magyar Telecom B.V. (Netherlands) – phone operator
- United Telecom Investment (Netherlands)

Manufacturing
- Audi AG (Germany) – engines
- Suzuki (Japan) – cars
- Sanofi S.A. (France) – pharmaceuticals and chemicals

Closed down forty years ago, the Budapest Stock Exchange, once the third biggest player in Europe, has been up and running again since 1990.

The investment pattern is typical of economies in transition – privatized industries (e.g. manufacturing), services (such as fast food outlets, photocopy chains, etc) and infrastructure development (e.g. telecommunications) – but other areas seem to be highly attractive as well. Biotech and medical technology, environmental services, information technology, construction, pharmaceutical, food and energy production, tourism and travel services are some of the most favoured fields.

Around two thirds of Hungary's imports and exports involve foreign-owned or jointly owned companies, which tend to rely on external markets, mostly in Germany, Austria, Italy, the Netherlands and the United States. However, most of the small and medium-sized Hungarian businesses tend to concentrate on the local market, and are therefore more sensitive to the domestic trade cycle.

To the degree though that multinationals embedded in the global market expand, the country's economy is becoming more dependent on processes outside its local context. The scope for independent monetary policy is limited by several factors, including the small size and openness of the Hungarian economy, and the convertibility of the forint, its currency. Hungary has been an associate member of the European Union since 1994, and full EU membership, with its opportunities and challenges for business and industry, is eagerly anticipated.

The grey/black economy is another significant element of the economy since, according to estimates, it accounts for one third of the GDP. Coping with inflation, unemployment and enhancing transparency in decision-making processes are some of the burning issues.

INTERPERSONAL DYNAMICS IN BUSINESS

More and more expatriates work side by side with Hungarians, often in the same company, sometimes as part of the same team. This process of group formulation may involve serious stress factors on both sides. To be able to work effectively and efficiently, you are likely to find it helpful to cultivate a strong sense of cultural sensitivity. Even the occasional hint of superiority in your attitude can seriously set you back in your interpersonal interactions and therefore damage your business.

Knowledge of the Hungarian Language and Culture

Many Hungarians in business speak a foreign language, or several even. However, your efforts to communicate in Hungarian will be very much appreciated. Indeed, some Hungarian language skill is often expected from expats staying for an extended period of time. If you fail to demonstrate at least some effort in this area, your Hungarian colleagues and partners may resent your attitude even if few are likely to actually say so.

Fluency in Hungarian is not really the issue; showing respect and goodwill by this gesture definitely is. Expat business people's lack of knowledge and understanding of Hungarian culture, language and the specific business context is likely to be seen as a sign of arrogance. This is not a helpful image to project if you are out to make your working relationship with the locals a success.

Hungarians may sometimes strike you as arrogant. Hence, you might infer that you cannot do too much harm by administering their own medicine to them from time to time. Well, it is indeed an option, but only if you prefer high-risk strategies. If this is not the case, any behaviour that can be interpreted as condescending is best carefully avoided.

Your Colleague as a Tolmács (Interpreter) at Hand

At first, it may look like a smart idea to attempt to 'shortcut' the linguistic and cultural problems by asking your Hungarian colleagues with English language skills to double as *tolmács* (interpreters) as well. Attractive and straightforward as it may seem, this is not really a feasible solution. It may easily generate resentment for several reasons.

To start with, managers often find having to act as an interpreter, i.e. servicing rather than managing others, humiliating. Having to act as a communicative bridge between two groups also adds an extra level of anxiety to the process at hand, not to mention the fact that most people are overloaded with their own work as it is. It is highly unlikely therefore that they will embrace the extra workload with glee.

It is also worth keeping in mind that the responsibility of interpreting is much more significant than it seems to those who have never dipped their toes in it. Almost everyone who has dabbled in professional interpreting can testify to just how stressful and draining that work can be.

Apart from being very demanding, interpreting is a profession in its own right. Since the wheels of business are oiled by communication, the quality of the communication process is of paramount importance. You can easily create costly miscommunication problems for yourself if you underestimate this process by making only ad hoc, informal arrangements rather than employ an experienced professional to do the job for you. One of the most serious problems is that, possibly, you may not even be aware of any communication failure at all for an extended period of time, and by the time you are, it may be far too late to repair the damage done.

Bizalom (Trust) and Sebezhetőség (Vulnerability)

Trust and efficiency are also fundamental conditions for business; both can benefit from your Hungarian language skills. On the one hand, Hungarians in your presence may well continue to make comments in Hungarian among themselves. If you cannot follow their discourse at all, you may feel shut out, or worse, end up feeling unnecessarily suspicious and jittery. On the other hand, although generally very friendly, Hungarian business people are not very likely to warm too easily to expat colleagues who display both distrust and vulnerability at the same time by constantly checking with English-speaking Hungarians what the rest of them are talking about.

Social Segregation

Speaking a little Hungarian and showing sensitivity can help you overcome one of the traps of expat business existence: social segregation. Socializing outside business is seen in Hungary as part of the process of doing business. It is valued as an opportunity to enhance the degree of openness and trust towards each other. For example, parties organized by expats solely for themselves is not the way to win the heart – and, more importantly, the goodwill – of your Hungarian colleagues. They are likely to take note of who is, and especially who is not, invited to such parties. It may take some extra effort but will be well worth your while to make sure that your parties and other social events cannot be construed as examples of social segregation.

Social Bonds

Social bonds may give support to individuals but they can also make the level of income a vital issue in their life. To earn a good living has a different interpretation from that in the West for many in Hungary. It is not uncommon for Hungarians to keep supporting their grownup children and their retired parents or other members of the extended family. This often imposes an enormous financial burden for the main provider of the family. A seemingly topnotch salary often has to go a much longer way than the uninitiated outsider might presume.

Social bonds within the extended family, and the financial responsibilities that can go with them, can play a pivotal role in the decision-making processes of individuals. But social bonds also carry a relatively significant weight outside the family context. The 'old boy's network' syndrome is not unknown here either. Social bonds – friendships, community loyalties, etc – can also impact on business people's role perceptions, handling of conflicts and decision-making.

Aktatologatás (Red Tape) as Control Mechanism

Most people in Hungary, business people in particular, are of the view that they have had more than their fair share of *bürokrácia* (bureaucracy) over the past few decades. Over-politicising and bureaucratising matters has been the order of the day for a long time. Notwithstanding the transformation of the economy, red tape is still doing rather well.

Many Hungarians in business expected having to do less paper-pushing after the changes, but this expectation seems to have proved wrong. Expatriate managers are often seen as increasing, rather than decreasing, the amount of red tape in the business procedures they introduce. The other side of this particular coin is that a Hungarian manager's aversion to bureaucracy can be framed in the expat mind as a lack of skill in structuring information, and in creating and adhering to procedures in general.

Bizalom (trust) and *kontrol* (control) are the primary issues here: paperwork overload can come across as an unnecessarily rigid control mechanism, reflecting lack of trust.

For example, you may think that the most efficient way of handling matters is creating written documents and issuing instructions to your Hungarian colleague. This may sound perfectly reasonable, and it is probably just that.

On the other hand, it may also come across, especially in lateral communication contexts, as an unhelpful imposition of control underpinned by lack of trust and possibly arrogance. This interpretation is quite likely if you and a colleague you have written to tend to run into each other on a regular basis, or have plenty of face-to-face interaction to discuss matters since your office is just a couple of doors away.

Circulars, memos and written records in general are just as important in the Hungarian business context as elsewhere. Nonetheless, it is best not to rely on issuing written communication only or mostly. Having written to your Hungarian colleague, you may reckon the matter at hand has been taken care of. It may have. Then again, quite likely it has not. Your letter is much more likely to be read with an open mind, and a willingness to cooperate, if you have taken the time to discuss the matter as well.

179

Üzenetek (Messages) and Válaszok (Replies)

Yes, you will, no doubt, meet many Hungarian business people who leave no communication unanswered, no promise undelivered, and would never ever *átver* (diddle) you in any way. Furthermore, they will always act with exemplary promptness, efficacy and flair. Before World War II, older generations can testify, Hungarian business practices were part and parcel of European business culture. This included letters answered scrupulously and in good time, calls immediately returned, and gentleman's agreements irrevocably respected.

On the other hand, also be prepared for situations that seem to subvert these honourable traditions. For example, if you have left a personal message for a Hungarian colleague, do not readily assume that it will have been promptly passed on. Instead, you may want to try to call again and again, until you strike lucky.

When you do, you may consider dropping subtle hints about your numerous unreturned calls, your tone of voice possibly betraying a pinch of resentment. Resist the temptation if possible: this strategy is not a winner. On the contrary, it is vital at this point that you act as gingerly as if you had already succeeded in whatever you had set out to achieve.

Generally speaking, replying to written communication, returning calls and, all in all, reacting to your interlocutor's initiatives in a speedy fashion is not something Hungarians are best at. In the business context, this situation tends to be better, but it is anything but perfect. If you really want something done, cultivating the virtue of patience and investing in regular and sustained face-to-face interaction are of the essence.

Keeping in Touch by Phone

Hungarians also love keeping in touch, as well as getting things done, over the phone. It is much more likely that they will call you than write to you. It is in the nature of business that it likes crossing boundaries of time and space. This also stands for the phone culture of Hungary.

Boundaries between the private and the public domain – home and work numbers – are not terribly clear-cut. If the context and the relationship make it appropriate, many Hungarians will welcome your calls at home about matters of business, even quite late in the evenings, early in the mornings or at weekends.

This is of course a two-way street; in return you are expected to take for granted that your phone at home will also act as a business number. If you would like to keep your boundaries more intact, you can do so by clarifying what your preference is from the beginning, and thus avoid a serious clash of expectations.

Aspirations, Timeframes and Workload

Sometimes expats in business stay for a limited period only, but do so with aspirations predicated on the attitude that the sky is the limit. They may feel driven to make an immense impact in a relatively short period of time. To this end, they may be tempted to create work schedules that assume weekend work for others. These schedules may also include assumptions about others readily working overtime – possibly on an unpaid or regular basis.

Now this could be quite feasible as far as people in (senior) management positions are concerned. It is important to bear in mind that, if they really feel part of an inspiring project, Hungarians can be very enthusiastic, generous and creative. If they identify with the goal and feel really part of the team, they can move mountains to achieve success. However, deadlines that assume regular, unpaid overtime by employees who are not in senior management positions may not be seen at all as reasonable from the Hungarian point of view as it may be from yours.

These sorts of conflicts are sometimes rooted in the potential discrepancy between the career-drives of expats and their Hungarian colleagues. Expats may be inclined to prove themselves while in Hungary, i.e. in a few years. Their local colleagues most probably want to do the same – but in a few decades or even a lifetime.

181

Compacting decades into a few years may be ideal for the former, but not necessarily for the latter.

An awareness of the rather different timeframes, driven by different circumstances, lifestyles and aspirations, can help mitigate frustration on both sides.

Munkastílus (Work-styles)

Change is anything but new to Hungarians – it has been their staple diet for most of their personal life as well as their history. The same is true for Hungarians in business. They have learnt to adapt to changes successfully – but it certainly helps if they see the point of it all. They are keen to have a clear idea about the *raison d'être* of a change, be it minor or major. The way in which a change is proposed to be implemented is also likely be thoroughly scrutinized. New procedures may meet with less resistance if local managers are first consulted about and committed to them. Introducing new management routines without further ado in the name of efficiency is likely to cause considerable irritation.

Stock responses and explanations will not solve the problem. For example, the argument that a given procedure has worked in the parent company, and therefore it should automatically work magic in Hungary as well, will not cut any ice.

A much better way to impress Hungarian managers is to regularly demonstrate your ability for reflective thinking. They will also notice and appreciate it if you have a broad knowledge of the context rather than just a very narrow specialization.

When is an Ígéret (Promise) a Promise?

Knowing just how much you can rely on a promise is crucial in business. 'Promise' is a relative concept. It is not always interpreted in the same way by different people, let alone by different cultures.

For example, you can stand on your head in creative desperation, yet the most you are likely to squeeze out of some English people is

a noncommittal "I'll see what I can do". This will not generally do in Hungary. The cultural difference between the concept of a promise as a performative speech act rather than a conversational gambit must be appreciated to avoid unnecessary frustration.

Hungarian gallantry seems to require routine face-saving when it comes to making promises. You may find yourself at the receiving end of energetic handshakes and even backslapping, which are meant to give more emphasis and authenticity to the promise (you think) you have just elicited. Hungarians may surprise even themselves by their commitment to a promise that seems important to their partner.

But it may turn out, after repeated prodding and pressing, that the particular promise you framed as a performative act of speech with due commitment may have acted for your Hungarian counterpart more like a conversational gambit to make social interaction smooth and enjoyable.

You may save yourself a lot of aggravation if you bear in mind that extracting a promise in Hungary is generally much easier than getting it delivered.

Only the Paranoids Survive

A healthy dose of scepticism and suspicion is vital to stay in business, and to do so with success. But just how much is a 'healthy dose' – not too little, not too much, but just right?

Since the 'ideal' degree of scepticism and suspicion is relative, it is helpful not to expect your own concept of them to tie in with what you experience in Hungary. You may find that some of your business partners tend to think that being a soupçon sceptical or a shade suspicious can make the difference between success and failure. What may come across to you at times like paranoia may be seen as a means of survival by some of your partners.

Keep Smiling?

Hungarians in business are just as fond of jokes and general merriment as the rest of the population. But too much demonstrative smiling is unlikely to be contagious with them.

Oozing optimism constantly is more likely to be seen as either a lack of authenticity or, perhaps even worse, naivety. Both of these perceptions will create distance and doubt rather than closer business relationships.

On the other hand, although the degree of optimism some of your Hungarian business partners display may not match your expectations, their commitment could still be rock solid.

Értekezletek (Meetings) and Tárgyalások (Negotiations)

To have some inkling as to what to expect in meetings and negotiations, it helps to bear in mind that Hungarians thrive on storytelling, anecdotes and jokes. They are also partial to the rhetoric of good arguments and greatly respect mental acuity. Display of broad knowledge is respected. Sustaining the floor by giving a monologue rather than taking turns in a dialogue is a quite common discourse activity.

All these have some way to go to explain why Hungarian meetings and negotiations are often the way they are. Undoubtedly, you will participate in many that are snappy, well-structured and properly chaired. Nonetheless, many of them may not be quite like that.

Mi újság?
So What's the Buzz, Tell Me What's Happening

To start with, meetings often kick off with a thorough warm-up to the exercise. For example, except for very formal meetings, people are likely to buttonhole each other for some chat, catch up with gossip and do some last-minute lobbying as they arrive.

When the lively buzz finally settles, the chair frames the debate by what may at times seem like an overly lengthy introduction.

Napirend (Agenda) vs Spontaneitás (Spontaneity)

If meetings sometimes end up going on forever, it is partly because debates are not taken too lightly. This may sound odd given that agendas may not be prepared and circulated to all participants in advance. Even if there is an agenda, it is not necessarily adhered to.

Different strategies for problem-solving and idea-generating meetings may not be clear-cut. Spontaneity as the main driving force of the meeting is not uncommon. People often feel compelled to contribute at great length, possibly several times. It is almost as if making a one-off, concise and to the point contribution is to run the risk of being cancelled out by the rest of the dynamic discourse.

Discourse in Meetings:
Térj a lényegre! (Get to the point!)

Participants may go off on what may seem like a tangent; they tend to cross-reference the flow of the debate and their own contribution by anecdotes to illustrate their point. The direction of the discourse may seem at times to be taking several loops, then it may start proceeding straight to the point until suddenly turning into a zigzag pattern again.

Although the tone of meeting may seem direct, even confrontational, often what is not discussed is just as, if not more, significant. Gaining and keeping respect, face-saving of self and others, and talking around delicate issues can be quite time-consuming.

Jegyzőkönyv (Minutes)

The protocol of starting a meeting by asking participants to confirm the minutes of the previous meeting is not something you can take for granted. Neither is the tradition of specifying who is responsible for keeping minutes for the current meeting taken as seriously as you might expect. Sometimes minutes are altogether replaced by a memo.

Tárgyalás (Negotiation)

Like meetings, negotiations can also take up more time than expected. Delegations may be relatively large. Be prepared to answer a plethora of questions, some of them hypothetical. Possible scenarios and options are often scrutinized with relish. Definitions of terms can assume greater significance than you would have imagined; details can be chewed over more times than you thought possible.

To mitigate the potential culture shock over what you may perceive as the 'fussiness' of your Hungarian partners, it may help to remember the broader context of business negotiations and contracts.

The legal tradition in Hungary is, as in many other parts of the European continent, that of Roman law. Now, if your own negotiating attitude is culturally rooted not in Roman law but in case law, you may be more used to its relative open-endedness, i.e. 'fuzziness'. Importantly, this implies that the degree of ambiguity you and your partners may welcome, and be happy with, can be quite different. They may perceive your document as fuzzy – needing further clarification. On the other hand, their process of seeking clarification may come across to you as fussy, unnecessary and endless.

Patience and awareness of the different legal traditions and their implications can help you to appreciate the different attitudes. Putting extra pressure to close the deal may instead end the relationship altogether. Impatience may be interpreted as a sign of condescension – a taboo if there ever was one. There will be more willingness to work out the differences and to do business with you rather than someone else if your Hungarian partner feels there is genuine, mutual respect.

PRACTICALITIES

Dress Code

When it comes to self-presentation, Hungarians in business tend to opt for refined elegance. Though the degree of formality depends on the subculture of the company, the time of day, the occasion and personal style, a quality outfit is seen as essential.

Vendéglátás (Hospitality)

Working lunches and dinners are very much part of the business routine. Hungarian business people tend to be friendly and hospitable, and they do appreciate the finer things in life, such as food and wine. It is customary for Hungarians to pride themselves on their legendary hospitality, and they may take offence if their invitation is not appreciated enough.

Dinners are usually rather formal occasions, with appropriately formal dress code. Do not expect to wrap it all up soon. The wining and dining is most likely to be done in style. Hence, it can take a lot of time and energy, not to mention money. This may be particularly the case if it takes place in the country and not in Budapest, where the pace of life is much faster.

Interruptions

Be prepared to sustain a dinner conversation even though its rhythm may be punctuated by mobile phone calls. Anybody who is somebody carries a *mobiltelefon* (mobile phone), or so it seems.

The Hungarian jargon for the mobile phone says a lot about its public perception at the time when it first made its appearance in Hungary. It was seen as a status symbol, and a negative one at that, so it was jokingly called *bunkófón*. It is a pejorative term, which roughly translates as 'the nerd's phone'. The judgmental message of the word originally referred to people who were perceived as having a lot of money to flaunt but not necessarily the taste to match it.

Névjegy (Business Cards)

Don't leave home without them ... When doing business with Hungarians, have plenty of this symbolic representation of yourself ready at all times, even if the occasion is social rather than business. Hungarians tend to distribute their *névjegy* (business card) generously, and expect you to do the same.

Hungarian business cards often signal the owners' attitude to boundaries between their public and private domain. The cards may include their home and business parameters, or they may present you with an extra card with their home contact details.

Nyitvatartás (Business Hours)

Hungarians normally get cracking in the office relatively early, around 8 a.m., and therefore wrap up sometimes as early as 4:30 p.m. These are the official business hours but people in business often work very late, and even during weekends. Long lunches are unusual unless it is an important working lunch. Afternoon siesta is not practised. The hours are not the same in various offices so it is best to double-check before you set out to get something done.

Friday afternoons are not the best time to do business. Many people finish around 4 p.m., sometimes even at 2 p.m. as in some ministries. If you need to visit your bank, you can usually count on it being open for customers between 9 a.m. and 1 p.m., although some of them would also be happy to receive you in the afternoon.

Generally you can do your shopping between 10 a.m. and 6 p.m. on weekdays. Thursday is usually the day for evening shopping, and a number of outlets operate 24 hours a day. Saturday hours vary.

Hungarians tend to take their holidays in June, July or August, so getting something done efficiently in the summer period could present a challenge. If you need to talk to several people, it may be difficult to schedule your different meetings for the same one or two-week period. It is likely that at least some of the people you would like to see are away for a few weeks. Business gets pretty serious though for the rest of the year, except from Christmas to the first few days of January, when the whole country virtually grinds to a standstill.

It is helpful to keep in mind that sometimes the timing of public holidays can be a bit unpredictable. They may be lumped together with weekends so that everyone can enjoy a longer break.

GETTING YOUR BUSINESS STARTED

The business climate favours the *külföldi befekteto* (foreign investor); government policies are business-friendly, and have encouraged the *külföldi toke beáramlás* (influx of foreign capital).

When you set out to set up your business, you are unlikely to feel constrained by either political or legal snags. The institutional framework for doing business has not only been established but is also in working order.

Banks and Pénz ügyek (Money Matters)

For example, as a foreign investor, you can *pénzt átutalni* (transfer funds), *tőke* (capital) or *haszon* (profit) freely in foreign currency. You will probably find that opening and maintaining *bankszámla* (a bank account), whether in forints (HUF) or *devizaszámla* (a hard currency account), is much the same process as in other parts of Europe.

Most of the time you can also rely on plastic money. Internationally known *hitelkártyák* (credit cards) such as American Express, Master and Visa and *bankkártyák* (debit cards) do not normally cause a problem.

Pénzváltás (exchanging money) can be risky if it involves street dealers, and it is safest done at the usual institutions such as banks, exchange offices and hotels. Forint (HUF), the Hungarian currency, has been *konvertibilis* (convertible) since 1996.

Most major commercial banks operate in Hungary, often with a network of local branches across the country. Some of the head offices include the following:

National Bank of Hungary
Szabadság tér 8-9
1054 Budapest
Tel: 269-4760, 302-3000; Fax: 332-3913

Budapest Bank GE Capital
Alkotmány u. 3
1054 Budapest, Hungary
Tel: 269-2333, 269-2358; Fax: 269-2417

Commercial and Credit *Kereskedelmi és Hitel Bank K&H Bank*
Vigadó tér 1
1051 Budapest
Tel: 267-5000; Fax: 266-9696

Hungarian Credit Bank *Magyar Hitel Bank*
Bárczi István u. 3
1052 Budapest
Tel: 266-6907, 117-1499; Fax: 266-6845

National Savings and Commercial Bank
Országos Takarék Pénztár OTP
Nádor u. 16
1051 Budapest
Tel: 353-1444; Fax: 312-6858

Postabank
József nádor tér 1
1051 Budapest
Tel: 318-0855; Fax: 317-1369

Hungarian Foreign Trade Bank *Magyar Kereskedelmi Bank MKB*
Váci utca 38
1056 Budapest
Tel 269-0922; Fax: 269-0959

Citibank Budapest
Szabadság tér 7
1054 Budapest
Tel: 374-5000; Fax: 374-5100

Hungarian Export-Import Bank Ltd
Nagymező u. 44
1065 Budapest
Tel: 269-0580; Fax: 269-4476

Central European International Bank CIB
Medve u. 4-14
1027 Budapest
Tel: 212-1330; Fax: 212-4200

Creditanstalt
Akadémia utca 17
1054 Budapest
Tel: 269-0812; Fax: 353-4959

Credit Lyonnais
József nádor tér 7
1051 Budapest
Tel: 266-1578, 266-9000; Fax: 266-9950, 266-7683

Internationale Nederlanden ING Bank
Andrássy u 9
1061 Budapest
Tel: 268-0140, 321-1320; Fax: 269-6447

American Express Hungary Ltd
Deák Ferenc utca 10
1052 Budapest
Tel: 235-4330; Fax: 267-2028

Multilateral Development Banks
EBRD European Bank for Reconstruction & Development
Rákóczi út 42
1072 Budapest
Tel: 266-6000; Fax: 266-6003

IBRD International Bank for Reconstruction & Development
Szabadság tér 7-9
1054 Budapest
Tel: 302-9581; Fax: 302-9586

Cégalapítás (Founding a Company)

To get your company going is relatively simple. All it is likely to take
for you to register it is a couple of hundred dollars, a few stamps,
filling in some papers and visiting a notary public. With the help of a
lawyer with local expertise, you could probably expect to wrap it all
up in a few weeks, unless you go for a complex operation. It is sensible
to get some expert advice from one of the Hungarian business
advisory bodies or one of the several well-known international
consulting firms. Check the list at the end of this chapter.

You are not restricted in your choice of company. You could, for
instance, get yourself an investment portfolio in Hungarian companies, enter a joint venture with a Hungarian partner or go for a
wholly owned subsidiary.

Some of the Hungarian business forms include the following:

* *Kft.* – *Korlátozott felelősségű társaság* (limited liability com-
pany)
* *Rt.* – *Részvénytársaság* (joint stock company of shareholders)
* *Bt.* – *Betéti társaság* (deposit partnership)

For the time being, acquisition of land and the defence industry are
no-go areas. In fact, if you have secured permission from the government first, you could buy land in certain cases. But again, if your
company is completely foreign-owned but registered in Hungary, not

even these restrictions apply. Fundamentally, foreign and local companies are treated the same if corporately based in Hungary and therefore regulated by Hungarian law.

The Business of Adók (Taxes)

As with banks and companies, the business of taxes is similar to what you would find, for example, in Western European countries.

Both *adók* (taxes) and *adókedvezmények* (tax allowances) come in all shapes and sizes. At the moment, some of the important taxes you may have to sort out include the following:

* *Jövedelemadó* – personal income tax
* *Társasági adó* – corporation tax
* *Adóelőleg* – withholding (dividend) tax
* *Vám* – excise tax (on export and import, depending on the product)
* *Luxusadó* – tax on luxury goods (e.g. on coffee, grape-wine, cars, gems and precious metals)

ÁFA VAT

If you would like to have a tax receipt for your business, you need to indicate that in advance by saying *ÁFÁS számlát kérek. ÁFA* (VAT) is generally 25 per cent on both goods and services. There are exemptions. For example, ÁFA is calculated at 12 per cent on books and some other goods. Sometimes, as in the case of financial or educational services, none is applied at all.

Then there are local taxes such as the communal tax of entrepreneurs and private individuals, a tax on building, land, tourism, industrial activities and the *gépkocsiadó* (vehicle tax) which is based on the weight of the vehicle.

The relatively high rates of personal income tax and a great variety of social contributions you can be expected to pay can come to a pretty substantial sum. For example, if you are an employer, you need to pay towards the cost of the social security system. These include a fixed, monthly sum as *egészségügyi hozzájárulás* (healthcare contribution) for your employee. On top of that comes 33 per cent of the gross salary of your employee as *társadalombiztosítási járulék* (social security contribution). The latter covers both the *egészségbiztosítási járulék* (medical contribution) and the *nyugdíjjárulék* (pension contribution). There are other costs as well, some of which are tax deductible.

The various taxes and social contributions you are expected to pay are only part of the picture. There are also several significant *beruházási adókedvezmények* (investment tax benefits) that are designed to act as *üzleti ösztönzők* (business stimuli). For example, if your company invests a substantial sum, say one billion forints, in production, it may benefit from the 50 per cent *társasági adókedvezmény* (corporate tax deduction). The Hungarian *társasági adó* (corporate tax) is quite favourable at the rate of 18 per cent, but you can receive a *teljes mentesség* (full waiver) of it for ten years in some cases. This can be the case if your *üzleti beruházás* (business investment) is in what they call a *vállalkozási övezet* (enterprise area), such as in and around Barcs, Makó, Mohács, Záhony and Zemplén.

Similarly, this *adómentesség* (tax waiver) also applies if you invest in one of the so-called *kiemelt körzet* (special regions) where the rate of *munkanélküliség* (unemployment) is higher than 15 per cent. You can *leír* (write off) a further 20 per cent from the *adóalap* (tax base) if the investment is for *kutatás és fejlesztés* (research and development).

Given the variety of taxes, tax allowances and social contributions, talking to an experienced accountant may be helpful to find out what exactly is appropriate and relevant in your particular case. You may also like to consult the website of the Hungarian Investment and Trade Development Agency at www.itd.hu.

Business Information Resources and Contacts
• *Investment and Business Guide to Hungary*. Hungarian Chamber of Commerce and Industry.

- *Who's Who in Finance*. Includes information about key movers and shakers in finance.
- *Equity Central Europe*. Stock market information for investors in the Central European region. *Budapest Business Journal*.
- *Book of Lists*. Company Directory.
- *City Guide Hungary*. Business information about major Hungarian cities.
- The Hungarian Investment and Trade Development Agency, ITD Hungary. Services include business matchmaking, information on business regulations, tax incentives, project development, company profiles, conference facilities, media and business relations. Regional offices around the country in Budapest, Győr, Veszprém, Eger, Debrecen, etc.
  Central Office Tel: 318-0051, 266-7034; Fax: 318-3732
  E-mail: itd@itd.hu
  Website: http://www.itd.hu
- Budapest Chamber of Commerce and Industry
  Magyar Kereskedelmi és Iparkamara
  Krisztina Körút 99
  1016 Budapest
  Tel: 353-3221; Fax: 214-1827
  E-mail: bgszi@bkik.hu
  Website: http://www.bkik.hu

Market Research Firms

Kopint-Datorg Rt.
Csokonai u. 3
H-1081 Budapest
Tel: 266-6722; Fax: 266-6483

Gallup Hungary
Fő tér 1
1033 Budapest
Tel: 250-0999; Fax: 250-0650

Trade and Industry Associations
Hungarian Chamber of Commerce and Industry
Kossuth Lajos tér 6-8
1055 Budapest
Tel: (36) (1) 353-3333; Fax: (36) (1) 269-4628

Hungarian Banking Association
Roosevelt tér 7-8
1051 Budapest
Tel: 312-5826; Fax: 331-1723

Hungarian Chamber of Database Suppliers
Kuny Domokos u. 13-15
1012 Budapest
Tel: 202-2998, 175-9722; Fax: 202-2894

Association of Hungarian Chemical Industries
Erzsébet királyné útja 1/c
1146 Budapest
Tel 343-8920; Fax 343-0980

Association of Hungarian Electronic and Informatics Industries
Szemere u. 17
1054 Budapest
Tel: 331-8986, 311-6271; Fax: 331-6320

National Association of Trading Companies
Kuny D. u. 13-15
1012 Budapest
Tel: 355-9689, 202-6574; Fax: 355-9689

Hungarian Franchise Association
Margit körút. 15-17
1024 Budapest
Tel: 212-4124; Fax: 212-5712

Association of Hungarian Insurance Companies
Deák F. u. 10
1052 Budapest
Tel: 318-3473; Fax: 337-5394

Joint Venture Association
Kuny D. u. 13-15
1012 Budapest
Tel: 212-2506; Fax: 156-2506

Ministry of Industry & Trade & Tourism
Honvéd u. 13-15
1055 Budapest
Tel: 374-2996; Fax: 332-9750

Ministry of Finance
József Nádor tér 2/4
1051 Budapest
Tel: 318-2066, 338-2633; Fax: 318-2570

Ministry of Environment and Regional Policy
Fő utca 44-50
1011 Budapest
Tel: 457-3300; Fax: 201-2846

State Privatization and Holding Co. (APV Rt.)
Pozsonyi út 56
1133 Budapest
Tel: 269-8600; Fax: 349-5745

Conferences and Conventions

Hungarian Convention Bureau
Sütő-utca 2
1052 Budapest
Tel: 317-9056; Fax: 318-9059
E-mail: hcb@mail.matav.hu
Website: http://www.hcb.hu

— Chapter Seven —

HUNGARIAN CULTURE AND SOCIETY

13/F HUNGARIAN CULTURE
12/F HUNGARIAN CULTURE
11/F HUNGARIAN CULTURE
10/F HUNGARIAN CULTURE
9/F HUNGARIAN CULTURE
8/F HUNGARIAN CULTURE
7/F HUNGARIAN CULTURE
6/F HUNGARIAN CULTURE
5/F HUNGARIAN CULTURE
4/F HUNGARIAN CULTURE
3/F HUNGARIAN CULTURE
2/F HUNGARIAN CULTURE
1/F HUNGARIAN CULTURE
G/F HUNGARIAN CULTURE
BASEMENT-STEREOTYPES

TRIGG.

OLD AND NEW TRAVELLERS ON HUNGARIAN CULTURE AND SOCIETY

The historical 'Grand Tour' that used to finish off the education of members of upper-class society did not normally stretch as far as Hungary. Nonetheless, from medieval to recent times, some travellers have been keen to go off the beaten track and explore Hungary, often finding themselves attracted to it like a magnet. Plans to stay for a day or two turned into weeks, months and years at times. Some of the writing published by travellers of past and present gives a fascinating insight into how Hungarian culture and society has been perceived over time.

"We continued two days travelling between this place and Buda, through the finest plains in the world, as even as if they were paved, and extremely fruitful, but for the most part desert and uncultivated, laid waste by the long war between the Turk and the Emperor ... Indeed, nothing can be more melancholy than travelling through Hungary, reflecting on the former flourishing state of that kingdom, and seeing such a noble spot of earth almost uninhabited."

— Lady Mary Wortley Montague,
The Turkish Embassy Letters, 1717

"I think Hungary is a noble country, which only wants navigations made across from the Adriatic to the Danube, to be one of the richest and best peopled countries upon earth."

— Elisabeth Craven, *A Journey through the Crimea
to Constantinople in a Series of Letters*, 1786

"The next day I attended the county meeting, and received every mark of civility and attention. It was a very brilliant assembly: the gentlemen were all in elegant Hungarian dresses. The debates were carried on in the Hungarian language; it was therefore by their looks, and not by their conversation, I was to learn what was going on. Some from the tone of voice I conjectured to be much out of humour: these frequently twisted their moustaches very rapidly between their fingers; but this did not signify, like the bull's rubbing his horns, or the boar his tusks, against a tree, defiance; business was peaceably transacted, and about two o'clock we sat down to a hospitable dinner, given us by the deputy lieutenant."

— Robert Townson, *Travels in Hungary,
with a short account of Vienna in the year 1793*

"The view which we enjoyed from the Observatory was truly superb. We overlooked even the fortress, and saw the town of Old Ofen [Old Buda], stretching along the banks of the river, to a great distance. On the opposite side of the river we looked directly down on the large city of Pesth [Pest]. Between the two flowed, at our feet, the majestic Danube, losing itself to the south in an endless plain, and, after being divided by finely wooded islands towards the north, becoming concealed amongst the broken mountains. The river was studded with numerous floating mills, and crossed by the long bridge of boats, which looked like a cord stretched between the opposite banks."

> — Richard Bright, *Travels from Vienna through lower Hungary; with some remarks on the state of Vienna during the congress in the year 1814*

"The Hungarian nation, ancient and picturesque, and peculiarly characterized as it is, appears to be at present little known, and perhaps still less cared for in England. Our indifference is singularly ungrateful; for there is scarcely a European country in which the Anglo-mania rages more fiercely than in that slighted land."

> — Catherine Grace Frances Gore, *Hungarian tales*, 1829

"Pesth [Pest] looks extremely well from the Danube. It is for the most part built in a modern style of architecture; several of the public edifices, and even of the private mansions are splendid."

> — Michael Joseph Quin, *A steam voyage down the Danube*, 1835

"The hills which bound the western coast of the lake [Balaton] produce Hungarian wines … A tour through the romantic valleys that intersect them will prove highly gratifying to the naturalist; the rocks are of the most dazzling whiteness, being principally composed of marine shells."

> — Edmund Spencer, *Sketches of Germany and the Germans, with a glance at Poland, Hungary and Switzerland in 1834 and 1836*

"Pest is a modern town, with wide, clean and well-paved streets, shops amply furnished with goods, many handsome public edifices, and a fine quay. The houses are almost invariably built of a light, porous stone, brought from the opposite side of the river. The university, which has acquired a high reputation, contains an excellent cabinet of natural history, and a good botanical garden."

> — Charles Boileau Elliott, *Travels in the three great empires of Austria, Russia and Turkey*, 1838

"Once launched on the Puszta, or vast plains which occupy nearly one third of Hungary, the traveler feels at once that he is in a new land; that another existence, a fresh order of ideas, are called into being by such a scene. Day after day he traverses at a slow pace the long flat, dreary, perhaps, to accustomed eyes, but to him teeming with novelty at every step."

> — George Edward Hering, *Sketches on the Danube, in Hungary and Transylvania*, 1838

"All persons travelling in Hungary must make up their minds resolutely to fling from them every feeling of hyper fastidious-ness, both as regards roads, horses, drivers, and accommoda-tion; to brave delay, disappointment, and every danger; and to prepare themselves to do battle with inconvenience of every description; when having so done, they will be certain to find natural beauty and interest enough to repay them for all the trials both of nerve and patience which they must inevitably encounter..."

> — Julia Pardoe, *The city of the Magyar, or Hungary and her institutions in 1839–40*

"When a Hungarian enjoys himself, he is sad. ... he will cast himself on to a bench, lean his arms on the table amidst the bottles and glasses, put his head down on them and sob audibly ... But this is only when he is having a good time and thoroughly enjoying himself; on other occasions you will find him a cheerful, practical, everyday sort of person, with a keen eye for business and no nonsense about him."

— H. Ellen Browning,
A girl's wandering in Hungary, 1897

"In summer, Balatonfüred [Lake Balaton] is delightful. The first time that I went there I arrived early on a July morning, thinking to go on to Budapest before noon. Actually I did not continue my journey till ten days later, by which time I had fallen completely in love with the place."

— Charles Cunningham,
What I saw in Hungary, 1931

"Margit Island, about two hundred and eighty acres in extent, is set not only in the middle of the Danube but in the middle of Budapest. You reach it in a few minutes by taxi, by bus, by tram or by river taxi, and at once you feel yourself removed from everything urban, for the Island is one huge park, one of the most charming in the world. It is as if the best of Maidenhead and Henley were situated in the middle of the river and transported downstream to somewhere between Westminster and Waterloo Bridge."

— John Brophy, *Personal impressions and an interpretation of the national character*, 1936

"I do not know whether I shall ever visit this plain [the Puszta], but even if I do I know I shall not feel that extraordinary sensation of being in another world for the first time. I shall have that scene forever photographed in my memory ...

"… for the man who can be content with one visit to Hungary ought simply to be led away to a quiet corner and shot. The place grows on you and grasps you and seems to squirt a divine soda water into your blood. Never shall I agree to leave Hungary alone. Never shall I agree to a final visit …"

— Christopher Sidgwick,
Whirlpools on the Danube, 1937

"I found on further acquaintance… the passion, the dynamic force which have made Hungary, its strange isolation, its strategic position in the centre of Europe, such a continually erupting crater, such a constantly humming powerhouse, which is also such a constant exporter of power."

— Edmund Wilson, *Europe without Baedeker*, 1966

"Life seemed perfect: kind, uncensorious hosts; dashing, resplendent and beautiful new friends against the background of a captivating town; a stimulating new language, strong and startling drinks, food like a delicious bonfire and a prevailing atmosphere of sophistication and high spirits that it would have been impossible to resist even had I wanted."

— Patrick Leigh Fermor, *Between the Woods and the Water: On Foot to Constantinople from the Hook of Holland – The Middle Danube to the Iron Gates*, 1986

"Budapest is the loveliest city on the Danube. It has a crafty way of being its own stage-set, like Vienna, but also has a robust substance and a vitality unknown to its Austrian rival. Budapest gives one the physical sensation of being a capital, with the urbanity and grandeur of a city that has played its part in history …"

— Claudio Magris, *Danube: A Sentimental Journey from the Source to the Black Sea*, 1999

Learning often encouraged from a very early age.

EDUCATION

Education is seen as a vital part of Hungarian culture. It has a fine reputation, and it is highly valued by Hungarian society. This is not at all reflected in teachers' salaries, which are often absurdly low, whereas their workload is just the opposite. In the light of this paradox, it is a mystery why the Hungarian educational system has been blessed with so many generations of inspirational teachers. Like their teachers, pupils also traditionally have a heavy workload, including tons of homework and regular in-class tests.

In principle, education is free, unless you opt for the burgeoning number of private schools. In practice, books and other school-related costs can make education a considerable outlay to reckon with in the family budget.

The Context

The development of the Hungarian education system was partly shaped by the ideological competition between the two major religious forces in Hungary: the Catholic and Protestant Churches. For example, famous denominational seats of learning include the first Hungarian school established in 996 by the Italian Benedictine monks of Pannonhalma, and Protestant schools and colleges at places like Sárospatak and Debrecen. In the mid-17th century, Comenius, the great educational reformer and an advocate of modern European mentality, wrote *The Visible World*, the first picturebook for children, while working in Sárospatak. From the 18th century, education became more a sociopolitical than a religious question.

The First Hungarian Universities

The first Hungarian universities go back to the 14th century. The oldest, the University of Pécs (1367), was founded by *Nagy Lajos király*, or King Louis the Great (1326–82), a Hungarian king of the French-Italian Anjou dynasty. It was the fourth oldest university in medieval Central Europe, after the universities of Prague, Cracow and Vienna. The University of Óbuda (1389) was founded by *Zsigmond*

király, or King Sigismund (1368–1437). However, its Schools of Law, Medicine, Philosophy and Theology did not seem to function by the time *Mátyás király* (King Matthias Corvinus) founded in 1467 the third Hungarian university: Academia Istropolis, the University of Pozsony (now Bratislava, part of Slovakia).

Many Hungarian-born Nobel Prize winners graduated from the famous Eötvös University in Budapest, although the institution itself has a somewhat bumpy saga. It started out as the University of Nagyszombat (Trnava, now part of Slovakia), founded in 1635 by Cardinal Péter Pázmány as a Jesuit educational centre in support of the Hungarian Counter-Reformation. The university was transferred first to Buda (1777), then to Pest (1784). It is now named after Baron Lóránd Eötvös (1848–1919), an outstanding physicist, president of the Hungarian Academy of Sciences, minister for culture and education, and well-known in the international scientific community for his Eötvös Law and Eötvös Torsion Pendulum.

He also initiated *Eötvös kollégium* (Eötvös College), in 1895, a legendary Hungarian school designed to educate the intellectual elite. The Hungarian educational system – and pedagogy – has traditionally been based on German models; Eötvös himself attended German universities. Nonetheless, *Eötvös kollégium* was set up as a centre for excellence in line not with the German tradition but the French educational model of the École Supérioure of Paris, with an emphasis on French culture. While a student of Hungarian and English literature and linguistics at Eötvös University, the author of this book also had the good fortune to enjoy studying French at Eötvös College.

Since the time of Eötvös, new universities have been established, especially after World War II and also after 1989 – including ecclesiastic and independent universities and colleges. One of the most famous independent universities, the Central European University, was founded in 1991 by György Soros, the Hungarian-born American businessman and philanthropist. CEU is a postgraduate school of social sciences, and its language of instruction is English.

Choice of Schools

Most children get their first social bearings at *óvoda* (nursery school) (age 3–6), which is compulsory from age 5–6 to prepare them for school. Serious studies start at the age of 6 at *általános iskola*, or primary school (age 6–14). Education is compulsory for 10 years, i.e. until the age of 16.

You can choose from many different types of primary school, depending on their field of specialization (e.g. music schools, experimental school for autistic children), pedagogy (e.g. Montessori, Waldorf) or the language of instruction (e.g. English, German, French) you want your children to be immersed in. There are plenty of denominational schools of all sorts, as well as special schools for children who are physically or mentally handicapped. International schools you can opt for include the Magyar-British International School, American International School of Budapest, Britannica School, International Kindergarten and School, and Super Kids.

The next major watershed is at 14, when students can continue at a *gimnázium* (grammar school), a *szakközépiskola* (vocational secondary school) or a *szakiskola* (vocational school). *Érettségi vizsgák* (matriculation exams) – like A levels – at age 18 is a truly momentous event in Hungarian students' lives.

Getting a Degree

University training lasts five to six years, college training three to four. Arguably, *egyetemisták* (university students) have never had it so good in some ways. For example, there is a plethora of *csereprogram* (exchange programmes) and *ösztöndíj* (scholarships) available to broaden their horizons with periods of study abroad. Many may not see it this way though, since the days when you could get your degree for free are also over. Many resent *tandíj* (tuition fees) at tertiary level, and fear that it will influence social mobility adversely.

After graduation, securing a *jó állás* (good job) is not a piece of cake nowadays. Hence it is not surprising if sharpening one's mind in the traditional sense is becoming less of a priority. The emphasis is shifting from educating oneself for 'life' to training for 'work'. Instead of the traditional focus on theoretical knowledge aimed at an all-round understanding of the world, there seems to be a tendency to concentrate on pragmatic and more specialized job skills.

Recently the system of university education has been through important changes. For example, more and more degree programmes are offered in English, German, French and Russian as the language of instruction. Several thousand foreign students graduate from Hungarian universities such as the Technical University and the Medical University in Budapest. On the other hand, thousands of Hungarian graduates go on to become internationally respected research scientists or musicians abroad where they are more likely to be able to get financial support for their work.

Some major Hungarian universities and their websites:
- *Budapesti Közgazdaságtudományi Egyetem* (Budapest University of Economic Sciences): www.bkr.hu
- *Budapesti Műszaki Egyetem* (Budapest Technical University): www.bme.hu
- Central European University: www.ceu.hu
- *Eötvös Lóránd Tudomány Egyetem* Eötvös (Lóránd University): www.elte.hu
- International Business School of Budapest: www.ibschool.hu
- Semmelweis University of Medicine: www.sote.hu
- Janus Pannonius University: www.jpte.hu
- József Attila University: www.jate.u-szeged.hu
- Kossuth Lajos University: www.lib.klte.hu

Some Private Schools
Montessori Educational Centre
Budapest, Gyömbér utca 2–4. 1213
Tel: (1) 277-0159
www.kih.c3.hu

Waldorf School of Óbuda
H-1037 Budapest, Bécsi út 375
Tel: (1) 314-2859

Budapest French Primary and Secondary School
Budapest, Mátyás király út 44–46. 1125
Tel: (1) 275-4296

Kinder Klub German Language Nursery
Budapest, Gárdonyi Géza utca 27-33. 1026
Martonvásár, Gábor Áron utca 20. 2462

Magyar-British International School, Budapest
Budapest, Somlói út 66. 1118
Tel: (1) 466-0589, 466-0590, 466-0595
Budapest, Pasaréti út 82–84. 1026
Tel: (1) 200-7571, 200-7572
Tel/fax: (1) 200-7573

Magyar-British International School, Székesfehérvár
Székesfehérvár, Széna tér 10. 8000
Tel: (22) 349-443

Austrian Hungarian Európa School
Budapest, Istenhegyi út 32. 1126
Tel: (1) 356-4657
Fax: (1) 356-4683

Deutsche Schule
Budapest, Cinege út 8/c 1121
Tel (1) 274-4212, 274-4228, 274-4229

Autism Research and Experimental School
Budapest, Delej utca 24–26. 1089

LAW AND ORDER

After several decades of highly controlled social existence with a relatively low crime rate, crime levels have risen significantly since the sociopolitical and economic changes. Consequently, people tend to feel more vulnerable, and both the media and the public talk endlessly about *rablótámadás* (violent robbery), *gyilkosság* (murder) and various Mafia activities. The *kábítószer-kereskedelem* (drugs trade) from the East to the West tends to use Hungary as a place of transit. Since drugs-related organized crime has become a serious issue, the general attitude towards drugs is not tolerant.

The Perception

When talking to Hungarians about these issues, remember that the public perception is at least as dramatic, if not more, as the problems themselves. Perception depends partly on what you have been used to – in Hungary's case, a relatively low crime rate based on personal memories. Perception also depends on your point of reference, which for Hungarian society is primarily Western Europe.

Being Street Smart

Budapest is a relatively safe city. For example, walking over *Lánchíd* (Chain Bridge) or *Erzsébet híd* (Elisabeth Bridge) after the theatre can be a singularly splendid experience. This is the case even if you happen to be a woman on your own. It is not uncommon to see people enjoying late night walks in the *Várnegyed* (Castle District) or in some of the residential areas in Buda.

On the other hand, Budapest is a major cosmopolitan city. As such, its urban jungle is not without the usual problems caused by city street gangs, *autótolvaj* (car thieves) specializing in *autólopás* (car theft), *zsebtolvaj* (pickpockets and purse-snatchers) and *késelés* (stabbing). The oldest profession, *prostitúció* (prostitution) is practically a legal activity. There are several *kaszinó* (casinos) in Budapest, where *szerencsejáték* (betting games) are legal, but doing the same in the streets is not, and you could be fleeced if you get involved.

As in many other major cities, when you make your way home by yourself late at night, it makes sense not to be in the wrong place at the wrong time. If you are alone at night and do not have sufficient knowledge of the area, avoid the temptation of exploring poorly lit, seedy-looking places such as certain parts of the *nyolcadik* and *kilencedik kerület* (8th and 9th Districts), which Hungarians sometimes refer to as *Csikágó* (Chicago).

Other sensible behaviour includes the usual urban precautions, for example, avoiding *pénzváltás* (changing money) in the street, and not displaying attention-grabbing valuables either in your car or on your body. When in crowded places such as some downtown streets (e.g. *Vörösmarty tér* – Vörösmarty Square), underpasses, popular tourist sights (e.g. *Margitsziget* – Margaret Island), the underground, and certain transport lines (e.g. *villamos* – trams 2, 4 and 6), beware of pickpockets, often working in teams, sometimes involving children.

Should you notice light fingers 'working' on you, shout *tolvaj* (thief). You can call the *zseblopási osztály* (police pickpocket department) on 312-3456, or file a report at the *rendőrség* (police station) in the *kerület* (district) where you think the *lopás* (theft) happened.

The Rendőrség (Police)

The *rendőrség* (police) is underpaid, overworked and lacks sufficient funds to compete with criminals. It also seems to suffer from corruption and poor image. Hungarian policemen are not famous for their foreign language skills, although some police stations may have an interpreter on hand to help you out if necessary. To make sure you are dealing with a real policeman or woman rather than an *álrendőr* (fake one), check the identification number on their police badge, and the photo, hologram and rank on their ID card.

Korrupció (Corruption) and Transparency International

According to Transparency International (TI), corruption is less of a problem in Hungary than elsewhere in Central and Eastern Europe. Hungary ranked 33rd in the TI corruption perception index in 1998.

211

Transparency of procedures is seen as the key strategy in fighting corruption. To increase transparency, workshops and conferences are held for institutions, civil organizations, legal experts, and journalists. Transparency screening projects have been launched to examine if current laws are doing their work in cracking down on corruption and tightening loopholes.

The Attitude: Presumed Innocent?

In England you are, or so it is widely believed, presumed innocent until proven otherwise. The traditional Hungarian attitude generally tends to be that of suspicion: rest assured you have a decent chance of being presumed guilty unless you can prove your innocence. The Hungarian way, as you will readily appreciate, undoubtedly has substantial benefits that are hard to beat: to start with, it provides run-of-the-mill activities with much-needed thrill and excitement.

Benefit of Doubt: Not On

Benefit of the doubt is a rare luxury. For example, in the naturally unlikely case of travelling on public transport without a valid ticket and bumping into an *ellenőr* (ticket inspector), be prepared to pay the fixed penalty without any further ado. Excuses and explanations, however imaginative or truthful, cannot get you off the hook.

Now, there was a time not so long ago when travelling without a valid ticket in England meant you simply had to buy a ticket from the inspector, or pay an excess fare at the exit, without being required to explain or pay a penalty. Your unblemished innocence was taken for granted: there must have been a good reason why you did not have a ticket, or not quite the proper one. And in all fairness, who could prove you were not going to sort out your ticket at or before the end of your journey?

Under the Hungarian system, you do not need to explain either. Whatever you say, the upshot of it all remains the same: that you cannot demonstrate your innocence is more than sufficient evidence for you to be deemed, rather doomed to be, inexcusably guilty.

Saved Against Your Will

It is also not worth your while arguing with the police who cruise Lake Balaton in patrol boats. They are there to protect you, and by golly they will, even in spite of your will if they deem it necessary.

In some other parts of the world, during a hurricane, alert swimmers and surfers have a whale of a time enjoying the huge waves, at their own risk. In Hungary, when a *vihar* (storm) is about to hit the deceptively calm waters of Lake Balaton, *viharjelző rakéta* (rockets) are fired and red baskets hoisted to warn holidaymakers to keep out of the water – signals to the adventurous, including those with a death wish and/or authority problem, to head for the lake as the waves build up to immense heights.

The police also seem to enjoy flaunting their machismo in attempting to control nature gone wild, since this is their preferred time for patrolling the lake. They fish out whoever they find enjoying the same game of trying to outsmart nature. There are 500 or so successful rescues annually, of which around 300 are credited to the police, the rest carried out by amateurs.

Regardless of your wishes, the police will do their utmost to prevent you in any attempt to raise the annual death statistics of Lake Balaton. With a death rate from drowning and cardiac arrest hovering around 50 souls per annum, Lake Balaton, despite its gentle image, is indeed sufficiently hazardous to deserve the accolade, *Magyar tenger* (Hungarian Sea).

My ID is My Bond

Just think of the continuous delight in being the proud owner of an identity card – an understatement for the hefty little booklet – with your very own card number as well as your own Personal Identification Number. Now, this PIN has nothing in common with the PIN you are used to as a private code to access bank cashpoints. It is no less than the people themselves you access with the PIN in Hungarian ID cards, on contracts and other such formal documents. A glance at a PIN will reveal a person's age and gender. [1] denotes men (who else?); [2] appropriately indicates 'second rate citizens', a.k.a. women. Anyone with a less rigid categorization of gender, including hermaphrodites, experiences a real challenge with this cut-and-dried system.

You must carry your ID, this precious document that clearly sets out the fundamental parameters defining you (thus saving you the trouble of having to orient yourself in this messy world), at all times, but in particular when smartly dressed in little more than your birthday suit for sunbathing, boating and so forth. Whatever the time or occasion, do not leave home without it, or you cannot prove your innocence, that you are indeed who you are, who you say you are, who you claim to be. Mind you, why accept only people's word, when you can trust what is written in their documents much more?

The authorities' intense fascination with documents does not stop with IDs. Drivers have the extra pleasure of having to carry their driving license as well, to prove their driving competence, whatever incompetence they have blatantly demonstrated.

Emergency Numbers

Mentők (Ambulance)	104
Rendőrség (Police)	107
Tűzoltók (Fire Brigade)	105

KEEPING IN TOUCH –
THE CULTURE OF TELECOMMUNICATIONS

The telephone system, or rather the lack of it, used to be one of the worst aggravations in Hungary. This has been particularly so since Hungarians, whether in business or private matters, are like high-flying American executives: the way they keep in touch is by getting on the phone rather than going to the trouble of dropping a line.

Thank-you notes are virtually nonexistent and, though not due to any commitment to save rainforests, Hungarians practise the birthday card ritual to a modest degree only.

"Hello, this is Dead Parrot speaking … get off the line!"

Hungary's fabulously restricted, low-tech phone network became seriously overburdened. Where else could a satirical sketch about someone trying to call a hardware store to enquire about a blender achieve cult status? Just like Monty Python's famous 'Dead Parrot' sketch, *Halló, Vasedény?* (Hello, hardware store?) became a big hit. So successful was it that the dialogue almost became part of the national consciousness: a word of this classic comedy act could be enough for people to fall about with hysterical laughter. And all this is about the simple yet, for most people, not straightforward act of picking up the phone.

Well, to start with there was not necessarily something to pick up. Hungarians used to register their names for a telephone, in line with the English tradition of registering newborn babies to secure a place for them at a top public (i.e. private) school. Some cynics attributed the remarkable abundance of doctors in Hungary to the policy of preferential treatment that used to be given to their phone application – for the benefit of the public at large, of course. Declaring that you are one of thousands of doctors who people need to get hold of on the phone in an emergency, used to be a justification for jumping the queue to have a line installed. But the divinely appointed day when the telephone was installed did not only trigger off 'hallelujahs' but sometimes profuse cursing as well. Potential irritation points included your 'twin' (another number, often a neighbour's, allocated to the same line) monopolizing the line, or knocking on your door to request you to stop chatting on the phone at once since they have business to conduct more urgent than yours can possibly be.

The hit cabaret sketch mentioned above capitalizes on the hilarious discourse and confusion created by several lines being unexpectedly linked. People totally unknown to each other, with very different character and purpose, found themselves teleconferencing, eavesdropping, and, inevitably, getting drawn into intimate discussions. In this popular Hungarian telecommunication game of *Szállj ki a vonalból!*

215

(Get off the line …!), stamina, patience and, above all, good humour used to be of the essence.

You also had to adjust the timing of your calls to a well-considered assessment of the hue and density of clouds in the sky, and not necessarily bother attempting to make a call, for instance, after a heavy shower. Many of the lines were flooded, but you did not worry since, with just a little bit of luck, it took only a day or two for them to be back to normal.

Fully Wired

The days of social factors – such as claiming membership of the prestigious medical profession – carrying weight in securing a phone ahead of others are now gone. So are most of the technical problems that made phoning such a deliciously unpredictable activity.

The sad news is that Hungarians have, for some time now, been gearing up for the most up-to-date and sophisticated telecommunications system. Hungary is now fully wired, and the telecommunications industry is one of the most rapidly developing fields of the economy. It seems destined to become just as boringly efficient and reliable as anywhere else in Europe, which will then take all the fun out of making a phone call.

The timeframe of the deal, though, may come as a slight shock if you are used to getting your phone installed within three days, if not the same day. In Hungary you are still likely to have a chance to exercise the virtues of patience and planning since it can take a few weeks to achieve the same result as giving a quick buzz to a telephone company in some parts of the world.

GETTING AROUND –
THE CULTURE OF TRANSPORT

KRESZ Highway Code

Generally speaking, you can expect to conform to European rules. To cruise Hungarian roads, you must have a valid third-party liability insurance, registration and, of course, a driving license. Front seat passengers and drivers must wear seatbelts and young children must take backseats. Illegal parking may land you with the costly inconvenience of your car being towed away or clamped. Crash helmets are mandatory on two-wheelers. You must not chat on your mobile while at the steering wheel, although many drivers seem to do just that.

Depending on what exactly you are used to, the subculture of driving in Hungary may give you a bit of a shock. Hungarian drivers may come across as not particularly sensitive souls, often with a strikingly short fuse. The style of driving tends to be macho. Demonstrating courtesy towards fellow drivers and other road users is not very common; shouting, cursing and using threatening body language is. Pedestrians: it is wise not to assume that oncoming cars will stop just because you are hovering at the edge of a zebra crossing.

On the other hand, Hungarian drivers and pedestrians alike often go out of their way if you are obviously in deep trouble, say if your car has broken down or needs a push. Crisis situations tend to trigger a more collaborative spirit than everyday routines, where many road cruisers seem to be of the view that driving is a competitive rather than a cooperative game.

Beware: *KRESZ*, the Hungarian Highway Code, takes the ultimate purist view on drinking-and-driving: drivers are not allowed even a single drop of booze. Zero tolerance is reinforced with frequent and random *alkoholszonda* (breathalysing). Even a glass of wine with your dinner or a sherry in the interval of the opera can be detected several hours later. Since you can expect the police to test your alcohol level at the most ungodly hours and unforeseen places, the risk of violating this law is not worth taking.

The problem this presents to Hungarians, who cannot imagine having a social gathering of any sort without alcohol of some sort, is considerable. The solution for many is to negotiate the driver's role while still sober. Since women are often delegated (read *relegated*) to this much sought-after role, the preponderance of female drivers on

Hungarian roads may be just as much a statement about male chauvinism as any achievement on the part of feminists – who, in any case, do not represent a dominant social force in Hungary.

Speed Enforcement with Artistic Flair

Speeding in cities as well as on motorways is taken seriously, if not by anyone else, at least by the police. They are a caring lot with an artistic flair: they may well surprise you with a lovely, unsolicited photograph of you in your car, with the date, time and speed stamped on the photograph, as hard evidence for the (doubtless, in your view, unwarranted) fine you have to pay.

In the extremely unlikely case your travelling companion is someone you would not want your partner to know about, you are advised to keep well within the speed limits.

Urban Orienteering

The heart of Budapest is off-limits to cars. The system of pedestrian zones and one-way streets makes the downtown experience – whether for shopping, eating out, entertainment or office work – a driver's survival challenge indeed.

First, you have to prove your driving credentials and general orientation skills while steering your way through one-way streets galore. Then you need to demonstrate alertness by hunting down and squeezing into a parking space in the narrow streets or in one of the parking garages. Sure, it can be done, and it is not terribly taxing either – but it is fun only if you welcome urban survival games.

Having done some fancy footwork to deposit your car, you are bound to enjoy letting your feet actually do the walking – the well-deserved, mostly pollution-free downtown experience.

Tömegközlekedés (Public Transport): Variety Is the Spice of Life ... or Is It?

Busz (bus), *troli* (trolley bus), *villamos* (tram), *vonat* (train), *metró* (underground), *libegő* (chair-lift), *fogaskerekű* (cable-car), river boat, horse and carriage. You name it, public transport comes in all shapes and sizes in Budapest.

Hungarians do not just have a *metró* (underground system) like any ordinary metropolis, but an underground line called *földalatti*, which was the first to be built in continental Europe.

The Hungarian answer to English double-deckers is the *csuklós busz* (articulated bus). This has one engine with two carriages loosely joined in the middle with some elastic and is great fun – especially for passengers standing in the seam – when the bus speeds along bumpy, winding roads.

What's more, regardless of its format, Hungarian public transport reassuringly displays capricious behaviour. If you have been waiting with a crowd of people for what seems ages, you can rest assured that at least four of whatever you are waiting for will suddenly turn up in double tandem.

The Hungarian answer to double-deckers: the articulated bus, two buses joined together, and run by one engine and one driver. Remember to hold onto the rails if you are standing in the middle of the articulated area, especially when the bus takes a sudden turn.

219

Line Up or Lounge About?

The Hungarian attitude to queuing for public transport is appropriately temperamental. The English passion for standing in an orderly line like slumbering sheep is too tedious and unimaginative for them. Instead, Hungarians lounge about in apparently haphazard fashion in the general vicinity of the *autóbusz-megálló* (bus stop).

This sort of 'loitering with intent', a criminal offence in England, is perfectly acceptable behaviour in Hungary, but should not delude you for a second. When the great moment comes, people lounging about suddenly spring into action and summon every ounce of adrenaline and creativity to jostle on the bus when you have just started to think about getting on. Don't despair though: with some focused practice to improve your reflexes and stamina, you should stand a reasonable chance of squeezing yourself on the next means of transport you wish to use.

Once you have actually managed to get on, do not expect to be able to buy your *jegy* (ticket). Most Hungarians have a *bérlet* (monthly or annual pass), or else buy their ticket beforehand at tobacconists or bus kiosks. The Hungarian travelling public is self-reliant, plans ahead and copes without the time-consuming and wearisome business of conductors, who have been replaced by little gadgets on buses and trams to punch the tickets with yourself.

In case you get stuck in the crowd too far from the ticket-puncher, you can count on the long-suffering loyalty and cooperation of your fellow passengers to pass your ticket from one to the other until it reaches its destination and is punched for you by a public-spirited fellow passenger. Now the validated ticket can happily start its journey back to you. And the further good news is that, normally, it should reach you just before you get off.

The occasional plainclothes *ellenőr* (ticket inspector) makes sure that the amount of revenue lost to fare dodging is a mere double or so that of more elaborate systems complete with armies of conductors. If by any chance you cannot produce a valid ticket or travel card on demand, it makes more sense to pay the on-the-spot *pénzbüntetés* (fine) in *készpénz* (cash) rather than do it later by *csekk* (cheque), which will cost you significantly more.

RETAIL RITUALS – THE ART OF SHOPPING

Nowadays, sophisticated shop-till-you-drop consumers can get almost anything and everything they could wish for – and more! Shopping has become simply a question of locating just where the secret object of desire is available, apart from the trifling issue of finding enough money to meet exorbitant prices.

Except for markets, the standard shopping paraphernalia in Hungary includes a *kosár* (basket). This is not something to trifle with. Most *bolt* (shops), including bookshops, have baskets at the entrance for your benefit, and taking them is by no means optional, not even if you simply dropped in *nézelődni* (to browse). Customer service is not necessarily what you would call impeccable but sales staff is bound to pay personalized attention to you if they notice you wandering around their premises with no *kosár*. Notice they will, so to pre-empt any confusion, the easiest is not to challenge the *kosár* principle: hang on to your *kosár* from the word go.

Boutiques, Malls and Markets

During the years of *butikláz* (boutique fever), sufficiently motivated shoppers could easily get rid of their monthly income in one go in any self-respecting boutique. This is still feasible, even if you are not a fashion addict, since these cramped private shops are boutiques with a difference: not just providing expensive homemade rags, but often a great variety of imported goods. Whatever your snobbery, or whatever junk your heart desires, boutique browsing – a dry version of pub crawling – is a safe bet.

Undoubtedly, things have improved in a big way, to the extent that Hungarians do not need a boutique any more to become skint: any of the growing number of posh, Western-style *bevásárló központ* (shopping malls) will do the trick. Many of these also perform the function of *szórakoztató központ* (an entertainment centre). It is not just about spending your money but time too. Apart from scores of sophisticated shops of all sorts, these centres will dazzle you with a multitude of fun things to do, including multiplex cinemas, bowling, fitness centre, mini-golf, garden, video games, billiards and squash. And to give you sustenance and support in all these activities, there are different bars, cafés and restaurants, not to mention the babysitting service offered at some of them. Some of the major shopping malls include the Budagyöngye, Duna Plaza, Lurdy Ház, Mammut, Pólus, Rózsakert and the West End complex.

Shopping at Hungarian *piac* (markets) is still an intoxicating and cacophonous experience. The sight of *fokhagyma* (garlic) and paprika garlands hanging everywhere in great abundance lives up to popular stereotypes about Hungarians. So too do the long sticks of *szalámi* (salami) and large bunches of all kinds of *kolbász* (sausage) – isn't it comforting to know you can rely on at least some stereotypes?

Many Hungarians and expats alike enjoy the *piac* (atmosphere) and especially the chance to meet the producers of goods. Besides butchers, fishmongers and other professional traders, farmers and peasant women sit at the rows of *zöldség* (vegetable) and *gyümölcs* (fruit) stalls, selling products from their own garden, which are often fresher and cheaper than other produce on offer. If you function well in the wee hours, you can benefit from the *nagybani* (wholesale price) at some of the markets around 4–5 a.m.

You can combine the *piaci bevásárlás* (shopping) at the market with a quick *tízóriai* (brunch) on the spot, fresh *hal* (fish) or spicy *kolbász* (sausage) perhaps with a wide variety of *savanyúság* (pickles). *Savanyú káposzta* (pickled cabbage) and *kovászos uborka* (kosher) pickles in dill, leavened cucumbers straight from the pickle seller's tub with *juhtúró* (curd cheese) can be amazingly delectable – really worth a try. The *piac* is also the place to encounter the famous *lángos*, one of the fast food icons of Hungarian dietary culture.

All in all, the *piac* experience is probably not something you want to miss. The many colourful markets to explore include the *Lehel piac*, the *Vásárcsarnok* and many others, usually named after the *tér* (square) they are located at, such as the *piac* on Battyány tér, Bosnyák tér, Garay tér, Hunyadi tér and the *Fény utcai piac* at Széna tér.

And what if you are not after delighting your stomach but your heart, which is set on antiques, second-hand bargains, art, craft and bric-a-brac? Well, you need to head for either the legendary *Ecseri* or the *Városligeti Bolhapiac* (flea-market) where you could find everything you do not really need but may still want to have. But if you crave to add some international flavour to your *piac* experience, then the *kínai piac* (Chinese market) is the place for you; traders there hail not just from China but various other cultures as well.

The Watermelon Ritual

When watermelon – *görögdinnye* (Greek melon) – is in season, you are in for an experience unlikely to be part of your stereotypical Hungarian shopping schema. Be alert, when driving and especially on foot, to spot in good time the enormous mountains of dark green melons piled high on the pavement, leaving you wondering when the huge heap is going to topple over to the four corners of the earth.

Since Hungarians always get their priorities right, they take the business of buying watermelons most seriously. This is one of the very few occasions when, believe it or not, they are actually prepared to queue and wait their turn, holding onto the particular watermelon they have selected. Making the right choice is a lengthy process of focused concentration, thoroughly examining dozens of melons by tapping them here, there and everywhere, listening for what is considered to be the perfect (i.e. deep, hollow) sound.

The real test, of course, is the actual *lékelés* (tasting) of the melon. Hungarians would not entertain the idea of buying one, unless they have tasted a bit cut out of the melon by the vendor. He takes a huge knife, plunges it into the melon, extracts a chunk with great panache and offers it for tasting as a precursor to buying. This annexed piece

223

Watermelon, garlic and red peppers are displayed in abundance at most Hungarian markets. The choice of görögdinnye *(watermelon) which is just right is a serious business for Hungarians.*

of melon will then be ceremoniously handed around each member of the family participating in the ritual. If, and only if, they all agree that the slice in question is sufficiently *mézédes* (sweet) like honey, does the deal go ahead. If it is a thumbs-down decision, other melons need to be cut and tested, in fact the whole ritual repeated, until either all parties are satisfied or sufficiently embarrassed/frustrated to call a halt to the game.

A Bagful of Medicine

Pharmacists in Hungary have miraculously managed to retain the status of medieval alchemists, along with all the mysterious paraphernalia that goes with it. The idea of walking into a common drugstore, let alone corner store, and taking what you need from the shelf is a relatively recent idea in Hungary.

Normally, you have to find the experts licensed to dispense their precious concoctions only in shops called *patika* or *gyógyszertár* (pharmacy) which tend to be exclusive places with wooden wall panelling, huge green plants, and the penetrating smell peculiar to an alchemist's den. Do not only look for the usual signs, such as a red or green cross, to indicate a *patika*; a snake curled around a pair of scales suits more the image of present-day Hungarian alchemists. Otherwise, shop windows full of overgrown plants ready to burst through the glass indicate the place you desperately need.

If an urgent problem strikes in the middle of the night on a Sunday or Bank Holiday, you simply search out the *ügyeletes patika* (duty pharmacy) in the neighbourhood, and keep ringing the bell until a bleary-eyed *patikus* (pharmacist) emerges to help you.

Locating a *patika* is only the beginning of your trials. The *gyógyszer* (medications) are often well-hidden in intricate systems of revolving drawers and suchlike, often made of ornately carved wood. The only things normally displayed and accessible to customers are a *kancsó víz* (jug of water) and some mundane *pohár* (glasses) on a tray. There is no way, therefore, you can figure out for yourself what you need. In any case, that would undermine the pharmaceutical profession. No, you have to wait your turn – another rare example of Hungarians queuing – to consult the expert in a white gown, safely distanced from ordinary souls by a high and wide counter.

Given the elaborate gatekeeping process you have to get through before you can get what you need, it is small wonder that Hungarians like to leave the *patika* with their shopping bags overflowing with enough pharmaceutical goods to sustain an army for a whole year.

225

Snake symbols by the entrance indicate that you have found a patika.

Since medicine and food are both *drága* (pricey), you may of course have to make the enviable choice as to which of the two you can afford to buy in the first place.

Sadly, it must be said that the first crack in the privileged position of pharmacists has already appeared. It used to be the ultimate head-shrinking experience for a man to go into a *patika* and bashfully ask the female pharmacist for some *óvszer* (condoms) with a queue of children and elderly people eagerly following the whole transaction. The fact that nowadays such fundamental goods are available even in grocery stores makes life markedly easier for foreigners with earthly desires but no Hungarian language skills. On the other hand, it's a real shame you don't need to demonstrate any more with body language what exactly it is you're after. Local Hungarians may feel unfairly deprived of what was a hilarious form of free entertainment.

If you are into natural remedies, look for a *herbária bolt* (herb store) or a *bio-bolt* (health food store). Herb stores are something like alternative pharmacies, selling mostly natural this, that and the other, but most of all teas and *gyógynövény* (herbs) you may have never heard of. Some health food stores also act as pharmacy, tea and bookshop, organic food and drugstore all rolled into one.

RECHARGING YOUR BATTERIES – LEISURE AND PLEASURE

Csak tiszta forrásból (Only from a pure spring)

Whether you are musically inclined or not, be prepared to act like a music lover or, better still, a musician to some degree or other.

You may prefer the music of Zoltán Kodály to that of Béla Bartók, but this preference may carry more meaning than you would expect. Kodály became one of the greatest Hungarian national institutions in his very long life and died one of the richest men in Hungary. By contrast, Bartók, appalled by the politics of the thirties, went to New York and died there prematurely in difficult financial circumstances. It is not necessarily a consolation that he became world-famous posthumously, recognized as one of the most outstanding 20th century composers. Not everywhere though. In Hungary, there was a time when, for example, his expressionist ballet music, the *Csodálatos mandarin* (Miraculous Mandarin) was declared cosmopolitan and immoral, and therefore banned.

An apparently innocent remark about musical preferences may be interpreted in ways not quite anticipated by the unwary. Bartók's music has influenced many musicians, including György Ligeti and György Kurtág, who are among the most significant composers of the international music scene today.

Nem élhetek muzsikaszó nélkül (No life without music)

Hungarians have an intimate relationship with music. The so-called *cigányzene* (Gypsy music) is only one of various musical traditions in Hungary, but it seems to be a hallmark of Hungarian culture – at least

227

in the eyes of foreigners. Indeed, it can prove a bit of a challenge for you to find a self-respecting restaurant that claims to be 'authentic Hungarian' without a Gypsy band stirring up your emotions while you are trying to cope with the burning sensation of spicy food.

Before entering such a mouthwatering establishment, you need to be prepared for some very personal attention from the *prímás* (first violinist) of the band. Whether you display any particular interest in the music or not is simply not an issue: he will in any case invade your privacy and play the most tear-jerking romantic tunes right in your ear. At such times you are supposed to look absolutely riveted by the performance, temporarily relinquish your food and sing along. To experience the ritual in its entirety, you can plant a large banknote, with the nonchalance of a medieval aristocrat, in either the bow or among the strings of the fiddle, or else, if you dare, on the forehead of the fiddler himself.

Some Hungarians, especially young city folk, tend to think this music is tacky, trivial and sentimental, and the ritual that goes with it is outdated. Then again, you could garner Brownie points for requesting the band to play a *nóta* (song) specifically for your table. For some Hungarians, this will demonstrate that you are a fun-loving, party animal, who knows how to *mulat* (revel). They may also make inferences about your intricate knowledge and appreciation of Hungarian and Gypsy folk music.

It is quite another matter of course that Gypsy music and Hungarian music are two different traditions. Gypsy folk music is vocal and sometimes percussive, but fundamentally not instrumental, uses no violins and is therefore unmistakably different from the music Gypsy bands have been traditionally so famous for in Hungary. The music Gypsy bands normally play is Gypsy only to the extent that Gypsy musicians perform it in their historic role as musical entertainers. In reality, this music is typically popular Hungarian music – *verbunkos*, *csárdás* and *nóta* – which is based on Hungarian folk-music idiom but is not in fact folk music at all: it is the product of mostly 19th century composers and also amateurs. Although the composers of this type of music included some Gypsy musicians, their music was part of the Hungarian, not Gypsy, musical tradition. For example, János Bihari (1764–1827), the virtuoso Gypsy violinist, is still famous for his *verbunkos*, and Pista Dankó (1858–1903) for his *magyar nóta* (Hungarian song).

One of the most popular and most often requested 'authentic Hungarian folk songs' is the *Pacsirta* (Lark). It is neither Hungarian (it is, in fact, Romanian) nor a folk song – but is nonetheless an invigorating tune indeed.

Should you confuse the Gypsy and Hungarian musical traditions, some Hungarians will despise you for your ignorance. However, usually in conversation with Hungarians, you can safely get away with this, since many of them make the same mistake – Liszt was no exception to this rule.

A Magyar tenger (The Hungarian Sea)

Most foreigners labour under the gross misapprehension that Hungary is a landlocked country. For a culture so obsessed with its history, it would be a tall order to expect Hungarians to do without, of all things, a sea. After all, no fewer than three – the Baltic, the Black, and the Adriatic – washed Hungary's shores as recently as the 14th century, during the reign of *Nagy Lajos király* (King Louis the Great), remember? Hungarians' obsession with the sea is well-demonstrated by the fact that Horthy, the leading political figure in the autocratic regime of the 1930s, was still an admiral at a time when Hungary possessed not a single sea. This tiny incongruity with reality didn't prevent him dressing up in his admiral's uniform and parading around on a white horse (incidentally, deeply symbolic for Hungarians) as a substitute battleship.

Hungarians have creatively reinvented their seas in the form of a glorious lake. Lake Balaton qualifies beautifully as a sea: after all, it is the largest lake in Central Europe, and the third largest in the whole of Europe. There are many superb advantages of Balaton being, strictly speaking, a lake rather than, as in Hungarian lingo, a sea. To start with, the lack of sharks and accompanying sensation of life-threatening danger is more than compensated for by the thrilling business of angling lackadaisically for bream and perch at dusk and dawn. Should you not find this strenuous sport exhilarating enough, you can always count on the famously hazardous Balaton storms to test your physical stamina and mental reserve to the limits.

Another advantage is that the water, being fresh, means you can deny yourself the pleasures of occasional salty mouthfuls while swimming, as well as the itching afterwards. Since the lake is relatively shallow, the water is warm, at times very warm indeed. On the one hand, it's safe and great fun for children to cavort and splash in for hours and hours; on the other, a hopeless enterprise trying to lure them out. Anglers, perched on tiny wooden rafts at dawn and dusk, also seem to be fatally attracted to the lake.

Yachters who like a challenge can test their sailing skills without having to compete with motor engines, which are not allowed on the lake. However, winds are unreliable: sometimes too light, sometimes too strong, sometimes nonexistent. Hundreds of sailing boats be-calmed in the middle of the lake for hours on end may make a quaint picture for onlookers, but tends not to be so inspiring for the sailors themselves.

Beginners in surfing can find no better place than the warm, shallow fresh water to accommodate their efforts while expert surfers get hooked on the gentle waves and brisk breeze in the glaringly corny sunset, complete with golden-red reflections across the calm waters of the lake. No picture postcard of Lake Balaton can be such perfect kitsch as reality itself.

If swimming is what you are into, head for the northern shores. Except, that is, if you long for a swim with a difference – one combined with hiking. On the southern shores, it takes some determi-nation, and what may seem like endless walking in knee-to-waist high

The shallow waters of the southern shores of Lake Balaton are an excellent playground – and not just for the youngest generation.

water, to reach a suitable depth for swimming. With children engaged in boisterous horseplay, teenagers throwing balls and frisbees, and surfers and boats crisscrossing your path, these walks are excellent for meditating and communing with nature. Once there though, your well deserved swim will be perfectly peaceful, since not many others are prepared to go to all this effort just for a swim.

Late night naturist swimming or floating to the rhythmic motion of the gentle waves can be fun but make sure you hang on to your swimsuit. It will sink, and retrieving it from underwater, while exhilarating, is not altogether a straightforward exercise. Also, spell-bound as you may be, it doesn't hurt to remember that if you hear others on the horizon, they will hear you too. If you have hang-ups about your privacy, recall your physics about the excellent sound-carrying faculties of water, and act accordingly.

In any of the above scenarios, you are guaranteed not to see your partner and/or family for most of the day – arguably, one of the reasons the annual Balaton holiday is a must for many Hungarians.

Spa Culture

Imagine you are in heaven, and it is winter. Snow sparkles and frost glitters wherever you look. It is freezing cold outside, and yet you are itching to get out. What is more, you can hardly wait to do that in nothing more than your swimsuit. Is there something wrong with you perhaps? Oh, no – not at all. You simply know the perfect secret: that there is nothing like floating in steaming hot water while nature around you is frozen.

Whether in hot or cold water, bathing culture is ancient and universal. Water is the source of life, and has been the focus of shrines and public spaces from prehistoric times in many different religions and cultures. Hot water – thermal springs – has made Budapest the European spa capital. Locals love it and visitors flock to enjoy Hungarian thermal baths and lidos (outdoor public swimming baths).

But how has this heaven-on-earth come about? Well, from heaven … so to speak. Strictly speaking, from the sky. Specifically, from the rain above. It seeps through crevices, percolates through limestone rocks and underground caves, and gushes to the surface as hot springs.

The Romans of Pannonia, passionate as they were about bathing, must have been delighted to find the medicinal springs of northern Óbuda. They started Hungarian spa culture in Acquincum (Óbuda), one of the 21 baths archaeologists have so far found. Here, you can admire the aqueducts of their public and private baths, and then pop into *Római-fürdő* (Római Baths), one of the many lido baths in Budapest, especially popular with families.

But it was not only the Romans who appreciated a good thermal spring when they saw one. The tradition continued. New baths – sometimes combined with hospitals – were built until the Turks arrived. They too set about making the most of the multitude of hot springs by building new baths in their own cultural and religious tradition. Many of their thermal steam baths are still ideal to recharge your batteries. For example, in Rudas Baths you can pick and choose from six pools to relax in, each with a different temperature; see if you prefer one of the hot air chambers or the humid steam chambers. Or treat yourself to a massage.

The thermal water of the 50 or so baths and open-air lidos in Budapest are rich in all sorts of minerals, so bathing in them is not just to gratify your senses and engage in social interaction at the same time. Swimming, bathing or getting a mudpack are also recommended for many different ailments such as arthritis, spine and joint problems and neuralgia. If it is your stomach you need to regenerate, you can still swim or soak in the mineralised water, but you must also be prepared to drink the stuff!

There are many icons of Hungarian spa culture around for you to enjoy, most of them with their own atmosphere and clientele. The *Lukács gyógyfürdő és uszoda* (Lukács Medicinal Baths and Swimming Pool), or *Lukács* for short, has 23 hot springs and is famous for the intellectual profile of its regulars – artists, actors and writers – who visit the place religiously, often every single day.

Be it summer or winter, regulars to the neo-baroque Széchenyi gyógyfürdő often combine an outing to the open-air pool with a game of chess in the steaming thermal water.

The baroque-style *Széchenyi gyógyfürdő* is for you if you like your baths to be grand – it is the largest of its kind in Europe. It also attracts chess lovers who, be it winter or summer, play al fresco while bathing. The thermal springs of Gellért Baths benefited many leprous and sick patients in the 13th century, but its elegant, Art Nouveau version today boasts of a guest list that includes Yehudi Menuhin, the Prince of Wales, the king of Nepal and Rabindranath Tagore.

Make no mistake – you do not have to limit yourself to Budapest when it comes to spa culture. The most famous ones outside the capital include Hévíz, Harkány, Balatonfüred and Hajdúszoboszló, but with more than 400 thermal spas around the country, making the right choice needs a long soak.

LITERARY CORNUCOPIA

Hungarians violently differ on almost everything, but they all enthu-siastically concur in their pity for the rest of the world deprived of the unparalleled and mostly painful pleasures of Hungarian literature. If only everyone else knew what they were missing out on!

This attitude is all the more painful for Hungarians since it is in stark contrast with their own awareness of European culture. Hungar-ians grow up with the classics of world literature as household names. For Hungarian children, Oliver Twist, Gulliver, Robinson Crusoe and Alice, along with other famous childhood literary heroes, are close friends. Indeed, were there one, Hungarian children would pass the examination in European Cultural Heritage Awareness with flying colours. They think that Winnie the Pooh, Little Prince, Asterix and all the others live just round the corner and speak – what else? – eloquent Hungarian.

How come then that dazzling Hungarian literary figures have yet to claim a place among the European canon? Two notable exceptions to this are George (György) Mikes whose humorous insights into English idiosyncrasies have appeared in numerous editions, and Arthur (Artúr) Koestler who is perhaps the only Hungarian writer to achieve the perhaps dubious distinction of having his *Darkness at Noon* enshrined in the English school syllabus. Small wonder then, if Hungarians feel justified in adding this point to their semiconscious list of resentments.

Shakespeare and suchlike are not so bad but there is, of course, no real comparison with some of the classical icons of Hungarian belles-lettres such as János Arany, Sándor Petőfi, Endre Ady, Attila József, Miklós Radnóti, Frigyes Karinthy, Dezső Kosztolányi – to name but a few of their heroes. Compared with these literary giants, English, French and German writers have simply been inexcusably lucky to write in languages traditionally accessible to relatively larger markets, thus ensuring their place in the universal literary consciousness.

The Open Air Book Festival is a truly fascinating feature of Hungarian culture and confirms its love of books. I have been to many book fairs (including Frankfurt), but the intimate informality and fiesta nature of the Hungarian event is rather different and special.

The Hungarian solution to this particular injustice is to trust their firm knowledge that in any case the Hungarian translation of foreign works is far better than the original piece. As for their own writers, there is no doubt whatsoever in their minds that if only others knew what they were missing, a great Hungarian language-learning craze would break out instantaneously.

For the moment, though, there is no such danger. Most Hungarian literature, thus much of its culture, is quite solidly stashed away in the enigmatic mysteries of the Hungarian language for the foreseeable future.

— Chapter Eight —

SETTLING IN

To start with, settling in involves – surprise, surprise – applying for various permits, securing certificates, having the appropriate documents translated and authenticated, attention to detail, probably some queuing and … a good dollop of patience.

Then there is the potentially more inspiring part of settling in – finding a home to actually settle into.

We will look at the various aspects of this process, but first let us get the paperwork out of the way.

THIS PERMIT, THAT PERMIT, THE OTHER PERMIT …

Vízum ügyek (Visa Matters)
If you are staying in Hungary for less than three months (90 days), your visit qualifies as a 'short stay', and the administration fees vary

accordingly. If you apply at the Hungarian embassy/consulate in your own country of residence, the current fee for a single entry visa to Hungary is US$40 (US$75 for double entry, US$38 for single transit). The same visa application at other Hungarian representations or at border crossings will cost you US$65 (US$100 for double entry, US$50 for single transit). In Hungary itself, the charge is HUF8,500 (HUF13,500 for double entry, HUF7000 for single transit). Again, if it is a multiple-entry or a multiple-transit permit that you are after, the charge will be different according to where you apply. (In May 2000 270 Hungarian forints converted to about one US dollar.)

An application for a temporary residence permit costs US$40 at Hungarian consulates/embassies, and HUF7,500 within Hungary; immigration visas cost US$30, and extensions of permission to stay, HUF3,000. An application to extend a temporary residence permit costs HUF3,000, but it is HUF4,000 if you are applying for the issue or extension of a long-term residence permit.

These are some of the fee options to tickle your fancy! The various administration fees come in all flavours of the month and change from time to time, but the details outlined above should give you an idea of the general structure and scale of the fees you can expect to pay.

Applying for Your Tartózkodási engedély (Residence Permit)

The list of items to submit may look at first a tad lengthy, complicated and intimidating, but you can make the process considerably smoother if you know not just *what* but also *how* things are expected to be presented, so that they are accepted without any further ado.

The following items must be submitted with requests for residence permits:

1. *Kérelem tartózkodási engedély kiállítására* – Residence Permit Application Form
2. *Szálláshely bejelentőlap külföldiek részére* – Residence Registration Form for Foreigners

3. Stamp duty of HUF4,000
4. Rental agreement or an affidavit about rent-free residence, or other relevant document about your housing arrangements
5. Document making clear the purpose of your stay, e.g. *Munkavállalási engedély* – Work Permit (see below)
6. Proof of finances to support yourself, and to travel out of the country at the end of your stay
7. *Orvosi igazolás* – Health Certificate (see below)
8. Two *Útlevél fénykép* – passport-size photos
9. *Érvényes útlevél* – valid passport

The first three items on the list are normally available at KEOKH (Alien Administration Department):

VI Budapest
Városliget fasor 46-48
Tel: 311-8668

The easiest way to get there is to take the Little Metro (M1) to *Hősök tere* (Heroes Square). The hours of KEOKH vary according to the nature of the enquiry.

Hours for requesting a residence permit for educational purposes:

Monday	13:00–18:00
Wednesday	08:30–18:00
Friday	08:30–12:30

Hours for requesting a residence permit for visiting, working and other income-generating activities:

Tuesday	08:30–18:00
Wednesday	08:30–13:00
Thursday	10:00–18:00
Friday	08:30–12:30

Numbers 4, 6, 8 and 9 on the list above are self-explanatory, although it is worth remembering that you might need to have your proof of finances authenticated, which will cost you at least HUF1,000.

Getting Your Munkavállalási engedély (Work Permit)

Now for number 5: *Munkavállalási engedély* (Work Permit). Well, to start with, you will be glad to hear that you do not need one if you are, for example, part of an educational exchange, work in the field of equipment installation and services, or happen to be a managing director of a *Korlátozott felelősségű társaság (Kft.)* – company with limited liability (Ltd) – or a director of a *Részvénytársaság (Rt.)* – joint stock company (Plc). Not part of this happy breed? Then read on.

Actually, getting a work permit should not be a major problem, since your local employer can get it for you. You will not be alone wading through this process – many foreigners work in Hungary, especially for joint venture companies. Your would-be Hungarian employer will probably apply for your work permit from the local labour exchange. Once obtained, you can relax for a maximum of one year, when it has to be renewed, and so the saga continues … To be able to proceed, though, normally you have to furnish your employer with a valid visa (see above) and a medical certificate, along with a certificate of your degree or qualifications, with its authenticated Hungarian translation attached. (More about translations later.)

You will be glad to hear, no doubt, that you will have a chance to familiarize yourself with your neighbourhood police station since you have to register your address with them.

Starting to Peel the Onion

For your expeditions to the holiest of holies, a.k.a. officialdom, on any of your red tape missions, recruit a friend with Hungarian language skills if you can. It is not necessarily 'the insolence of office' you have to team up to combat, although that is not altogether impossible either. The reason tends to be less sinister and more asinine. You would think, wouldn't you, that public servants dealing with foreigners would see it as part of their job description to be able to communicate with them in some foreign language? But this would make too much sense, so it is wise not to count on it.

As elsewhere around the world, to get what you want in the kafkaesque realm of government bureaucracy, you need impeccable preparation, lots of time, even more patience and a good dollop of humour into the bargain. Losing your control, thumping the desk and turning purple while you argue your case in your own language – or, for that matter, in Hungarian – will not help. On the other hand, immersing yourself in a good book will help, if nothing else, to while away the time – and retain your mental health.

Be it in Asia, Europe or elsewhere around the globe, completing all the paperwork necessary to start integrating into a foreign culture is, more often than not, seriously draining – but, at the same time, educational. You can look on it as part of the challenge: starting to peel off the onion of culture.

Or Delegate the Peeling ...

But if you cannot make the time or simply prefer to delegate dealing with bureaucrats and paperwork to others, that is also possible.

Some companies specialize in obtaining residence and work permits, registering your car or your company, clearing your belongings with customs, and even finding you an office or a home. Unless you hear about a reliable one through the grapevine, or your office deals with one in particular, you can have a look at the adverts in, say, the *Budapest Business Journal*. These specialist companies normally advertise under 'Business Services'. Here is one, for example, which claims to deal with all the paperwork 'quickly and inexpensively':

World Services International
Tel: (06-30) 424-343
Fax: (06-23) 312-521

What to Look for in Employment Contracts

Once you have your work permit, the contract of employment should not hold too many surprises since the Hungarian Labour Code is much like its Western European counterparts. It applies equally to you whether you are a Hungarian citizen or a foreigner, unless you are working in Hungary for a foreign employer based outside the country.

To check if your contract is in line with the Labour Code, see if it specifies contractual period (fixed or indefinite); your remuneration (not less than the minimum wage); location of work; your tasks and responsibilities; your working hours (normally not more than 40 hours per week, with statutory limits on overtime); annual leave (minimum 20 days, maximum 30, unless you have a young child or unhealthy working conditions, both warranting a longer period).

Should you or your employer wish to terminate your contract, either party can do so by giving a minimum of 30 days' notice, although this could be much longer, depending on the length of service. You cannot be simply dismissed without a reason, and if you are, you can seek compensation from your employer in the courts.

Securing Your Orvosi Igazolás (Health Certificate)

Number 7 on the list on page 239 looks straightforward enough but it deserves some attention if you are to pre-empt unnecessary frustration. So let's dive into the details below.

If you are staying for more than a year, you will have to submit a health certificate proving that you are risk-free from the point of view of public hygiene, along with the other documents in support of your application for a long-term residence permit. You can obtain this certificate from your local doctor or medical institution before travelling to Hungary if you plan ahead – not too far ahead though, because the medical certificate must have been issued within three months of your application.

Alternatively, once in Hungary, you can get it from the *Állami Népegészségügyi és Tisztiorvosi Szolgálat* (State Public Health and Medical Officers' Service):

XIII Budapest
Váci út 174
Tel: 329-0490

Please note: if you get your health certificate outside Hungary, it will be accepted there only if it meets certain requirements. To start with, there is the issue of timing and the shelf-life of the documents, mentioned above. Then, not surprisingly, it has to state the name and address, and bear the signature of the doctor issuing the certificate, as well as the name of the medical institution of the doctor. Oh, and of course, it simply must sport the official stamp of the issuing physician – Hungarians are used to decorating their documents: the more stamps, the more authority vested in it. When in doubt, have your certificates and documents stamped, just in case. Thrice over!

As for its content, the certificate has to state specifically that you do not have AIDS, TB, leprosy, syphilis and/or are not a carrier of such pathogens, or of typhoid and paratyphoid bacteria. It has to confirm as well that the doctor signing the certificate performed the tests and the examinations, and to this effect, all the test results must be attached to the certificate.

You might like to compare the costs of these tests at your local medical institution with the amount this procedure will set you back in Hungary. Here is the current fee for each test in forints: AIDS test HUF4,000; syphilis serological examination HUF2,000; leprosy (dermatological examination) HUF4,000; Stool test (typhoid, paratyphoid) HUF2,000; tuberculosis screen test HUF2,000.

Fordítás és hitelesítés (Translation and Authentication)

Once successfully obtained, the health certificate, along with some of your other documents, needs to be translated into Hungarian and authenticated by the Hungarian consulate or diplomatic mission in the country where the certificate was issued.

Alternatively, once in Hungary you can have your documents translated and authenticated all in one go by the *Országos Fordító és Fordításhitelesítő Iroda RT* in Budapest or in one of its local branches across the country. The name translates as the 'National Bureau of

Translations and Translation Authentication', but since its transformation into a company in 1994, it is normally referred to simply as OFFI Rt.

OFFI Rt. prides itself on being the first translation and authentication company of its kind in Central Europe – it was founded in 1869. Assuming your mastery of Hungarian is not topnotch as yet, and since authenticated translations are vital in the settling-in process, here are some of the current contact details of the OFFI Rt. network in Budapest and in two major cities, Győr and Székesfehérvár:

Budapest
VI Budapest
Bajza u. 52
Tel: (269) 573-0269-54-18
Fax: (1) 2695-184

Győr
9021 Győr
Szent István utca 5
Tel: (06-96) 316-675
Tel & Fax: (06-96) 316-686
Hours: 8:00–11:30 and 12:30–16:30

Székesfehérvár
8000 Székesfehérvár
Marx tér 1
Tel: (06-22) 311-001
Fax: (06-22) 311-438
Hours: 8:00–16.00

Further details about their offices around the country are available from the Budapest office or OFFI's website (www.different.hu/offi/irodak). Considering that this is a website of a translation company, it may come as a surprise that the site seems to be only in Hungarian. But you can work out the details if you remember the following:

irodák means offices, *cím* address, *félfogadás munkanapokon* opening hours on weekdays, *hétfő* Monday, *kedd* Tuesday, *szerda* Wednesday, *csütörtök* Thursday and *péntek* Friday.

FINDING THAT HOME, SWEET HOME ...

Unless your company makes arrangements for you, you are faced with what may at first seem a daunting part of settling in: finding a home in a foreign country where, however foreign it may be, you can still feel at home. The challenge is serious but manageable if you are armed with appropriate insights into the real estate situation in Hungary.

Buying a Property

If you are staying for an extended period, the decision you need to make is whether to rent or buy a place you can call your own. Real estate purchase in Hungary may well be a smart move. Property is still relatively cheaper than in, say, Vienna, which is only a few hours away. As the linchpin between Eastern and Western cultures, trade and travel, Hungary has always been the place to be. It may even work as a sensible investment since property prices have been rising and are expected to rise considerably further in the next few years.

Yes, but how complicated is it? you may wonder. Well, it is easy sailing, at least compared with the earlier situation. Whether you would like to buy property as a foreign individual or a company, you are fully entitled to do so. This is the case even if the company is one hundred per cent foreign-owned as long as the property is an integral part of the company's operation. To comply with this condition, some real estate activity can be included in the deed of foundation when you register your company.

Procedures for buying property have been relaxed: for example, you do not even need to apply for the approval of the Ministry of Finance any more. The local administrative authority's approval must be obtained though, to make sure the purchase is not in conflict with or harmful to the interests of the local community; that it is not a listed property or in a preservation area; and it is not on agricultural land.

Relaxed or not, it easily takes around two months or more to wrap up the red tape around the purchase. The necessary documentation includes the application, along with the appropriate amount of stamp duty (currently 50,000 HUF), a notary-authenticated copy of your passport, a bank statement showing sufficient funds available for the purchase, a copy of the contract stating your intention to buy that bears a lawyer's signature and an official stamp, a copy of the property ownership registration and a copy of the valuation certificate.

To keep the frustration level to a minimum, it is worth remembering that the last two documents should be less than three months old. You are not expected to attach the local mayor's permission any more.

More and more foreigners, many of them private individuals and large investment institutions, choose to buy property in Hungary. In Budapest more than fifty different nationalities have already done so. Most of the buyers are Germans, Austrians or Swiss, with an increasing number of Israelis, Romanians, Chinese, Russians and Ukrainians also making purchases. Several thousand applications are issued per year, with only a couple of hundred rejected, for example if the purchase involves agricultural land or the documentation is incomplete.

Patterns of Renting and Buying in Budapest

> "Budapest is the loveliest city on the Danube. It has a
> crafty way of being its own stage-set, like Vienna, but also
> has a robust substance and a vitality unknown to its
> Austrian rival."
>
> — Claudio Magris, *Danube*

Say you join the increasing number of foreigners buying a Hungarian home, the thorny issue of location has then to be decided. Apart from the size, condition, age and outlook of the property, location is a fundamental factor in the price of Budapest properties. A helpful rule of thumb is that the higher on a hill, the higher the price.

Generally speaking, properties with the highest prices are concentrated in districts II and XII. Decisive factors in rental costs are the type, quality and orientation of the property and its furnishings. However, as usual in this business, location is the single most important factor. For example, there seems to be a much stronger correlation between the location of the property and rent levels than between its size and the cost.

Overall, the pattern of top quality rental housing follows the pattern of the property market for sale. Though it did not used to be the case, now there is a large supply of residential accommodation for rent. Except for the *Belváros* (City, district V) in Pest, top quality rental properties are mostly on the Buda side: in the *Budai hegyvidék* (Buda hills) (district XII, II, hilly parts of XI), and the *Várnegyed* (Castle district, district I). For example, the monthly rent of a studio in district XII can be HUF80,000 or more, and twice the amount for a one-bedroom flat. A three-bedroom flat could cost you around 400,000 HUF; a house with the same number of bedrooms can be more than HUF600,000 per month. The rent of the large houses in this area, say with four or five bedrooms, can be anything from one million HUF monthly. Or, if you are looking for a recently built, large family house with a relatively moderate rent, you may want to consider the southern parts of district III or the northern areas in district II (often referred to in the property business as IIA).

Outskirts such as the *Rózsavölgy* (Rose Valley) in district XXII on the Buda side, and *Zugló* (district XIV) in Pest, and parts of district XVI are also becoming sought after for house construction since they require a smaller capital investment.

Then again, if you have children attending certain schools, moving to the school's vicinity may be worth considering.

But when it comes to finding a home, for many people the choice is also that of lifestyle. So where to look for your would-be home then?

As in many other metropolises, Budapest neighbourhoods vary immensely in atmosphere, shopping and recreational facilities, architectural style, leafiness, crime rate, access to public transport, degree of air and noise pollution – and therefore, in price.

Here are some of the areas foreigners – as well as many Hungarians – tend to be attracted to, and that you may want to consider too.

BUDAI HEGYVIDÉK (BUDA HILLS)

If you are planning to settle in Budapest, as indeed most expats do, it helps to know what the prime locations are. One of the most favoured, if not the overall favourite, is the *Budai hegyvidék* (Buda hills): district II, hilly parts of district XI, and district XII, where properties costing 20–30 million HUF are seriously sought after. As for the quality rental market, most of it consists of flats, but grand villas and impressive representational space with quarters for domestic staff are also available at around HUF2,000 per square metre per month.

It is a good idea to take note of the date the house was built, even before viewing it. Generally speaking, prewar or recently built villas are more likely to be of higher quality than family houses built in the 1970s or '80s. There may be drastically different prices for the same type and size of house, in the same street even, depending on when they were built.

Hills, Meadows and Valleys

Sas-hegy, Hűvösvölgy, Normafa, Rózsadomb, Szabadság-hegy, Svábhegy, Széchenyi hegy, Pasarét, Farkasrét are just some of the popular areas in the Buda hills. You have an idea of what to expect if you realize that all these names refer to nature in some way or other: *hegy* (mountain), *völgy* (valley), *rét* (meadow), *fa* (tree), *domb* (hill). Thus *Sas-hegy* is Eagle Mountain, *Szabadság-hegy* Freedom Mountain, *Farkasrét* Wolves' Meadow, *Hűvösvölgy* Cool Valley and so on …

History is also evident in the name of *Sváb-hegy* (Swabian Mountain) where many Swabian Germans came to settle and culti-

The Buda hills are a unique benefit of Budapest living. Many regulars pop into the Sport Park in Buda, before or after work, to soak up the sun on the gentle slopes and do their laps in the pool nestling in the valley.

vate their vineyards after the Turkish invasion; or in *Pasarét* (Pasha Meadow) which refers to the Turks themselves – *Pasha* being a high-ranking title, something like Governor, of the Ottoman empire. Already then, foreigners clearly favoured this area.

Beware: *Budai hegyvidék* is a generic term – you have not seen it all when you have explored one of the hills or the valleys. When you get to know more of them and more intimately, you will see that the various hills and valleys have their own character.

Living with History and Botany Intertwined

One of the oldest and most prestigious is, for example, *Rózsadomb* (Rose Hill). *Rózsadomb* long ago transcended the confines of geography and became a sociocultural term in its own right, denoting the classiest class in the category of gracious living space.

But for those in the know, *Rózsadomb* has never really been a purely geographical term; the name, as almost everything in Hungary, is pregnant with history, if not historical disaster. You see, the first roses in Hungary were actually planted here, by a Turk, Gül Baba, whose name means 'the father of roses'. *Rózsadomb* abounds in roses because this Turkish dervish made it his priority to set about planting a rose garden here – right after partaking in Buda's invasion in 1541 but before going to meet Allah the same year.

Therefore the roses on this hill are a thing from the past but not of the past: there are plenty of them, including the rose garden of Gül Baba himself, which you can visit and enjoy, along with its serene views of the river. A grateful and tolerant lot as Hungarians are, Turkish invader or not, Gül Baba even has a street in the area named after him – more likely for his horticultural hobby than for his military escapades.

Dawn Chorus and Late Night Concerts to Cope with

Some of the lush and leafy areas of the Buda hills feel like the best of Mediterranean holiday resorts: verdant garden restaurants and often steep, sleepy streets lined with truly exquisite old villas and lavish new mansions. Although close to the centre, and very much within the bounds of Budapest itself, living in this oasis offers you fresh air, fair views and no pressure-cooker atmosphere of metropolitan existence.

The polluted and busy bustle is only a couple of bus, tram or 'cogwheel railway' stops away, and yet life here seems essentially calm and gentle. Here you have the much-craved, but mighty rare, post-modern commodities called peace and quiet. Well, almost quiet, except for the *madárkórus* (chorus of the birds) waking you inconsiderately at the crack of dawn.

If you like something more dramatic in your everyday routine, imagine making your weary way home after a long day's work, weighed down by heavy shopping … when suddenly mammoth dogs seem to leap at you from the dense dusk. Well, it is no doubt all your fault – you have ignored the *A kutya harap* (Beware of the Dog) signs, and actually took the street to be public domain.

Although 'The dog bites' – the verbatim translation of *A kutya harap* – sounds rather more direct, not to say brutal, than its vague and subdued English counterpart, there is no major reason for the adrenaline overflow. Fences provide normally solid boundaries between you and the dogs, whose job is simply to scare the living daylights out of innocent passers-by such as yourself in a laudable effort to keep trespassers out. The good news is that you can count on the drama to play itself out every night, since it is unlikely for the dogs ever to acknowledge familiarity with you.

Not to mention late night concerts performed by the *tücsök zenekar* (cricket orchestra) that makes sure all the tranquillity does not get to you by being all too tranquil. You can easily acquire your private musician, if by chance a cricket makes its way indoors, possibly behind your bookshelves, keeping all the family busy for days trying to locate and gently relocate the green instrumentalist where it belongs. (It happens!)

But relax, there is respite in sight. Late at night, when the crickets have already turned down their volume, and the birds have not yet tuned in, the same dogs, dating through the ether, entertain you with their songs as undulating as the hills around them. Then there are the cats … but you get the picture.

The Simple Joys of Life

Seasonal delights of the *Budai hegyvidék* lifestyle include many simple joys of life, most of which come free. In spring, you can pick lilac as you lose yourself in the spicy aroma of the alleys and valleys. Posy, berry and cherry picking, along with tree climbing and reading in the treetops take over in summer. Come autumn, primeval activities like descending deep down the Buda caves, gathering nuts and making bonfires of autumn leaves are on the agenda. Then there is the ultimate elation: sleighing or tobogganing downhill in the palpable stillness of the midnight snowfall, listening to your heartbeat in tandem with the crunch of snow under the sleigh. Can you resist standing in the whiteness of the night, observing the branches' white fur-coat grow by the second, and leaving your marks in the untrodden snow? Not to mention the euphoria of shovelling the same uphill the next morning.

The last exercise can be more dramatic than you would think. Snow, in its heavy, heavier and heaviest versions, is the delight and desperation of the Buda hill dwellers. You may end up locked in your home by a solid snowfall for a good part of the day ... or more, unless you are a skilful snow shoveller with the right amount of stamina, determination and good humour.

ÓBUDA (OLD BUDA)

Or you can opt for *Óbuda*, which is also on the right side of the river, just north of Buda. It includes Aquincum, the remains of the first century Roman settlement, and stretches along the Danube around *Árpád híd* (Árpád Bridge). Óbuda, Buda and Pest (see later) merged and became known as the modern capital, Budapest, in 1873.

Tower Blocks Cheek by Jowl with Roman Ruins

To the uninitiated, at first glance Óbuda (district III) may look much younger than Buda. Industrial buildings and housing estates with tower blocks – not exactly pretty – dominate a lot of the landscape here. But if you have come to accept that vertical architectural expansion is part of modern city living, this may just be the place for you.

Óbuda's current contours conceal the fact that it is a very old part of the city – hence the archaic *Ó,* signifying 'old', in its name. Aquincum, city of water, as it was called between the middle of the first century and the third century AD, already functioned as an important Roman garrison and settlement. Indeed, it was already a capital long before *Árpád fejedelem* (Prince Árpád) and his conquering Magyars made their appearance around 896. Later, they buried Árpád here – hence the name Árpád Bridge.

Considering its credentials then – being the capital of Lower Pannonia, for example – it is no surprise if you come across the visual remains of history among the trappings of modern, industrial life if you choose to live here. You bump into not particularly well-preserved but quite significant Roman ruins wherever you go: one of the amphitheatres could probably hold around 16,000 spectators.

Properties are 20–25 per cent cheaper than similar ones in the Buda hill districts II and XII and in most of the hilly areas of district XI. If you prefer prewar flats and houses, then the area to explore is bounded by the following streets: Bécsi út, Flórián tér and Árpád fejedelem útja. There is a direct correlation between the proximity of the property to district II and its price, although the 20 per cent difference tends to prevail.

Many choose to build a new home in the Óbuda hills of *Tábor-hegy, Remete-hegy, Arany-hegy* and *Testvér-hegy*. If you prefer to be by the river rather than up in the hills, you may consider looking for a house or flat in one of the tower-block developments in the riverbank areas of *Csillaghegy* and *Római-part*. Medium-priced houses of 150–200 square metres can cost anything from 30 to 60 million HUF. Also, prefabricated or not, the demand for flats in the housing estates around here tends to outmatch what is available.

Water as a Way of Life

And now lifestyle considerations in Óbuda. Are you or would you fancy being a 'boatie'? Do water sports give you a thrill? Well, if the answer is yes, *Csillaghegy* (Star Mountain) and *Római-part* (Roman Riverbank) may be the house-hunting place for you. The riverbank is lined with *csónakház* (boathouses) and boat clubs. This is the area to look for a home if you are planning to pursue something as robust and potentially romantic as rowing up the Danube at weekends or even in the early evenings after work.

Beware: *evezés* (rowing) in this context is not about paddling along here and there with one member of the crew doing the work while the others keep up the chatter, flirt, picnic and admire the sun setting on the river. Should you adopt this strategy, you will drift downriver, leaving Budapest far behind and hit the Black Sea in no time.

But seriously, though rowing upriver on the Danube is great fun, you need to be in reasonable condition to assert yourself against the slow but determined flow of the river. It does no harm either to know what you are supposed to be doing with your paddles, especially in the aftermath of big ships creating massive waves in their wash.

The romantic 'roughing it' subculture of Danube boathouses is a world of its own. It is certainly worth trying if you decide to live in this area, are keen on outdoor exercise on your doorstep and appreciate a chance to meet new, like-minded people.

Being an Óbuda resident comes with the privilege of having your very own island, so to speak. The northern part of *Óbudai sziget* (Óbuda Island), or *Hajógyári sziget* (Shipyard Island) as it is some-times called, is north of Árpád Bridge. It can be reached by boat, bus or local railway from other parts of Budapest – but it is only a leisurely stroll away if you live in certain parts of Óbuda. It's not as refined *as Margitsziget* (Margaret Island) – the central island on the Danube in Budapest. Nonetheless, its extensive green stretches of park-cum-playground delight children with their truly gigantic slides, while parents play tennis on the courts nearby.

Canoing and rowing are popular on the Danube. Boathouses line the banks along the Óbuda stretch of the Danube, but you can join in the fun in other places as well, such as in Győr, a northwestern Hungarian city. This rowing crew has just arrived from a day trip on the Danube.

Depending on your musical preferences and just how alternative you like to get, an added attraction of this area is that in August, the island on your doorstep hosts the Hungarian answer to Woodstock – a pop festival of sorts, lasting for several days.

A BELVÁROS (THE CITY)

But how about the eastern side of the river, I hear you ask. Well, on the left side of the Danube, in Pest, district V in particular – the *Belváros* (City or Downtown Budapest) – and parts of districts VI, VII and VIII are popular with foreigners. Quality flats with impressive views will meet your expectations if your lifestyle is urban and you have the proximity of your office rather than schools to consider.

Pest Versus Buda Side of the Danube

By now you have a general idea of what Buda and Óbuda feel like. Now, Pest is as different from both Buda and Óbuda as it can be.

Historically speaking, Pest too has had its own history as a separate town since Roman times. However, the really dramatic development of Pest as a commercial and industrial city, when it emerged as the hub of the region, is relatively recent – in the 19th century. If you wanted to be in the focal point of action in Roman times, you went to Óbuda. Come the Middle Ages, your place would be in Buda. And it is over in Pest where the pulsing rhythm of city life would get you going from the second part of the 19th century onwards.

Geographically speaking, if Buda and Óbuda are rugged, Pest is little more than a flat urban landscape. It is centred around the revamped pedestrianized area of its downtown streets, many displaying sumptuous turn-of-the century architecture. The atmospheric streets swarm with chain stores, boutiques and tourist traps, offices, banks, eateries, cinemas, concert halls and theatres. The aura is vibrant, the atmosphere redolent with action, business and money, and the air with pollution.

Dunakorzó (The Promenade) and a Room with a View

Do your lifestyle priorities include leisurely, late evening strolls or brisk early morning jogs along the misty *Dunakorzó* (The Promenade), catching every now and then the breath of the robust river rolling by?

How about browsing through morning papers over your steaming espresso, savouring evening meals in one of the many eateries overlooking the Danube and then pub crawling without having to do much crawling at all? Does the waterfront atmosphere of moored boats inviting you on deck to dance, wine and dine or take off on a river cruise – locally or as far as to Vienna – appeal to you?

Do you fancy the *joie de vivre* of reading, courting or even fishing on the steps of the embankment, with languid waves lapping your ankles? Are you an amateur anthropologist, keen to observe others, or someone who likes to be seen? Do you prefer to be within walking distance of where the action is?

Or will it be love at first sight, as for countless others, when you set your eyes on the panorama of Buda from the Pest embankment, compelling you to obtain a room with a view to admire its magic at your leisure – preferably from your bed?

Everything on Your Doorstep but …

Well, to indulge yourself regularly in the finer things in life, and meanwhile be an actor on the exuberant stage-set of Budapest, the seductive splendour of the *Belváros* and some of its neighbourhoods are your terrain to explore. Here, you will have almost everything, and more, on your doorstep.

Having said that, to enjoy living right in the vibrant heart of it all, and to do so on a long-term basis, it helps to be good-humoured about crowds pulsing, tourists flocking, seedy sections crumbling, city crime spurting, and easy parking and relaxing gardens lacking.

To feel at home in the *Belváros*, it may also help to already have, or at least cultivate, an appreciation of the temples of conspicuous

Many Hungarians cherish the hustle and bustle of the Dunakorzó, the top promenade in Budapest, which stretches along the Danube, with its many restaurants facing the river and the Buda hills. People-watching is a popular pastime while taking a rest on one of the many benches of the promenade.

If you are into angling, you can indulge yourself right in the middle of Budapest, for example at the foot of one of the many bridges.

In the summer street vendors and street artists congregate on Vörösmarty tér, a popular meeting place in the heart of Belváros, downtown Budapest.

259

consumption: stores and restaurants. Some of them are enticing and elegant, others touristy and tacky; nonetheless, you can expect heftier than usual bills either way, be it glamorous or glitzy.

If you can live with these pleasures of downtown life, then it may make sense for you to look for a flat in or around the *Belváros*. A smallish flat may cost 5–10 million HUF.

MORE THAN JUST A WEEKEND IN THE COUNTRY

An increasingly popular alternative is to migrate out of the city and to settle down in some of the green areas not too far away from Budapest.

A Hop Away from Budapest

Many people choose to move out of the city and commute from *Budakeszi, Adyliget, Tök, Leányfalu, Tahitótfalu, Zebegény* and *Kisoroszi*.

In *Budajenő, Telki, Páty* and *Zsámbék* you can find houses from around 6–12 million HUF, whereas in *Budakeszi,* a house may cost around 20–50 million HUF. Some of the areas around Budapest, such as *Budakeszi*, are virtually overflowing with people moving out from Buda in search of some 'country living', complete with house and garden.

Szentendre is an atmospheric and famous artist colony on the riverbank, within reasonable commuting distance – consequently, swarming with crowds in the tourist season.

Lake Balaton

In some areas around Lake Balaton foreigners own more than 10 per cent of properties. If you consider this an option, think about your needs and priorities first, since the choices available offer a great variety.

The microcosmos of Budapest reflects the macrocosmos of Hungary: you have the choice between the part packed with unruly hills and the reassuringly flat side right opposite. Facing the Buda hills on the western riverbank, you have flat Pest on the east. This geographical and visual contrast, with all its atmospheric, practical and lifestyle implications, is mirrored on a large scale by the contrast between hilly *Dunántúl* (Transdanubia) in the western, and the prairie land of *Nagyalföld* (Great Plains) in the eastern part of Hungary. Similarly, at Lake Balaton, the hilly versus flat contrast is there for you to consider. The only difference is that it is not an east-west, but a north-south divide.

Pick Your Favourite Shore

Accordingly, families with young children may well prefer the flat southern shore of the lake, where you have a large stretch of shallow water that warms up very quickly in summer. Here, you have the added bonus of the panorama of hills opposite.

If, on the other hand, you are a hill-person, cherish relative seclusion, vineyards, etc, and do not mind peregrinating half an hour to the shore for a swim and then climbing back uphill afterwards, then the areas to search for property are the northern villages of Balaton.

Many people buy houses in *Hévíz, Keszthely, Gyenesdiás, Vonyarcvashegy* and *Cserszegtomaj*. Prices vary enormously, depending on the location and the quality of the property: it can be anything from around 100,000 to 30–40 million HUF.

Other Hot Spots around the Country

Western areas of Hungary, such as *Győr-Moson-Sopron megye* (Győr-Moson-Sopron county), are also sought after, as, to a lesser degree, are *Somogy és Zala megye* (Somogy and Zala county).

PROPERTY AGENTS, INFORMATION AND IDIOSYNCRASIES

Having acquired the gist of what to expect in the area you plan to find a home in, you will probably want to go on a walkabout there. Reading, talking to people or looking at photos can certainly help sort out your potential preferences. But neither the best of descriptions, nor the best of estate agents or photos can replace your personal explorations of the streets themselves, preferably at different times of day, on different days.

Ingatlan Ügynökök (Estate Agents)

Training in real estate is relatively new in Hungary. The recent development of the property market has created and driven the demand for professionals in this field with appropriate qualifications. As a result, the Technical University of Budapest, the Budapest University of Economics, and Nottingham Trent University jointly offer the first Hungarian programme in real estate, with an internationally transferable degree recognized by the RICS (Royal Institute of Chartered Surveyors).

Whether renting or buying, if you decide to look for professional advice, there are more and more real estate agencies in Hungary to help you find the home you envisage. You can also consult the *Who's Who in Real Estate*, a bilingual guide to real estate professionals in Hungary. Here are a few contact details to get you going:

Who's Who in Real Estate
Tel: 374-3344; Fax: 374-3345

Kala and Eppel
I Budapest
Csalogány utca 6-10
Tel & Fax: 212-4756
E-mail: kala@mail.datanet.hu

Biggeorge's International
XII. Budapest
Városmajor utca 20
Tel: 202-6080; Fax: 202-7735
E-mail: info@biggeorge.hu
Website: www.biggeorge.hu

Quality and Service Real Estate Agency
XII Budapest
Krisztina körút 23
Tel & Fax: 202-0121, 212-9271
E-mail: qands@mail.matav.hu

Where to Look for Further Information

It is also worth checking out adverts in English-language papers such as the *Budapest Sun* and *Budapest Business Journal*. Then there is *ReSOURCE-Ingatlan Info* (ReSource-Real Estate Info), a bilingual listings guide:

V Budapest
Szent István krt. 11
Tel: 374-3344; Fax: 374-3345

Ingatlan (Real Estate) is another magazine devoted to the property market, with lots of adverts, many of them with colour photos. Although it is in Hungarian, you could try to navigate through it.

The adverts normally start with the name of the location. Some of the key words that may help you understand the gist of the ads are as follows: *vételár* (sale price), *MFt* (million forint), *irányár* (price in the region of ...), *méret* (size of property), *nm* or *négyzetméter* (square metre), *eladó* (for sale), *bérbeadó, bérelni* (to rent), *szoba* (room), *érdeklődni* (contact), *venni* (to buy), *eladni* (to sell), *lakás* (flat), *ház* (house), *telek* (land), *parkoló* (parking), épült (year built in), *kerület* (district).

Another place to check is the website of this magazine where people can advertise for free: www.ingatlan.com

Square Metre Versus Number of Rooms

Unlike in Britain, in Hungary the property is most often priced and advertised in square metres. The size of the property, i.e. its overall area (in square metres), is usually considered much more important than the number of rooms. This may take some getting used to if you tend to think in number of rooms rather than the size of the whole property, in square metres to boot.

Another point to remember is that a two-roomed flat may have one or two bedrooms, a three-roomed house two or three bedrooms, and so on, the reason being that, unlike in some other parts of the world, in Hungary traditionally the living room is included in the number given. This produces a potentially ambiguous situation. It is worth checking out if it is a matter of some importance that, for example, your would-be one-room flat has a separate bedroom rather than one room all in all – i.e. a studio or bedsit.

If you need a base in Budapest while you explore the rental and property market, you could consider staying at Millennium Court, an apartment block operated by Marriott in the heart of the city. Stays are for a minimum of three weeks and a maximum of six months.

Millennium Court
V Pesti Barnabás utca 4
Tel: 235-1800; Fax: 235-1900

Shifting the Stuff
And then, when you have found the place you will call home while in Hungary, your belongings need to be shifted to the new place. Here are a couple of contacts in Budapest you may like to try:

CORSTJENS Worldwide Movers Group
Tel: 261-2651; Fax: 263-0797

Euromove
Tel: 382-0990; Fax: 204-3572
E-mail: EuroMove@csi.com

Interdean
II Budapest
Szállító utca 4
Fax: 277-2877

AGS Worldwider Movers
Tel: 204-8674; Fax: 204-8670

Apart from relying on the expertise and contacts in this area within your own company, or from your estate agent, if you look at the *Budapest Business Journal*, you are likely to find many more removal firms.

CULTURAL QUIZ

SITUATION ONE

You and your Hungarian colleagues have just ordered some foamy-fresh draft beer in a *söröző* (brasserie/beer garden). Since on previous outings to restaurants you noticed just how obsessively Hungarians are into clinking glasses, you decide to please your friends by showing off your cultural awareness. Before anybody has a chance to grab their mug, let alone clink it, you hasten to clutch yours, and demonstratively clink it with everybody else's around you, starting with the person sitting the furthest from you.

You expected to generate some enthusiastic remarks and appreciation of your efforts to integrate culturally with Hungarians. Instead, an exchange of knowing looks follows among your friends. You are amazed and wonder what went wrong.

A   Hungarians clink their glasses but not their mugs. Since the beer was served in mugs, you shouldn't have clinked at all. It would have been OK though, had it been served in glasses.

B   Hungarians do clink both their glasses and their beer mugs, but only if the beer served is bottled, not draft.

C   You started the 'clinking ritual' with the person sitting furthest from you, when in fact your immediate boss was sitting right beside you – your gesture clearly violated social hierarchy. You should simply have started by turning to her first, and then your clinking would have been appreciated.

D   Hungarians are into clinking glasses of anything and everything, except beer, which is a taboo for historical reasons.

Comments

The correct answer is *D*. By now, you may be aware of the prime role history plays in the Hungarian psyche. Still, you may never have imagined, even in your wildest dreams, that a historical disaster could manifest itself in such a relatively mundane ritual as the beer drinking procedure. Nonetheless it does.

Finer details vary, but the important idea to remember is that this particular taboo is linked to the Hungarian Rebellion in 1848. The glorious rebellion against the Austrians ended at Világos, followed by ruthless reprisals. For Hungarians, the historical and psychological significance of the failed rebellion of 1848 ranks equal with the lost battle of Mohács in 1526. Hungarian mythology holds that the victorious Austrians were clinking their beer glasses while the Hungarian generals were being executed. So Hungarians will happily clink glasses of wine, champagne, spirits or, if worst comes to worst, even soft drinks – but clinking beer glasses is a taboo rooted in mythologized history.

SITUATION TWO

You have never considered yourself a feminist per se but observing, let alone experiencing, sexist behaviour in Hungary is rapidly turning you into a forceful advocate of the cause. You find yourself acting in the grip of two irresistible impulses: you feel compelled to enlighten your Hungarian woman friends and colleagues, and you cannot resist giving men a piece of your mind about this issue. It does not take too long before you find that you are being studiously avoided by colleagues of either gender.

A   Hungarians never welcome interference or any sort of comment concerning their private life. They are eminently private people, and they expect you to respect that.

B   It is OK to enlighten women but you should avoid intellectual banter about gender-related topics with men.

C   You have alienated people around you simply because your line of argument was too abstract and rational.

D   You have come across as if you thought you knew the answers to their problems.

E   Feminism is taboo and should never be discussed in public.

Comments

Respecting privacy is not a particularly obvious cornerstone of Hungarian culture. Quite the contrary, in Hungary gossiping is a much cherished pastime – indeed, a widely cultivated popular art form. Even topics that in some cultures would be considered questions of intimacy rather than privacy may be discussed by Hungarians, often quite publicly and with admirable fervour.

Banter about gender relations is generally quite OK, as long as it stays light-hearted and no 'educational intent' can be detected.

You may find it difficult to win the hearts of some Hungarians with overly abstract and rational arguments. It may be helpful if you cultivated your skills at collecting anecdotes related to, and supportive of, your line of argument. Make sure, though, that you present them with a knockout punch line and a heightened sense of drama.

Feminism is a complex and sensitive subject in Hungary albeit not a taboo per se. It can be raised and discussed but only with due care, at the right time, with the right people. And, most importantly, in the right style: try not to come across as if you thought you knew the answers to the problems. In any case, if you allow yourself to explore the matter with a sufficiently open mind, you may find that some of its concerns may be quite different from what you would expect were you firmly established in the tradition of Western-style feminism. It is helpful to assume that feminism, as with other social movements, has its various versions implanted in different sociocultural and economic contexts. Jumping to conclusions that may seem self-evident to your eyes may not help you to achieve the results you are after. So *D* is closest to the right answer.

SITUATION THREE

You have invited your Hungarian counterpart and her family to visit your home. The family arrives and you are happy to see that the children are lovely and reasonably well-behaved. You make a throw-away remark about bringing up children, which triggers the parents to launch into an extensive elaboration of their children's respective gifts. You listen patiently as one charming anecdote unfolds after the other. Finally, when you feel you can risk changing the topic, you do so.

In the meantime, one of the children gets somewhat hyper and starts rushing around like a wild horse. When she knocks over a vase which has great sentimental value to you, you tell the child kindly but firmly to cool off a bit. The get-together feels less and less 'together'; the chatty and cozy atmosphere seems to have evaporated. You wonder why.

A It was wrong to extend the invitation to the whole family. Hungarians do not like to mix family and business matters in general.

B You did not compliment the parents on their children.

C You demonstrated no genuine interest in the stories about them when you reset the evening's agenda by switching topics abruptly.

D   Your patient listening came across as distant and passive, even aloof.

E   By telling the child to stop running around, you have interfered with the family's privilege to discipline their own offspring the way they think appropriate.

Comments

In general, Hungarians are much in favour of mixing family and business matters.

Many Hungarian parents, and especially grandparents, dote on their (grand)children to a degree that may be surprising to the unaccustomed eye. Therefore, inviting the whole family was a good move. Your culturally appropriate gesture, however, was not authenticated by your overall behaviour in the course of the evening.

Praising the children could have provided a better start. Then, rather than changing the topic abruptly, it might have been better to

An intimate chat between grandfather and grandson. It is common for children and their grandparents to have a close relationship.

actively engage the discussion about children by matching your guests' anecdotes with a few well-chosen family stories of your own.

At times, Hungarian parents may come across as unusually protective of their children, especially when it comes to them being disciplined by somebody other than the parents themselves. Perhaps paradoxically, this predisposition does not imply that in turn you can expect them to abstain from commenting on or interfering with your way of dealing with your own offspring. You may find that sometimes even passers-by in the street or fellow commuters on the tram seem to feel compelled to offer you their approving or disapproving comments on the parent-child conflict at hand.

Nonetheless, telling other people's children off, however tactfully you imagine you do it, is a high-risk activity – try to steer clear of it or be prepared to suffer the consequences. So *A* is wrong. On the other hand, *B*, *C*, *D* and *E* have all contributed to the relative failure of the get-together.

SITUATION FOUR

You have just been appointed the new business advisor to a Hungarian company. You launch yourself into the job with panache, spreading valuable advice enthusiastically whenever possible. You illustrate your points with a plethora of illuminative examples and intricate theories. You focus on being articulate and authoritative. You invite the team to business lunches, and offer toasts to the success of the joint effort. In spite of it all, you feel you have not really been accepted; but cannot fathom why.

A You are not accepted because you cannot speak Hungarian. Hungarians cultivate a lifelong love affair with their much-treasured mother tongue. Small wonder if the language gap acts as a communication barrier.

B Your authoritative, well-rehearsed discourse style is perceived as patronizing.

C Spending less time on giving advice and more on listening to what your Hungarian colleagues think they have got to contribute may be a good start.

D You project yourself as *the* authority whereas Hungarians often have a problem with authority figures.

Comments

Some knowledge of Hungarian, albeit limited, albeit coloured with a heavy foreign accent, will no doubt help rather than hinder you. Hungarian is not the devilishly difficult language it is often made out to be. It is simply different. Once you have accepted that you cannot take your well-worn grammatical concepts for granted, you are on your way to having fun with the language.

The more knowledge of Hungarian you can demonstrate, the better. Try not to stop at saying *Jó estét!* (Good evening), *Köszönöm szépen* (Thank you very much) and *Egészségedre!* (To your health/ cheers!) Repeating the same old words over and over again may turn out to be more irritating rather than impressive, so building up and practising your knowledge base is a smart move.

Having said that, the fact is that many Hungarian business people are quite fluent in one, and often in more than one language. There-fore, it is highly unlikely that the root of your problem is your inability to converse in Hungarian.

The key issue may well be anchored in your style of interaction: *B, C* and *D*. Hungarians tend to be quite proud and consider them-selves smart – if not smarter – than anybody else. Suffering fools gladly is not a popular pastime – they take the view that they have had more than their fair share of that in the course of their history. Now being thought of as patronizing is a particularly unpalatable version of being considered a fool. So it may be advisable to scrutinize your own image and work towards eliminating any verbal and nonverbal messages that may be perceived as stuffy or snooty. Maybe you sound just a tad too well rehearsed? Or perhaps just a pinch too authoritative? What's the ratio of your listening and speaking time? You may get through to your Hungarian partners more if you make them feel that you understand this relationship to be a two-way process. This way, you may be less likely to be perceived as an outsider with a missionary zeal, arrogant enough to imagine you have the keys to wisdom and administering advice to the uninitiated.

It may help to remind yourself occasionally that any self-respecting Hungarian takes pride in thinking of himself as rebellious by nature. In the light of this Hungarian self-image, be careful not to be perceived as ramming yourself down their throat as an authority figure, however impeccable. This is more likely to pique rather than stir them into cooperative action.

SITUATION FIVE

Your Hungarian business partner has invited you to the opera. You go there straight from work and therefore cannot change your clothes. Still, you get there just in time. Your colleague is already inside; your ticket is left with the usherette. Rather than queuing at the cloakroom, you take your coat with you, greet your colleague and discreetly stash your folded coat under the chair. In the interval you offer your host some drinks.

The show is splendid but draining, so you are relieved you only have to fish your coat from underneath the chair, thank your colleague for the evening, and dash off to get horizontal as soon as possible. As you are about to leave, you seem to detect a vague sense of disappointment in your colleague's face. You wonder what the matter could possibly be. Perhaps you:

A were not dressed for the occasion and, in subverting the dress code, insulted your host.
B put extra pressure on your host by not getting there earlier.
C stashed away your coat under the chair – bad manners.
D stepped on your host's toes by offering her drinks. The evening was her treat, including the interval drinks.
E disappointed your colleague by not inviting her to dinner after the show.

Comments

When in Budapest, in matters of style it might be a good idea to act as if you were in Paris or in New York. Hungarians in general, and Hungarian business people in particular, have an acute sense of style, especially when it comes to fashion. Appearance is of prime importance; first impressions are vital; grand styles are favoured. Spending hard-earned cash on high fashion is often seen as an investment in self-presentation. Expenditure on anything for public display is not money down the drain, however ephemeral, provided it projects the appropriate image.

Whether you are a woman or a man, the quality and cut of your clothes will be scrutinized to the last button. The way you present yourself will be commented on and well remembered. Dressing down is not a recommended option. You may consider erring on the side of caution; if anything, be a touch overdressed rather than a tad under. It makes sense not to underestimate the Hungarian flair for fashion, and to respect their sense of occasion.

Although Hungarians may seem to be in a manic state of rush, people do tend to make an effort to be on time, especially in business and professional contexts. Generally speaking, do not expect the Mediterranean, laissez faire attitude to time in Budapest. It is a vibrant, pulsating city where time is money and business people will not judge you favourably if your attitude to time is overly relaxed, i.e. more relaxed than their own.

You were right to offer your host a drink in the interval. But stashing your coat under the chair was not a cool idea. It is perfectly acceptable, say, in the London Opera House, but it is simply not done in Budapest, unless you do not mind coming across as uncouth.

Pre-show and post-show dinners and drinks can be stylish occasions and perfect opportunities to do some bonding, business or otherwise, in a mellow ambience. Budapest, remember, is a human-scale city compared with London, New York or Tokyo. Distances are manageable; you can get from one end of the city to the other within a reasonable time. Unlike in most other metropolises, in Budapest you can go to a show without the major stress of having to rush right after (or even before) the end of the performance to be able to get the last tube to a suburban satellite town. So treating your host to dinner after the show is a recommended option. However, if you are really serious about the invitation, it is best arranged in advance.

SITUATION SIX

You are having an early morning business breakfast in a relatively small Hungarian town. The aroma of espresso is afloat, the table is loaded with food but ... no sign of any cereal or porridge, your regular diet in the mornings. Along with the steaming espresso, you are also offered a glass of something that vaguely looks like water. Recalling your coffeehouse experience in Budapest (see the chapter on Food and Wine), you boldly take it to be water to wash down the bitter aftertaste of the espresso. You venture a generous sip and discover, to your utter shock and horror, that what you are expected to drink at the crack of dawn is *pálinka*, the famous – or, to some, infamous – Hungarian brandy.

- A Not wanting to offend your hosts, you quickly down the whole lot, to get it over and done with once and for all.
- B You make apologetic noises about not being used to imbibing the fiery booze first thing in the morning, and take small sips.
- C You put the glass back nonchalantly, as if you have not even noticed it.
- D Firmly but kindly explain that for, say, medical reasons you cannot drink spirits.
- E You praise the excellent qualities of the drink but stand your ground and do not touch the rest.

Comments

If you quickly quaff the whole lot, you will be gently – or not so gently – forced to drink more. And more. And then again some more. So the ordeal will not be over; on the contrary, that will only be the prelude to the generous Hungarian insistence on making you enjoy the blessed stuff to their satisfaction – extensively. So *A* is not an option unless you intend to become a *pálinka* devotee. This of course you can contemplate only on the condition your body can be counted on to rise to the occasion, i.e. it can handle the ferocious fuel first thing in the morning without ousting the solid elements of your morning intake.

Squirming apologetically is generally unlikely to cut much ice with Hungarians. In this case, for example, your apologetic noises, with or without making halfhearted gestures of sipping, might just generate endless explanation as to why it is so beneficial to your health and general wellbeing to down this magic potion.

Probably one of the best options is a shrewd combination of *D* and *E*: being positive by praising the *pálinka*, and demonstrating your views by making appreciative noises; at the same time, being firm (and non-apologetic) and making it clear that you cannot and will not drink the rest.

SITUATION SEVEN

You are in a coffeehouse, having a tongue-wag with your Hungarian friends. The chitchat turns into an intense discussion, this time with a focus on literature. You:

A are impressed by your Hungarian friends' knowledge of European literature, but you keep your views to yourself.

B cheerfully admit that, like most foreigners, you know absolutely nothing about Hungarian literature, and ask them if there is anything at all you should have read.

C inquire about the best translations they can recommend for you to have a better sense of the incredibly rich literary heritage you are aware of.

D make comments about the fact that they seem to know much more about European literature than you do, and wonder why this should be so.

Comments

If you go down the road of the alternative proposed in *B*, be prepared not to make many friends. Quite like the Hungarian language, Hungarian literature is a strikingly powerful part of the Hungarian identity. Admission of your ignorance in this particular field may well be taken as an insulting disappointment rather than a gesture of sincerity.

You may be forgiven – at a pinch – if you do not have an overview of Hungarian literature. However, it is imperative that you can at least pronounce the names of such classical authors as Dezső Kosztolányi, Attila József, Frigyes Karinthy, Miklós Radnóti, Endre Ady, János Arany and Sándor Petőfi – to mention just a few of the absolute 'must'. So, option *C* is a viable alternative, especially if you throw in some of these names for good measure.

Options *A* and *D*: If you find that your Hungarian friends have an impressive knowledge of European literature, you risk offending them by complimenting them for being so exquisitely erudite. Hungarians who are well versed in European culture will often see this knowledge as something taken for granted, almost a prerequisite to calling oneself a European. If you show surprise by complimenting them, the subtext of your comment may be interpreted as an insult, i.e. that you had not anticipated them to be proficient about this in the first place.

SITUATION EIGHT

You have just spent a relaxing week in the summer cottage of a Hungarian friend by Lake Balaton. Your friend asks you some questions about your home in your native country. You:

A take the questions at their face value and give him the information he is asking about.
B understand the illocutionary force of the questions to be an indirect request for an invitation to stay at your house next time your friend and his family are in the area.

C clarify details of any travel plans he may have, and how he generally arranges accommodation for his family.
D make it abundantly clear that your house is too tiny to host visitors.

Comments

It may be tempting to accept an invitation to stay as a guest in the home or the holiday cottage of Hungarian friends. Before accepting though, it is perhaps a good idea to elucidate what the expectations are on both sides. It may or may not be the case that in return for the invitation the tacit expectation is a payment in kind, so to speak. It is not altogether impossible that you will be expected to reciprocate the hospitality by inviting your hosts to sojourn in your house or holiday home at some point. If, for some reason, this is not a viable option for you, it is perhaps best clarified in advance. This way, anticipations and realities are realigned, and the likelihood of disappointment and frustration is minimized.

If you have already accepted the invitation of hospitality without having previously explored and matched each other's schema of things, the situation is more delicate. If you follow option *A*, you may be seen as disingenuous, whereas *D* may come across as ungrateful and blunt. In *B* you are making assumptions which may or may not be warranted, whereas *C* will provide you with relevant information for dealing with the issue more appropriately.

SITUATION NINE

You have been invited to a Hungarian home for Sunday lunch. All sorts of colourful and enticing food are being served – Hungarian hospitality is unleashed, as usual, with a vengeance. At a closer look though, you discover that all the mouthwatering sustenance on offer seems to contain at least some meat. You are vegetarian. Everybody else is relishing the feast immensely; repeatedly, they encourage you to join in. How can you get out of this sticky situation, you ask yourself. You:

A simply say you are vegetarian and cannot consume any of this.

B nibble at it as a gesture.

C refuse to comply with the pressure put on you, and quit in disappointment, fuming that no vegetarian alternatives have been prepared.

D claim you are not hungry since you ate brunch not so long ago.

Comments

Here, you may have become the victim of your own cultural assumptions. Where you are coming from, it may be customary to either ask guests about their dietary preferences well in advance, or else take it for granted that some guests may be vegetarian and prepare the choice of diet accordingly. Neither of these attitudes is terribly common in Hungary – a carnivorous society in a big way. In some ways, not to prepare meat for a special meal, such as a Sunday lunch – especially when guests join the table – may be seen as very inappropriate. Indeed, it may be construed as being stingy or unable to afford meat.

So, if vegetarian diet is of paramount importance for you, the best strategy may be to alert your hosts to this in advance, making it easy for them by specifying the sort of things you are happy to eat. If this precaution is not an option for some reason, you might wish to consider tasting some of the food offered as a gesture that may be appreciated by your hosts.

Option *D* is very offensive – how could you possibly have eaten just before coming to join them for the ritual of sharing food? Do not be surprised if you are not invited again.

SITUATION TEN

You are about to visit a Hungarian family you would like to get to know better. You decide to get some presents from your local shop on your way to their home. During dinner, there is a rambling discussion about all manner of things, touching at times on issues of religion and politics. This you take as a signal that you are free to ask probing questions about these topics. At the end of the evening you are puzzled as to why the evening was not quite as successful as it could have been. You reckon:

A   asking about people's religious beliefs and political affiliations is taboo.

B   it is OK to ask about political beliefs but not about religious ones.

C   your presents were not well chosen.

D   it was wrong to take presents to your hosts. You should have taken a bottle of good quality wine instead.

Comments

Historically speaking, asking questions, especially probing ones, about religious and political beliefs can be a really delicate business in Hungary. Nowadays, these issues may not be the full-fledged taboos they used to be, but close enough. Points of reference such as one's political affiliation and spiritual disposition may act as sources of more general extrapolations about a person's character and trust-worthiness, based on perceptions of their value and belief systems.

Stating one's religious, cultural or political background may trigger rigid frames of references in your Hungarian interlocutor's mind. For example, your claim to support a particular political party or subscribe to a particular religion or, for that matter, religion in general, may be construed as something more wide-ranging and significant than a mere identification with a political or religious agenda. On the bases of your stated preferences in politics or religion, you may be attributed an intricate value system about life in general. Beware: even what you may consider a relatively minor issue of expressing personal likes or dislikes about a public or even a private figure may generate far-reaching and complex judgements about your own character as a whole.

It may be a good idea to wait until your hosts actually volunteer information, either directly or indirectly, about matters of religion or politics. Once you have been initiated into the inner workings of their mind, then, but only then will they be likely to engage such sensitive issues in your company. At that stage, they will be happy to do marathon probing-sessions with you.

Option *D*: to take a bottle of high quality wine is fine, but it is not the only option. Elegant bouquets of flowers, plants, boxes of fine chocolate, some exotic fruit can also work as gestures of appreciation.

Presents (although not sweets) for children are always welcome and seen as signs of warmth and caring. Something cheap and cheerful is unlikely to do though. It is advisable to pick something of fine quality – otherwise you may be judged as selfish and superficial.

SITUATION ELEVEN

You are driving home from work when the Hungarian police stop you. They wish to see your passport and various other documents to prove your identity. When it turns out you do have all the required papers on you except for your passport, they make it clear that they will take you to the local police station. You:

A take a deep breath, release it to the count of eight, and demonstrate cooperation.

B insist that they call your husband who can locate and show them your passport.

C demand to see a lawyer, and do not budge until they agree to comply with your request.

D make it clear that you consider this incident a major infringement of human rights.

E create a scene in an attempt to make them accept the other documents in place of the passport.

Comments

Probably *A* is your most feasible option. Documents in general, and proofs of identity in particular, are no trifling matters in Hungary. If you want to avoid being hassled, you *must* have them on you at all times, even if you are, say, canoeing on the Danube, dressed in little more than your birthday suit.

SITUATION TWELVE

One day you are busy running errands downtown when you run into a Hungarian friend of yours and her husband. You are delighted to see each other and start chatting about old times. She and her husband suddenly suggest having dinner in a place nearby where they are regulars. You trust her expert advice in ordering the meal for you too. Unfortunately, you cannot join them in tasting some exquisite wine since you have to slog away that night.

The waiter knows them well and presents them with the bill. You:

A   make a quick calculation in your head, and pay for what you have eaten, adding ten per cent for your share of the tip.
B   oay one third of the bill and of the tip.
C   let them pay, and express your appreciation for their generosity.
D   insist on paying the full bill.
E   invite the couple for dinner the week after, thank them for the meal, and leave.

Comments

Option *B* is probably the best way to go about this. Had your friend and her husband meant to be the host for the evening, they would have indicated this to you. The waiter gave them the bill simply because they did the ordering, so you came across as their guest.

Paying specifically for the items you had could be OK, although you may come across as a cheapskate. This may be the case even if you drank only water while your friends consumed a considerable amount of fine wine.

SITUATION THIRTEEN

You bought a quaint but dilapidated house in desperate need of a total makeover. A colleague of yours recommends a highly skilled and reliable team of workers. They look trustworthy and experienced so you trust them with the job, and agree on a clearly specified date and cost, with half of the money paid as deposit.

Several months after the agreed deadline, the job is still not done to your satisfaction and the bill you are presented with is hiked up to double the amount originally agreed upon. You:

A yank your colleague in on the crisis and rely on him to tackle it. After all, he was the one who recommended the team to start with.
B contract a lawyer in moral outrage.
C take the matter in your own hands by investing your creative energies in the ancient art of haggling.
D put together meticulously an itemized list of costs and fees as you remember them, and ask the team to do the same.

Comments

The correct answer is *D*. It is not advisable to do away with the fussy business of written, signed and dated itemized estimates in any circumstances. Even if your colleague recommends some tradesmen, it is essential to stick to jotting down everything concerning job details, timeframe and financial implications. You can expect your colleague neither to take responsibility for the crisis, nor to carry out the damage limitation exercise on your behalf. The best you can hope for is comparing the itemized lists, and getting it checked out by a registered trade organization. Then, and only then, is the time to have a crack at bargaining with some reasonable chance of success.

Should you take the matter to court, you can count on a lengthy and costly battle draining not just your money, but time and energy as well.

SITUATION FOURTEEN

You and your family live in a house with five other flats. Life is quite dense, you are often tense and mostly in a hurry. You:

A whizz off in the small hours and return quite late in the evenings, without having any contact with anybody else in the house. Anyway, they do not seem to mind since they too seem to have lots on their plate.

283

B occasionally make time during weekends to be around the house and gossip with families living there.

C invite some of the families over for tea or coffee to suss each other a bit.

D smile and stop to exchange a few words with neighbours when you run into each other in the hallway.

Comments

It may be efficient in the short term, but may well backfire in the long term to isolate yourself from your immediate Hungarian community. Hungarians tend to put a high premium on personal relationships. You do not really want to alienate everybody else in the house by projecting an insouciant, let alone frosty and aloof image. You may reckon your neighbours are content with hardly knowing your name but in fact this may well not be the case.

Option *D* is the best if you and everybody else around you is also hard-pressed for time. The trick is to take those few moments of incidental encounters and make the most of them by establishing at least a minimum degree of trust by acknowledging each other's existence. A couple of words about children, for example, provide a neutral ground to share views and feel less distanced.

Options *B* and *C* are much more time-consuming but, who knows, may turn out to be time well spent in the long run. Even if you are not lucky enough to strike up real friendships with your neighbours, you might get just a bit more under the skin of the culture you live in.

SITUATION FIFTEEN

Your business assignment includes creating a project team to establish procedures. You:

A highlight the shared objectives, delegate responsibilities and expect everybody to cooperate as a team from that point onwards.

B make clear who the boss is and expect the rest of the group to be deferential to her.

C foreground the detailed structure of linear management, and exert pressure on everybody else to conform to the prescribed hierarchy.

D place a premium on individuality and engage in regular ego-stroking of your team members.

Comments

Naturally, as all peoples and cultures, Hungarians too display an endless variety of personalities. And yet, like others, they too will demonstrate at the same time a predilection for certain characteristics in their interpersonal interaction. These patterns are often ambiguous, and imply powerful tensions pulling in opposite directions.

On the one hand, Hungarians will often be seriously committed individualists and, as such, not the best team players per se. Historically, conformity and bowing to public pressure are not perceived as positive attributes. Therefore, neither management by paternalistic or peer pressure, nor leadership by the sheer evocation of team spirit offers readily available keys to success. Hungarians tend to be thoroughly impatient with authority and conformity as well as with team members at large. Falling in line is often construed as following the crowd, revealing weakness and sheep instinct.

On the other hand, there is also a strong tendency in Hungarian culture for autocratic, demanding behaviour. Expecting obedience from others in general, and subordinates in particular, is an attitude not altogether without tradition. Hungarian procedures and regulations, carefully set up to control people and processes, are complex and plentiful. An authoritarian and paternalistic discourse style is not uncommon in most walks of life: parents with children, teachers with students, managers with 'managees', doctors with patients, etc. Titles, status, protocol are vital if for nothing else than for the sheer pleasure of subverting them. The symbols and styles as well as the essence of authoritarianism are alive and well.

And in spite of, or perhaps precisely because of this, authority is highly likely to be disparaged demonstratively, and regulations circumvented creatively. Hungarians may be just as meticulous in working out minutely detailed procedures and rules as, say, some Germans are. Then again, they will also pride themselves in being inventive in finding ways of not following the same procedures if they were to impinge on their own delicate and much respected individuality.

So, options *B* and *C* may not get you very far; they would probably only provoke resistance and generate hostility. If you take, however, the course of action suggested in *A*, the project may well fall apart by the time you realize that a major assumption on your part – team spirit – is not functioning in the way you had expected.

Ego stroking – option *D* – may well be helpful in your effort to reconcile just the right degree of authoritarianism with due respect to individualism, rather than opting for any clear-cut, unambiguous approach.

SITUATION SIXTEEN

You have just been to the movies with a group of Hungarians, and are debating the film you have just seen. The discussion heats up in a few seconds to a level you are not accustomed to in your own culture. You:

A tell them they are dogmatic in their views and are behaving like 3-year-olds.

B adopt their combative style – join the debate by retorting with dogmatism of your own.

C clam up, intimidated and appalled.

D manoeuvre to reset the agenda.

E leave in disgust at what you see as an uncivilized style of interaction.

Comments

Blunt criticism is unlikely to win you Hungarian friends. Hungarians themselves may come across as blunt – or even brusque at times – the way they criticize others; nonetheless, they do not necessarily excel in taking well much of the same. Option *A* is touch-and-go: it may well violate the proud and sensitive Hungarian ego.

The white intensity of a Hungarian debate may be truly alarming at first but you will have to try to get used to it. People are often highly demonstrative about their feelings, whether it is seething anger or passionate affection. Even supposedly dispassionate, cerebral debates tend to be imbued with emotions.

Option *B*: If dogmatism is not your second nature, then being sufficiently tenacious in presenting your argument can be draining to uphold, and may come across as unauthentic. So it may not work in the long run.

Opting out by clamming up or leaving the scene is an option of course, should you be content with cutting yourself off from the group. If, however, you are striving to be accepted as a member of it, you may try to set the agenda yourself, and pick a topic where you feel sufficiently at ease to stand your ground with energy and panache. Whatever the topic, your impeccably argued case for pragmatism, with a pinch of emotional rhetoric, can be a step towards successful membership into the group of your choice.

FURTHER READING

History and Travel Writing

Anger, Per. *With Raoul Wallenberg in Budapest: Memories of the War Years in Hungary.* Translated by David Mel Paul and Margareta Paul. New York: Holocaust Library, 1988.

Dunn, Seamus and Fraser, T.G. eds. *Europe and Ethnicity.* London: Routledge, 1996.

Everyman Guides: Budapest. London: Everyman Publishers Plc, 2000

Fermor, Patrick Leigh. *Between the Woods and the Water: On Foot to Constantinople from the Hook of Holland – The Middle Danube to the Iron Gates.* London: Penguin Books, 1986.

Garton Ash, Timothy. *The Uses of Adversity: Essays on the Fate of Central Europe.* New York: Random House, 1989.

Gerő, András. *Modern Hungarian Society in the Making.* Budapest: Central European University Press, 1993.

Johnson, R. Lonnie. *Central Europe: Enemies, Neighbours, Friends.* Oxford: Oxford University Press, 1966.

Lukács, John. *Budapest 1900: A Historical Portrait of a City and Its Culture.* New York: Weidenfeld & Nicolson, 1988.

Magris, Claudio. *Danube: A Sentimental Journey from the Source to the Black Sea.* London: The Harvill Press, 1999.

Smith, A.D. *Nationalism and Modernism.* London: Routledge, 1998.

Wilson, Edmund. *Europe without Baedeker.* New York: Farrar Straus Giroux, 1966.

Culture and Communication

Hall, E.T. *Beyond Culture*. New York: Anchor Press, 1976.

Moore, D. Jerry. *Visions of Culture*. Walnut Creek: AltaMira, 1997.

Scollon, Ron and Wong Scollon, Suzanne. *Intercultural Communication: A Discourse Approach*. Oxford: Blackwell, 1995.

Sperber, Dan. *Explaining Culture*. Oxford: Blackwell, 1996.

Young, Robert. *Intercultural Communication: Pragmatics, Genealogy, Deconstruction*. Clevedon: Multilingual Matters Ltd, 1996.

Economy and Business

Bögel, György et al. *Hungary since Communism*. London: Macmillan, 1997.

Turnock, David. *The East European Economy in Context: Communism and Transition*. London: Routledge, 1997.

Learning Hungarian

András, T. László and Kövecses Zoltán. *English-Hungarian Dictionary of Slang*. Budapest: Maecenas Publisher, 1991.

András, T. László and Kövecses Zoltán. *Hungarian-English Dictionary of Slang*. Budapest: Eötvös University Press, 1994.

Törkenczy, Miklós. *A Practical Guide to the Mastery of Hungarian: Hungarian Verbs and Essentials of Grammar*. Chicago, USA: Passport Books, 1997

Hungarian Writers and Writings

Ady, Endre. *The Explosive Country: A Selection of Articles and Studies, 1898–1916*. Translated by G.F. Cushing. Budapest: Corvina, 1977.

Esterházy, Péter. *The Glance of Countess Hahn-Hahn: Down the Danube.* Translated by Richard Aczél. London: Weidenfeld & Nicolson, 1994.

Faludy, György. *My Happy Days in Hell. 1962.* Translated by Kathleen Szasz. Toronto: Totem Press, Collins Publishers, 1985.

Fisher, Tibor. *Under the Frog.* Edinburgh: Poligon, 1992.

Füst, Milán. *The Story of My Wife.* Translated by Ivan Sanders. New York: Vintage Books, 1989.

József, Attila. *Selected Poems and Texts.* Translated by John Bátki. Cheshire: Carcanet Press, 1973.

Karinthy, Frigyes. *A Journey Round My Skull.* Translated by Vernon Duckworth Barker, 1939. Budapest: Corvina, 1992.

Koestler, Arthur. *Darkness at Noon.* London: Vintage Classics, 1994.

Konrád, György. *The Case Worker.* Translated by Paul Aston. New York: Harcourt Brace Jovanovich, 1974.

Kosztolányi, Dezső. *Anna Édes.* Translated by George Szirtes. Budapest: Corvina, 1991.

Mikszáth, Kálmán. *St. Peter's Umbrella.* Translated by B.W. Worswick. Budapest: Corvina, 1962.

Molnár, Ferenc. *The Paul Street Boys.* Translated by Louis Rittenberg and George Szirtes. Budapest: Corvina, 1994.

Móricz, Zsigmond. *Seven Pennies and Other Short Stories.* Translated by G.F. Cushing. Budapest: Corvina, 1988.

Örkény, István. *One Minute Stories.* Translated by Judith Sollosy. Budapest: Corvina, 1994.

Radnóti, Miklós. *The Complete Poetry.* Translated by Emery George. Ann Arbor: Ardis, 1980.

Szász, Béla. *Volunteers for the Gallows: Anatomy of a Show Trial.* Translated by Kathleen Szász. New York: W.W. Norton and Co., 1971.

MUSIC

Some CDs to Get You Going

Bartók Album. Muzsikás with Márta Sebestyén and Alexander Balanescu. Muzsikás, 1998.

Béla Bartók. *Music for Strings, Percussion and Celeste. Divertimento.* Liszt Ferenc Chamber Orchestra, Budapest. Hungaroton Classic, Budapest, 1994.

Béla Bartók. *Dance Suite. Hungarian Sketches. Two Pictures. Divertimento.* Chicago Symphony Orchestra. Deutsche Grammophon, Hamburg, 1995.

The Best of Márta Sebestyén. Traditional songs from Hungary and Transylvania. Rykodisc USA, 1997.

Boldog szomorú dal. Folk music from Hungary and Transylvania. Csík Zenekar. Fonó records, 1996.

Ferenc Liszt. *Études d'exécution transcendante.* György Cziffra, piano. Hungaroton Classic, Budapest, 1994.

György Kurtág. *Song Cycles.* Quasi Una Fantasia. Ensemble Modern. Sony Classical, 1990.

György Ligeti. *Concertos for Cello, Violin and Piano.* Ensemble Intercontemporain, Deutsche Grammophon. Hamburg, 1994.

A Night in the Garden of Eden. Central European Yiddish Folklore. Budapest Klezmer Band, 1995.

Szól a kakas már. Muzsikás. Hungarian Jewish Folk Music. Hungaroton-Gong Kft., 1992.

Zoltán Kodály. *Háry János.* Hungarian State Opera Chorus and Orchestra, Hungaroton, Budapest, 1982.

ABOUT THE AUTHOR

The author, Zsuzsanna Ardó, is Hungarian by birth, English by existence, human by inclination and humorous by nature. Her books and articles on management, communication and culture have been published in Germany, Hungary, Russia and the United Kingdom.

She has a Masters degree in English and Hungarian Literature and Linguistics from Hungary, and an English Major in Canadian Studies from Canada. She was an associate professor at the Budapest Business College and did research in intercultural communication in the United Kingdom and Japan. Her broadcasting experience includes directing and presenting the live, Europe-wide satellite television series on communication and management from the studio of King's College London.

For several years she has been lecturing in English Language Studies and intercultural communication. Her cultural satires on Hungarians are English and Hungarian parallel texts: *How to Be a European: Go Hungarian* and *Love Blues: Hungarian Rhapsodies*. She is the editor of HASnotes, the book reviews editor of the London regional newsletter of ITI UK; a member of PEN, ITI and the Society of Authors UK; and the Chairman of the Hampstead Authors' Society.

Her current projects include translating films, working with a composer on a libretto, and writing a film script.

Zsuzsanna Ardó can be contacted at ardo@pobox.com.

INDEX